UNTIL ANTIETAM

S. B. Richardson

UNTIL ANTIETAM

The Life and Letters of
Major General
Israel B. Richardson,
U.S. Army

Jack C. Mason

Southern Illinois University Press
Carbondale

12 11 10 09   4 3 2 1

Frontispiece: An early Civil War portrait of Israel B.
Richardson, by L. Prang & Co. of Boston, that was
published in newspapers in fall 1861, as the national
news media promulgated accounts of the new leaders
of the Union Army. (Library of Congress)

Library of Congress Cataloging-in-Publication Data
Mason, Jack C.
Until Antietam : the life and letters of Major General
Israel B. Richardson, U.S. Army / Jack C. Mason.
     p. cm.
Includes bibliographical references and index.
ISBN-13: 978-0-8093-2947-2 (cloth : alk. paper)
ISBN-10: 0-8093-2947-6 (cloth : alk. paper)
1. Richardson, Israel Bush, 1815–1862. 2. United States.
Army—Officers—Biography. 3. United States. Army of
the Potomac—Officers—Biography. 4. United States—
History—Civil War, 1861–1865—Campaigns. 5. United
States—History—Civil War, 1861–1865—Biography.
6. Mexican War, 1846–1848—Campaigns. 7. Mexican
War, 1846–1848—Biography. 8. Generals—United
States—Biography. I. Title.
E467.1.R54M37 2009
973.7092—dc22
[B]   2009010532

Printed on recycled paper. ♻
The paper used in this publication meets the minimum
requirements of American National Standard for
Information Sciences—Permanence of Paper for Printed
Library Materials, ANSI Z39.48-1992. ∞

Contents

Illustrations

Photographs

Maps

Preface

Like Israel Richardson I am the sum total of my lifetime experiences. As a history fan, I came across the vague story of a seemingly down-to-earth, but aggressive, fighting general who sacrificed his life for his country at the Battle of Antietam. Although Richardson's exploits during the first year of the war were very important to the cause he fought for, personally, he has become just a footnote in the multitude of writings concerning our American Civil War. Living near his last home and final resting place of Pontiac, Michigan, I was fortunate to discover old, forgotten sources enabling me to piece together his career and to set forth his story in a way that will help us understand why Israel Richardson turned out to be the man he was. In another perspective, I tried to focus not just on Richardson's deeds but also on the leadership styles of other officers who, while serving with the man as friends and comrades, directly affected the development of Richardson's own manner of leadership from the beginning of his army life as a cadet to the end of his service as a major general.

My theory that President Lincoln might have considered Richardson as a possible candidate to replace George B. McClellan can be debated by Civil War scholars much more distinguished than I. The notion surfaced several times in my research of postwar writings of soldiers of all ranks connected with Richardson, and probably had its roots in the comments of Captain Charles S. Draper, Richardson's aide-de-camp, who was also wounded at Antietam and shared a bed in the same room. He was the only witness present when the president visited Richardson to pay his respects after the battle. If I accomplished anything with this book, I would hope that history will look more favorably on this old soldier and give him a greater recognition for his actions and service to the nation.

In the beginning my goal was to research enough information to publish an article in one of the military's professional development journals or a Civil War history magazine. But over the course of several years, my search became a sort of detective hunt in which one source led to another. My service as an officer in the U.S. Army Reserve at Fort Benning led me to microfilmed personnel returns of U.S. Army Infantry regiments dating back to the 1840s. This interesting source shows how closely some of the most senior opposing commanders during the Civil War worked together on a daily basis within a regiment, and often within the same company, during their Old Army careers.

Fort Leavenworth was an excellent source of materials describing the difficulties faced by Richardson in the days following the Mexican War. The U.S. Military Academy at West Point was very helpful in supplying records of Richardson's early years. I was constantly amazed at the historical connections I uncovered between the army of Richardson's day and our army today. I am sure that Israel Richardson would be satisfied to know that the disciplined regulars of Company E, U.S. 3rd Infantry Regiment, which he commanded in arguably his most gallant act, charging up the steep hill of Cerro Gordo, still performs its duty today, guarding the Tomb of the Unknown Soldier at Arlington National Cemetery. In personal character, these two armies, separated in time by more than 150 years, are not far apart.

My friend Thomas Lane and I worked together to transcribe close to one hundred personal letters written by Richardson that spanned his whole career in the army, from his days as a cadet at West Point to his last prophetic letter as a major general to his wife three days before his mortal wounding. These private letters, held for many years by Mr. Lane's grandfather, D. Duffy Lane, are a historical treasure that enables the reader to draw out the honest, unpretentious character of the man and help make his past come alive. The letters are also a confirmation of descriptions noted by officers and men who served at his side throughout his army career. Also included with these letters was a one-hundred-page manuscript, titled "Twelve Years Service in the U. S. Army." Richardson probably began this project in the late 1850s, after his resignation from the army. The Civil War interrupted his hobby but left his enlightened opinion on the advantages and faults of strategy taken by senior leaders during the Seminole and Mexican Wars.

I quoted many of these Richardson letters verbatim. The tone of his unpublished letters and rarely referenced after-action reports, produced immediately following an event, go a long way in honestly describing the motives and actions of the soldiers involved in a way that popular literature written with the advantage of hindsight cannot. I hope the reader will gain more from Richardson's honest written description of an event (sent privately to family, without concern for political correctness) than from any paraphrasing of his general thoughts.

I was fortunate to find several histories written by close associates that mirror his career. The campaigns of the U.S. 3rd Infantry Regiment in Florida, Mexico, and the New Mexican frontier are covered in autobiographies by his old regimental commander, Ethan Allen Hitchcock, and a fellow company commander, William S. Henry. Richardson's experiences raising and training the 2nd Michigan were related by Charles B. Haydon. The rest of Richardson's career as a division commander on the Peninsula, and at Antietam, is covered by journals written by soldiers in each of his three brigades. Pieced together, they do a good job judging Richardson's performance as a leader from a private's, a sergeant's and a junior officer's perspective. Finally, the *National Tribune*, a newspaper published in Washington, D.C., after the Civil War until the 1920s, was a great source of veterans' anecdotes and comments. The majority of these vignettes were commonly by junior officers and enlisted men who were present during the course of the war and were not shy in offering their opinions on the great captains and events of the day.

I owe many thanks to all the library and museum experts who took the time to assist me in my efforts and steered me toward other pertinent sources. A critique from William C. Davis was helpful and reassuring, and Mike Musick at the National Archives was quick to respond to my request for help. Ted Alexander, of Antietam National Battlefield Park, also provided suggestions and references, and a special word of thanks must go to Charlie Martinez and the Pontiac Historical Society, where this project began. Finally, I thank the Lane family for their Richardson Document Collection, whose contributions to this effort helped me confirm many facts I had investigated from a combination of other sources.

Introduction

Throughout its history, the American army has cherished its heroes and held their exploits as examples for future generations of leaders to follow. On a national level, everyone recognizes the names of Washington, Lee, Pershing, Patton, and MacArthur. At a more specialized level, military professionals and historians draw inspiration from the episodes of Joshua Chamberlain at Little Round Top or Phil Sheridan at Winchester. Within the army community, legends of soldiers' deeds have made for spellbinding conversation around campfires since the birth of its organization. Many of these characters have been obscured over the years, but their stories are important because they capture the mood of the army and show how it has evolved over time. As has always been the case, our army reflects the prevailing attitude of our society, and knowledge of American army folklore is another way to understand the history of our nation.

This is the story of one of those soldiers. Israel Bush Richardson was a talented and fearless infantry leader in the Civil War who has been denied the recognition that he deserves for his performance as a brigade and division commander in the Army of the Potomac. Tragically, he died just as his aggressive leadership was being recognized by the highest levels of the government. Although he played a short role in comparison with the great scope of events during the Civil War, he was held in high esteem by his soldiers and his peers for many years after. His duty to his country can be measured by his participation in twelve active campaigns over the course of three conflicts during his military service. His early death, from a wound at the Battle of Antietam in November 1862, robbed his country of his experienced, commonsense leadership just as President Lincoln was searching for a solution to his nagging leadership problems within the Union army.

By looking back through Richardson's military career and his personal letters, it is possible to trace how he was mentored by superiors and events during his

1

almost twenty years of service in the army before the Civil War. The hard lessons young Richardson and his generation learned during this period shaped their views of strategy and the handling of an army. Those lessons, as well as their moral values, have gone far in determining the heritage of our country's armed forces today. By the end of the Mexican War, Richardson, as a company grade officer, had more combat experience than most of his peers in the army. This experience is key in how he came to regard his duty and develop his character, courage, and competence.

Through the expression of Richardson's private thoughts to his family, which at times differed from the recognized doctrine of the army, we can begin to trace the professional arguments that always start when frontline units attempt to put professional theory into practice. He was quick to point out in his letters, often years before it became accepted truth in his profession, that the army was successful in Florida because of a change in small unit tactics and that later, in Mexico, the greatly outnumbered American army was victorious due to superior training, tactics, and discipline.

As both sides of our nation mobilized for war in 1861, many men motivated by pride, patriotism, and politics rushed to fight for their country. Key leaders in both armies did not understand the dynamics of logistics, the training of large numbers of volunteers, and aggressive new tactics that complemented the greater lethality of new weapons. The few men who did understand, and who rose to the top on both sides of the conflict, tended to be young professionals from the Old Army. This group, like Richardson, entered the army around the time of the Mexican War and drew their first and lasting lessons of leadership from older officers who had spent careers of thirty years or more leading soldiers and fighting battles along the expanding frontiers of their country.

To fully understand the character of Israel Richardson, one must know his mentors as well. A few of these personalities are well known, such as Winfield Scott, Zachary Taylor, and William Harney. Others, successful in their own careers but not as famous, including Edmund Alexander, Ethan Allen Hitchcock, Louis Craig, and William Henry, are equally inspiring. As Richardson's life unfolded, his own leadership style began to reflect bits and pieces of the success he witnessed in the actions of his old commanders. The accomplishments of many great generals from both sides of the Civil War had their roots in the teachings and lessons from these now obscure soldiers.

1

Novice

"I always had a greater taste for the active duties of the field than for the monotonous and sedentary life in garrison"

In the early 1800s, a young boy spent his childhood in the quiet community of Burlington, in northern Vermont. His life as part of a large family supported by the legal profession was a fairly easy one. The days combined play among siblings with lessons from both parents, which would help stimulate the children to become more aware of their heritage and encourage them on to greater accomplishments as they grew into adulthood.

By the light of the fireplace, the youngster begged his father to tell another tale from the many notable adventures in the life of a legendary local hero. Over time, he heard how the neighbor came to prominence in his community by tracking down and killing a wily old wolf that had plagued the village for years. During the course of one night, this wolf was responsible for killing more than seventy sheep and goats. Finally having pursued the predator to a small cave, which even the dogs were afraid to enter, Israel Putnam grabbed a torch and pistol and crawled into the dark unknown until he came face to face with the animal, which he shot dead.

During the French and Indian Wars, Putnam, although thirty-seven years old, became a respected company commander in the independent volunteer light infantry unit known as "Rogers' Rangers." The talk around the ranger camp, "that Rogers always *sent,* but Putnam *led,* his men into action," was an indication of his ability.[1] During a skirmish in 1755, Captain Putnam saved Major Robert Rogers' life during a hand-to-hand fight with the French. In 1758 Putnam was wounded and captured near Fort Edward. When Indians attempted to burn him alive at the stake, a French officer appeared and cut him free as the flames grew higher around him. Sent to Canada, Putnam remained for a time until he was exchanged. In recognition of his service, he was promoted to lieutenant colonel and commanded a battalion under General Jeffrey Amherst during the capture of Fort Ticonderoga and Crown Point. For several years after the war, he lived in New Salem, next door to Richardson's grandparents, and had a lasting impact on the family. Richardson's father was named Israel Putnam Richardson in honor of their courageous family friend.

During the Revolutionary War, "Old Put" proved a reliable leader, serving as a major general, second in seniority only to Washington himself. With these stories as inspiration, the young Israel Richardson was determined to become a man who could lead by example and build a legend of his own one day.

Israel Bush Richardson was born in Fairfax, Vermont, on December 26, 1815, the second of seven children born to Israel Putnam Richardson and Susanna Holmes Richardson. His father had graduated from Dartmouth College in 1804 and started a law practice in Fairfax in 1807, becoming one of the most prominent lawyers in the state. He partnered in the law office with a cousin, Origen D. Richardson, who had served in the army and participated in the Battle of Plattsburgh during the War of 1812. For a time, Israel P. Richardson was employed as an attorney for the state of Vermont, and the younger Israel spent an uneventful childhood with his three surviving sisters, Susan, Marcella, and Marcia, living successively in Cambridge, Fairfax, St. Albans, Swanton, and Burlington. He grew into manhood dreaming of the military events that his ancestors participated prominently in during the Revolution and before.

After Israel completed preliminary study at St. Albans, the Richardson family sought an appointment for him to the U.S. Military Academy at West Point. In March 1832, at sixteen years of age and of "firm constitution and good moral character," Richardson was sponsored by the leading citizens of Burlington for appointment as a cadet. Congressman Swift, apparently a political enemy of the Richardson family, wrote to discourage the appointment: "Of young Richardson, I have no personal knowledge which will enable me to judge his qualifications, but I have been long acquainted with his father, who is in the practice of law, and is a man of wealth, amply able to educate this (and only) son, at any college in the country, and I think it not improper to add that a very considerable portion of his wealth has been gained by holding lucrative offices under the United States, and few men in Vermont, if any, have shared more largely in the bounty of the government than he, and few who know him would desire to see his son educated at public expense."[2]

That first attempt failed with the selection of Stephen H. Campbell, a "very meritorious young man who has not the means of an education in the ordinary way."[3] That Richardson pursued his goal of a military career over the course of several years attests to his determined efforts to follow in his famous neighbor's footsteps.

Richardson's childhood dream was realized when he was admitted to the academy on July 1, 1835, at the age of nineteen years and six months. As the academic year started, however, he ran into problems with the study of mathematics. During the New Year, Richardson became one of a dozen cadets admitted to the hospital during an epidemic of the mumps. He recovered soon enough but, writing his sister, admitted that he "got clear behind in my studies, and expect to fall as much as 20 this month in mathematics, but think I can get up at the next examination."[4] It also appears that his fellow roommates at the academy were not helpful in furnishing an environment conducive to study.

"One of my roommates was tried by a garrison Court Martial the other day, and his charges were, cooking after taps. It seems that on the 21st of last month, one of the January graduates from our room, and one from another room, got up at 10 o'clock to steal chickens, which they brought to our room, and came to wake me up, but I lay in bed. In about 15 minutes, Lieutenant Burbank, who was inspecting Barracks, came into the room. 'Gentlemen, what is going on here? Cooking, Sir. Cooking what? Chickens, Sir. Who is the orderly of the room? Mr. Hamilton, Sir. Lieutenant Burbank then came into the back room where I was in bed, and examined the room very closely, and then went out. The next day the two January graduates were ordered off the Point and Cadet Hamilton placed in arrest.'"[5]

At his semiannual examinations held in January 1836, midway through his freshman year, he failed his math portion and was found officially deficient in that subject. Every cadet who found himself in such a position had to appear before the academic board, where his future status would be decided. In each case, the instructors would gather to discuss the merits of the individual to determine whether the cadet would be allowed to retake the exam or asked to leave West Point.

Records of the board meeting show that although his instructors agreed that as a student he had "little" aptitude in the field of mathematics, they also felt his study habits were "good" and his general conduct was "very good." Shortly after the meeting adjourned, Richardson received the dreaded news. He was recommended by the academic board for discharge from West Point. However, a letter from the Engineer Department, Washington, dated January 29, 1836, announced that the secretary of war directed several cadets recommended for discharge after the January examination, including Richardson, be allowed to resign and reappointed the following year. The good conduct of the four individuals whose cases were handled in this matter was cited as the reason for the secretary's decision.

Richardson was readmitted to the academy on July 1, 1836. He was not a brilliant student, and his weakness in mathematics came back to haunt him, as he was once again found deficient in that subject in June 1838. Subsequently, he was turned back again to repeat his sophomore year. After spending five and a half years at the military academy, he became a member of the celebrated class of 1841, which contributed twenty-three generals to the Union and Confederate armies during the Civil War.

It would be safe to say that young Richardson struggled through the academic portion of his training at West Point. After a disastrous beginning, hard work was evident as he slowly improved his class standing. He wrote his father, on July 26, 1838, to explain the bad news of his math exam: "The examination is just done and I have passed in all branches except in Mathematics. That I failed in this branch was very unexpected to me as I had the best mark in the section from Jan. to June. And my professor told me before the examination that there was no danger, and that I would pass if any one in the section passed. The whole class is well satisfied that it was not my fault that I was found deficient, but that of my professor."[6]

With another close brush at dismissal, Richardson redoubled his academic efforts and his grades slowly but steadily improved. He wrote to his sister on October 6, 1838, "All the deficients of our Class were dismissed but myself and one other. I intend to get high enough this year, if possible, so as to be in no danger again while at the Academy."[7]

As a senior, his class ranking was twenty-fourth in engineering and thirty-second in geology. However, his grades in ethics (forty-fifth), artillery (forty-first), and infantry tactics (forty-ninth) helped to fix his class academic standing to the lowest quarter. Being close to home and the support of his family, Richardson probably spent a pleasant time during his stay at West Point, where he ranked thirty-eighth in his class of fifty-two when he graduated on July 1, 1841.

While he toiled at the intellectual tasking at the academy, he discovered one of his great strengths was his adaptability to the disciplinary aspects of military life. While future illustrations in his career proved he was not a rigid follower of rules for the sake of regulations, his record at West Point shows that he quickly adjusted to the type of conduct expected from cadets. In each of his five years at the academy, Richardson finished in the top quarter of the general conduct roll, which listed the number of demerits accumulated throughout the academic year.

The system that Sylvanus Thayer established at West Point was designed to rate everything a cadet did, both academically and on the drill field, as well as during personal, off-duty time. This system of demerits meant that class rankings would be based on the whole-person concept, because no matter how brilliant a cadet was, his class standing could be low if his behavior was poor. Richardson found that system to be an advantage to him, as his good behavior was able to bring his class standing up to a respectable finish. It was the "devotion to duty" aspect of Israel Richardson's character that allowed him to graduate above the bottom quarter of his classmates.

Upon on his return to West Point, Richardson commented to his sister, "There are now 130 cadets here in the 4th Class, and it is said to be one of the worst for devilry that has been here for a good while. They say there will be a few eliminated in January."[8] His prediction was low: fewer than half of his classmates would receive their diplomas four years later. While his class grew a reputation for unruliness, Richardson managed to keep a low profile. A sampling of the type of behavior that Cadet Richardson was found wanting was mild for the expected behavior of boys and young men in their late teens and early twenties. Bayonet out of order at inspection, talking in ranks, sitting in shirtsleeves in quarters, and coat collar not hooked in church were specific examples found in the academy demerit book. However, an entry on July 28, 1838, "setting fire to combustible fireworks in camp,"[9] shows that the young man was not without a sense of humor.

Living and studying at West Point was still a spartan affair, but Richardson gave credit to the new superintendent, Major Richard Delafield, for improving the quality of life. "Major Delafield has made a great many alterations since he came to the Point. The fare is much better than it used to be, and the Secretary of War has ordered that we shall have iron bed-steads, instead of sleeping on the floor. Each Cadet will pay 20 cents a month until they are paid for."[10]

Writing his mother on December 20, 1839, Israel described the sudden death of his friend William H. Heath. They had sat next to each other for a year and a half, and were together in a drawing class when Heath suffered a seizure and died shortly afterward of what was then called brain fever. His letter laments, "The examinations will commence in about a week, I do not feel much like preparing for it, and indeed, the Second Class never is prepared for it."[11]

As Richardson struggled with the scholastic aspects of West Point, he continued to improve in the leadership aspect of his military training. He described the duties of the senior class to his father: "The course of studies in the First Class is by far easiest of any here, and it is more use than that of the other 3 years put together. From reveille, which is beaten at 10 minutes before 5 o'clock, until 7 A.M., the broad and small sword exercise & Infantry drill. From 8 until 9 A.M., morning parade, from 9 till 10, riding; from a quarter past 10 until half past 12, Artillery drill, mortar firing, and laboratory work. From 4 until half past 6 P.M. fencing, broad sword, and Infantry drill. From 7 until half past 7 evening parade.

"Our class is excused from guard duty as private sentinels, and mount guard as Officers of the Day, by turns. We also go to Infantry drill as officers and carry a sword instead of a gun, which by the way, is much easier. I am the Officer of the Guard today and take this opportunity to write home, since the Officer of the Guard is allowed a table to write upon. It is now 20 minutes past 11 P.M., and the only light in camp is at this tent, and at that of the Officer of the Day. . . . Our class is permitted to walk all day on the public lands when not on duty, a privilege which has never yet before been given to any class. . . . Uncle John was here on the 3rd, and remained nearly all day, during which I went around and showed him the principle places upon the Point. He says he never saw a place so lonesome where so much money had been expended."[12]

His letters home always showed an honest confidence as to how he handled his duties as a cadet at West Point, as well as a dogged persistence toward achieving his goal of becoming an officer. "Our class has commenced riding and learning cavalry tactics. I have got so as to ride pretty well to what I could do at first. The horse I ride throws almost everybody except myself. I expect I do not ride so well as some others, but think there is not a horse among them that can get me off. I have not yet been thrown."[13] He also found the student projects in the laboratory fascinating. Each cadet was required to make blank cartridges, rockets, priming tubes, canister shot, quick and slow match, ball cartridge, buck shot cartridge, and buck and ball shot.

With the end of his goal within sight, Richardson demonstrated his commitment to the support his family had given him throughout his West Point experiences. "I shall have three hundred dollars coming to me when I graduate, which I shall be happy to let Father have, if he wants, as I shall have no need of it myself. I mean to say by letting him have it, he can have 300 of it and I shall never want the return of it, as I expect he wants it more than I shall."[14]

When Israel Richardson received his diploma in June of 1841, he achieved something that very few young men of his country had earned. His good aptitude and high interest in engineering studies guaranteed him a career in the rapidly expanding railroad industry, if his future as a soldier would ever change.

Upon graduation, Richardson, along with the majority of his classmates, was commissioned a brevet second lieutenant, or acting second lieutenant, with the salary of sixty-five dollars a month. The army, by law, had no way of adding new officers to its ranks in a given year. Since there was no effective retirement system in place, and since all promotions were based on seniority, an officer had to literally wait until someone resigned or died before he could be promoted. After graduation, Richardson traveled to his family home in Burlington for a three-month furlough and to await his first assignment as a commissioned officer in the U.S. Army. Orders duly arrived, assigning him to the 3rd U.S. Infantry Regiment and instructing him to join the escort of eight hundred new recruits leaving New York and to report to his new unit in the northern portion of the territory of Florida, where it was engaged in operations against the Seminoles.

The Seminoles, who had been scattered but not destroyed by General Jackson in 1818, continued to chafe under constant pressure from white settlers who wanted more land. The Second Seminole War had been under way since Major Francis Dade and 104 of his 107 soldiers were massacred near Fort King in 1835. When American troops arrived in force, the natives retreated into the Everglades and had been conducting a guerilla war with the army and settlers ever since. Six years into the conflict, the U.S. government and the public were becoming increasingly frustrated at the lack of a decision, and the popular support of the war was starting to erode.

On the voyage to Florida, aboard the *Benjamin Azmar*, the new lieutenant displayed the ability to take decisive action even though lacking experience. He recounted the episode to his sister. "On this day we had a row with the recruits. Three of them got drunk and fell upon the sergeant; . . . I was sitting with one of the Lieuts., on the quarterdeck. Soon a gathering of 40 or 50 of the troops on the main deck, and I told the other officer we had better go down and stop the scrape; and he, supposing there was no trouble stayed where he was and I went forward into the crowd. I . . . saw the sergeant raise a windless bar and strike a large man on the forehead cutting a deep hole in it. I ordered the man tied up to the timberhead.

"The men, by this time, began to crowd around so thick, a person could hardly stir. I ordered the guard to form a line on deck and charge them with their bayonets. The men retreated back a few paces, and the second man who had been at the sergeant retreated down the fore hatch and got his bayonet and swore he would kill the first man that came near him.

"I told the corporal of the guard to have him tied up, and the men began to press up again and I told the guard to keep them back or I would have them all tried for mutiny; and told the corporal to charge the man down the fore hatch, 'and don't be afraid to use your bayonets.' The men went down again, the corporal struck the man in the face with his musket, the man fell heavily backwards. All three men were then tied up to the timberhead and kept there until sober. The large man was a pugnacious fellow, had a large scar on his forehead before; and the windless bar made another in the same place. He looks as though he would as soon eat a man's throat as not."[15]

Richardson reported for duty at Fort Stansbury, located on the Wakulla River, twelve miles south of Tallahassee. He was named executive officer of Company K, under command of Second Lieutenant Thomas Jordan. The fact that his new company commander had graduated the previous year from West Point was an indication of a shortage of company grade officers in the 3rd Infantry. Richardson and Jordan had been friends and classmates just the year before, and their familiarity made for an easy relationship between the commander and his executive officer.

Jordan was born on September 30, 1819, in Luray, Virginia, and entered the U.S. Military Academy in the summer of 1836. While not a bright student, (he was ranked forty-one of forty-two in his West Point class of 1840, where he had been William T. Sherman's roommate), he was a steady leader who constantly improved his skills throughout his career. Richardson described Fort Stansbury as a typical Florida outpost. "These different military posts were generally built upon the same plan, one line of log huts for the soldiers, and another parallel to it some 80 or 100 yards for the officers, and a square formed by filling up the other two sides with the guardhouse, commissary and quartermaster buildings with a parade ground in the center sufficiently large for drill and parade." Without sawmills, nails, or glass, the buildings were crudely built. "The open space between the logs was filled up with pieces of wood called chinking. The cracks in the floor served as the ingress for fleas, to which there was no end in number or measure, and the holes between the shingles admitted rain, which in the summer was endless.

"These posts were generally built and finished in about two months after being commenced; only one half of the garrison working upon them, the other half being employed on scouting parties against the Indians. I speak, of course, of the effective garrison; which would be reduced as low as one third of the original strength, the other two thirds down with the chills and fever, a prevalent sickness here."[16]

The 3rd Infantry regiment carried out constant patrolling into every part of the country known or thought to be occupied by the Seminoles. In the campaigns of past years, the swamps had been avoided, and hence had been used as a sanctuary by the Indians. Slowly the net was being tightened around them by more aggressive scouting. Within weeks of arriving in Florida, Richardson found himself conducting offensive operations against the Indians. "Nothing could have suited me better; for I always had a greater taste for the active duties of the field than for the monotonous, and sedentary life in a garrison."[17] He describes his activities in a letter to his sister. "I have been on a scout with 10 men since I wrote before. Started at reveille in the morning with two days rations on our backs besides our arms and a blanket each. . . . heard plenty of bears and wolves; but no Indians. . . . Col. Worth's order now is that 2/5 of the troops at every post in Florida shall be constantly employed in scouts or movable camps, detached from the main garrison, having 3/5 at the garrison to relieve the others, and while the relief is going on leaving 8 or 10 men at the fort."[18]

After serving several months at Fort Stansbury, a vacancy within the regiment led to Richardson's promotion to full second lieutenant and a transfer to the company at Fort Pleasant, on the eastern extreme of the regimental sector. Under the command of Captain Wheeler, Richardson began to learn his craft as a soldier in the field. "As we carried not tent or camp equipment with us, we bivouacked at night with nothing but our blankets in the open air. Capt. Wheeler, being an old campaigner, would allow no fires after dark for fear of giving notice to the Indians of our presence in their country."[19]

The young lieutenant found these missions frustrating; "the troops not only had been up against stern difficulties which were full enough of themselves, but were expected to find and fight the Indians, who after committing an outrage on the inhabitants, would probably not be seen again in that vicinity for months." Richardson believed these tactics were ineffectual: "Ten days supply of provisions on the men's backs was, I believe, the largest quantity taken out by any scouting party; and this together with musket, ammunition, and blankets so loaded down the soldiers that he could with difficulty make 20 miles per day through the swamp; and at the end of the day might well be farther from the Indians he was in pursuit of than when he started. The swamps afforded them protection where a white man could not follow; and an Indian could travel day after day."[20] He was correct in that the Indians were hardly ever caught while in "hot pursuit," but the constant harassment of the patrolling was effective in lowering the number of attacks on settlers.

The heat during summer months and exposure that the troops were subjected to, combined with contaminated water and spoiled rations, created an unhealthy environment. At Fort Stansbury, which Richardson considered a "healthy" post, ten 3rd Infantry soldiers had died in the previous five months, but only one of the deaths was from combat. In the summer of 1842, Richardson, now stationed at Charles Ferry, in eastern Florida, reported he suffered from chills and the "fever" for five straight days before taking a quinine treatment, which cured him. Army medical records at the time showed that out of six hundred men under Colonel William J. Worth's command, 130 were sent to the hospital, unfit for duty.

The inexperienced second lieutenant struggled to find a way to discipline his men in a harsh climate and small-unit atmosphere. He related his hard lessons to his family: "A great many of the soldiers run away from camp, a mile or two and buy liquor from the citizens, or *crackers*, as they are called. I am very severe with drunken soldiers. I had twelve men of the company in the guardhouse at one time for getting drunk. One man I let off lightly, twice for his promises. Well, one day as I was hunting about a mile from camp, this man was passing me about 10 or 15 rods off with two jugs full of liquor, and I called him to stop and bring me the liquor, but he kept on and I called to him again, but he kept going on as fast as he could and looked at me once in a while.

"Now, I had a double barrel shotgun with fourteen buckshot in each barrel and told the man if he did not stop I would shoot him, and accordingly got it all ready to fire and was just about firing when the man came towards me to give up the whiskey. I certainly would have shot him if he had not. Well, I emptied the man's whiskey out on the ground very coolly and lectured him about fifteen minutes and concluded by ordering him to report to the sergeant of the guard, and stay in the guardhouse until I got through hunting and came into camp.

"The man, instead of obeying, went towards camp, laid down and was picked up drunk by the sergeant. I had the man kept in the stocks the rest of the day; and every day since, which is about a month, having had him chop wood with the sentinel over him in the daylight and in the night have him in the guardhouse. I expect he will be kept the same way for a month longer. There is no use punishing soldiers lightly. If so, they only laugh at it afterwards; as for lying, they will lie as far as a dog can trot—"[21]

The method of strict discipline practiced by Richardson and his fellow officers, however effective, was also dangerous and had to be enforced evenhandedly. This necessity was evidenced by an episode in a neighboring company concerning Richardson's classmate, Don Carlos Buell. During an engagement with the Seminoles, Lieutenant Buell led a charge. Buell received a shot, which cut his belt in a manner that dropped one end of his scabbard, entangling it in the brush and throwing him to the ground. Immediately he said to the fellow officer, "That shot did not come from the enemy." To which the quick reply was, "You may be sure it did not come from any friend."[22]

Another aspect of learning his craft as a soldier came with camp management. An onerous duty, usually given to the most junior officer, dealt with supply. Richardson explained his additional duties to his sister: "I go to Fort Pleasant tomorrow with an escort and wagon for commissary stores for this post. I have a great many papers to make out every month for the quartermaster and commissary at Washington. I have to give receipts for every article of provisions and quartermaster stores turned over to me for the use at this post. I make out a certified list of expenditures and provisions for the month and a great many others, making a very large package. Every ration of pork, flour, hard bread, beans, sugar, coffee in the commissary dept. and in the quartermaster dept. every horse, saddle, bridle, blanket, wagon, mule train, wagon cover, water bucket, axes, hatchet, tent and many other articles too numerous to mention, have to be accounted for, and if lost, the quartermaster has it to pay—"[23]

For Israel Richardson this first year of soldiering was the perfect building block for the rest of his career in the army. In Florida he learned the importance of taking care of his personal health, as well as that of his men. In the future he would lead his men as he was taught by the old regulars from the 3rd Infantry: by example, with firm standards, but with care and compassion.

In later years, he would look back nostalgically to his first experiences in leading troops. "The soldier, besides his proper equipment of musket, cartridge box, containing forty rounds of cartridges, blanket, knife spoon and tin cup for cooking, was loaded down with his possessions; without which he was unable to travel for any length of time. The possessions, blanket and cooking utensils of the officer were packed upon a packhorse or mule which was led by one of the party; the officer always marching with his men on foot. Not withstanding their privations, for the short time I was in the country, I never remember having a complaint or murmur among the troops, and the men seemed to enjoy themselves as well as afterwards in regular garrisons."[24]

"I am absolutely sick of this country"

On October 10, 1842, the new commander of the 3rd Infantry arrived at Fort Stansbury and inspected the regiment. He was a seasoned leader who left an immediate impression on young Richardson that would continue for the next five years. Lieutenant Colonel Ethan Allen Hitchcock, the grandson of Ethan Allen of Vermont, was a soldier who had spent his whole career as a trainer in the army. Hitchcock was a graduate of West Point in 1817, during its earliest days, and served as an instructor and later as commandant of the corps of cadets. A visiting officer remarked, "It's a delight to watch Hitchcock handle his men."[25]

Hitchcock emphasized training while the 3rd Infantry were in cantonment, with ample attention given to parades and exercises. Drill and ceremonies were pursued so energetically that the unit earned a reputation as being a "crack" regiment. The tradition of precise drill and discipline was established and maintained by the unit for years, extending even to its service in Mexico.

Tactics changed to longer-range scouting expeditions. Richardson described one patrol deep into Seminole territory: "During this trip of a month's duration, although constantly traveling either on land or water, we never even got sight of an Indian. On one or two occasions we came on to their camps which had just been abandoned, where they left their fires burning, and fish boiling on the coals; but the secret of the whole was they were always on the lookout, saw us before we could find them, and owing to the swamp, which skirted all along the banks of the rivers, and their perfect knowledge of the country, they always succeeded in eluding our pursuit, the water leaving no trail for us to follow."[26]

However, by August 1842, constant patrolling pressure on the Seminoles forced one of the last remaining groups, led by Tiger Tail, to surrender. This event led Colonel Worth to declare to the troops that the war was near an end. Rumors of troop movements were a subject of one of Richardson's letters home: "Col. Vose tells me that the 4th Infy is expected to go out soon. I hear the 8th Regt. is expected to go too, leaving the 3rd Infy, which is the last to go. If it does not go out by this time next year, I should like to resign and go home for I am absolutely sick of this country and firmly believe I never should like it, from the first day I saw the land from the ship nearly a year ago. The water which we drink is of the color of rum and molasses, exactly like the swamp water of the north. . . . I had another attack of the chills and fever since I last wrote you from Charles Ferry, but got rid of it by taking plenty of quinine."[27]

As the wheels were in motion for the withdrawal of the army from Florida, Lieutenant Colonel Hitchcock left Fort Stansbury in December of 1842 to pursue the last large group of Seminoles left in the northern portion of the territory. Two friendly Creeks accompanied the expedition and, within four days, returned with the senior Seminole chief, Pascofa. After a week of negotiations, the last ragged band of fifty Indians came to terms and the Seminole War was closed for the last time. In his diary, Hitchcock wrote, "I have succeeded quite beyond my hopes. By a little show of kindness, which is very easy to show when it is felt, I have won Pascofa's heart. General Worth says I have saved the government fifty thousand dollars."[28]

The long-awaited orders arrived from Washington on March 20, 1843, transferring the regiment to Jefferson Barracks, on the Mississippi River. With this, the first chapter of Israel Richardson's apprenticeship in leadership was closed. In less than two years since his graduation from West Point, he had participated in his first active operation, one characterized by long patrols deep into enemy-held land, resulting in either short, violent actions or frustration. During this campaign, the 3rd Infantry lost three officers and sixty-five enlisted men in action or to disease. Assigned temporarily as company commander since January 26, 1842, Richardson had to quickly learn the art of small unit leadership. His company of sixty-two soldiers contained no other officers and only four sergeants to help him learn his task.

Jefferson Barracks was the U.S. Army's command and logistical base on the edge of the western frontier. The news was thrilling to Richardson, who wrote his family, "From New Orleans we shall go up the Mississippi River in steamboats. I anticipate much pleasure during our passage from Port Leon to Jefferson Barracks. . . . I had some attacks of the chills and fever lately, but expect to get over them on leaving the territory. I think the majority of the officers are pleased at leaving this country. As for myself, I shall pray for a keel propelling gale to get away from this land as fast as possible."[29]

As the Florida climate was becoming increasingly unhealthy for Richardson, he was grateful for the new assignment out west and put aside his thoughts of resignation. Embarking on two riverboats, the *Maria* and *Ben Franklin*, the regiment traveled north, briefly stopping at Natchez, Vicksburg, and Memphis before reaching St. Louis five days later. Arriving in Jefferson Barracks, Richardson applied for and received a six-week furlough from General Gaines. Traveling east, he spent several weeks with his sister Susan and Uncle John who were living in Pontiac, Michigan, before continuing to Burlington to visit the rest of the family.

Returning to duty, Richardson occupied his time with military amenities, social diversions, and a continued effort to sustain the proficiency that the regiment gained in Florida. A captain from the regiment was court-martialed and dismissed from the service during this period, and the event was noted in Lieutenant Colonel Hitchcock's diary: "This is the last of a set of men who were all drunkards. We have not now a regular drinker left in the 3rd Infantry, and but few who touch liquor at all."[30]

Jefferson Barracks, one of the largest army installations in the country, gave Richardson the opportunity to expand his circle of friends and role models from outside the regiment. Ulysses S. Grant and James Longstreet, with whom he became particularly close, were lieutenants in the 4th Infantry, and George Sykes had recently been assigned to the 3rd Infantry. Another friend of Richardson, Lieutenant Richard S. Ewell, gave an indication of the priorities of these young officers in a letter to his brother in August 1844. "This is the worst country for single ladies I ever saw in my life. Except for the Miss Garlands (daughters of the regimental commander of the 4th Infantry) I have not seen a pretty girl or interesting one since I have been here."[31]

Colonel Stephen Kearny, the post commander, along with Lieutenant Colonel Hitchcock and Lieutenant Colonel John Garland of the 4th Infantry, were great mentors to the junior officers. The training stressed not only drill and discipline but also theory and "high mental culture" and gave the two regiments the reputation of being the premier units in the army at the time.

The schooling was intense and kept the regiment busy throughout the week. "Here now commenced a system of drill and discipline which was to prepare the troops for again taking the field," wrote Richardson. "Two drills every day except Sunday were kept up during our stay there. Company drills in the morning and battalion drill in the afternoon, with a parade in the evening."[32]

"The kind of service which is coming, is the kind which I like, and have been anxiously waiting for"

On April 20, 1845, Richardson's quiet garrison duties came to an abrupt end. The 3rd Infantry was ordered to Fort Jessup, in southwestern Louisiana, within twenty miles of the Texas frontier. "All was now enthusiasm, confusion and preparation for departure," wrote Richardson. "The cumbersome full dress uniform worn by the troops in garrison, which, by the way, was neither useful nor ornamental, was thrown off, and after being packed in boxes and turned over to the quartermaster department, the sky blue undress uniform for the field was substituted in its place. Within two days after the arrival of our orders, we were on our way."[33]

The 4th Infantry followed a month later, and for the remainder of the year, regiments from all over the country gathered as the diplomats argued. President Polk chose Zachary Taylor to command the expedition. "Old Rough and Ready" was always prepared to do anything that he asked his men to do. Taylor's distaste for military pomp and ceremony was legendary; his casual dress made him look more like a farmer than a general.

The 3rd Infantry wintered at Camp Wilkins, adjacent to Fort Jessup, now filled by the 2nd Dragoons commanded by Colonel David Twiggs. The fort was austere, with Richardson complaining that "the officers have few amusements except what the library affords, there is a billiard table here and the theatre is open twice a week, although the actors are very indifferent. Our prospect for Texas, is at present, very fair."[34] On March 1, 1845, Congress voted to annex Texas. Taylor's Army of Observation changed to an Army of Occupation.

On July 7 the 3rd Infantry marched from Fort Jessup to the Natchitoches River and boarded the steamer *Alabama*, accompanied by General Taylor, bound for New Orleans. Writing his mother, Richardson told of his excitement: "Well, here we are, at last encamped under the sheds at the lower cotton press of the Crescent City. We are only a mile and a half from the St. Charles Hotel, I have wandered nearly every street in the city, although we have been here but a week. We have just returned from the funeral of Col. Vose of the 4th Infantry. He died about a minute after leaving drill at the barracks."[35] The death of Colonel Josiah H. Vose was another symptom of the lack of a military pension system. As old and decrepit as Vose was, Lieutenant Grant was proud his commander was "not a man to discover infirmity in the presence of danger."[36] Vose forced himself out of his rocking chair on the parade ground where he gave two or three orders, grew faint, and died.

Leaving New Orleans bound for Texas, Richardson arrived at Corpus Christi and found the area quite agreeable. "I have fine times here fishing, and have caught red fish weighing 10 pounds, as fast as I throw in my line. . . . shade here is not necessary, as the trade winds from the south blow fresh and steadily without intermission during the whole day and night and our tents are quite comfortable."[37]

The site grew into the main staging base for the American army as it prepared to enforce the government demand of the Rio Grande border. By the first of October, there were almost four thousand soldiers in camp. Officers and soldiers known only to each other by their reputations in the far-flung army now were able to become personally acquainted, and silently measured each other up. Richardson wrote to his father that he was now serving with the best-known soldier from Vermont, Captain Martin Scott, so famous throughout the army for his marksmanship that the story was told of a raccoon, realizing that he was the intended target of the famed sharpshooter, came down out of his tree and voluntarily surrendered.

On October 23, Richardson along with other officers from the 3rd Infantry had a chance to organize a three-day hunting expedition along the Nueces River. Hunting separately, Richardson left his pony to shoot a deer and after butchering it was unable to find his horse. He returned to the hunting camp after dark on foot, marking his way with geese that he shot on his return to mark the trail back to his pony the next morning.[38] Later on the trip, in the company of Lieutenant Barnard Bee, Richardson claimed the pair "killed at a single shot from our guns, upwards of ninety snipe of different sizes and returned to camp with a horse packed down with game of different kinds."[39]

The U.S. Army, except for the few hundreds who served in the successful but undistinguished campaign against the Seminoles, had known almost no activity beyond peace-keeping duty in widely scattered frontier garrisons. The four thousand men gathered on the Mexican border represented the largest single army command since the days of George Washington, seventy years before.

Since the War of 1812, the army had been forced to divide its regiments into small detachments manning more than one hundred posts throughout the country. Regiments had been divided up for so long into smaller units that large-unit training had ceased. The plight of the senior leadership was summed up by Lieutenant Ewell's command philosophy: learn all there was to know about handling fifty men and forget everything else.[40]

During their first attempts at large-scale maneuvering, neither Taylor nor Colonel William Whistler could form a brigade into line. Lieutenant Colonel Hitchcock noted, "Whistler cannot give the simplest command, and Garland could not possibly dispose the brigade for battle. Egotism or no egotism, I am the only field officer on the ground who can change a single position of the troops according to any but a militia code. I can do anything with the 3rd Infantry, for every officer and every man knows his place and duty."[41]

It seemed that most of the inhabitants of Corpus Christi had some motivation to flee Texas for one reason or another. Lieutenant Abner Doubleday noted that the citizens of Corpus Christi were men who found even the freedom of the Lone Star State too much for them. "Isn't it strange," he commented, "that every gentleman I have been introduced to, has killed somebody."[42] Writing his father, Richardson described how the camp of Taylor's army had begun to take on a life of its own. "All is quiet here, except a murder now and then; I wonder why Gen'l Taylor don't proclaim Martial Law in the town, as there is no civil law in force there and murders are continually perpetrated, and the authors escape with impunity—this place, which consisted at our arrival here, of only a dozen houses and stores, now contains some two hundred of different sorts. A theatre is now in operation and affords some amusement—Although the people of the town are ruled among themselves by such a murderous and revengeful spirit, I have noticed in general, that they are very civil and polite toward the officers."

He went on to boast about his own living conditions. "Our situation here, exposed in tents to blasts of cold Northerners, would be comfortless in the extreme if we had not hit upon a novel method of getting warm—And I lay credit to myself of having had the honor of originating in our Brigade. I made a fireplace at one end of my tent of sods and logs, a chimney of barrels by driving the ends of three into each other—In one day the sods became as hard as bricks and my chimney works admirably well, and I can keep as warm as I please—Within a week, nearly all of the officers followed my example, and I am writing to you, sitting by a good fire in very cold weather."[43]

After wintering at Corpus Christi, Taylor was ordered to establish a base on the north side of the Rio Grande, across from the Mexican town of Matamoros. Richardson was elated by the news and sent word to his family: "The troops are ordered to march; and now 'Huzzah' for the Rio Grande. . . . The army is in a fine state of discipline and all except the sick are in fine spirits—My health was never better and I am perfectly delighted with this march. The kind of service which is coming, is the kind which I like, and have been anxiously waiting for sometime—Give my love to all the family."[44]

In an adjoining company, Lieutenant Robert Hazlitt wrote his family, "A better little army than this never took the field. This move of the army is a sad blow to Corpus Christi, it rose with the army and it will fall without it. The streets are deserted, and the public places no longer resound with mirth and revelry. The theaters are closed and the gamblers are gone. Thus lament the Corpus Christians, the worst set of Christians under the sun. Many of them will 'take up their beds and walk' to the Rio Grande to prey on us."[45]

Richardson's Company H, along with Company D, 4th Infantry, led the army, marching out early to establish a depot of provisions and forage at a river crossing on the San Getrudes, about fifty miles south of Corpus Christi. On March 28, 1846, as the army arrived on the Rio Grande two hundred yards opposite the town of Matamoros, Taylor ordered the regimental colors unfurled and the fifes and drums to play as the army marched into camp along the banks of the river. Both armies were now poised in front of each other, and only time would tell whether the Mexicans would accept the forced annexation of Texas.

Some indications were given on April 6 to that outcome, as Richardson wrote that one of General Taylor's spies, a soldier named Clegg from the 8th Infantry, had just returned to camp after spending four days within Mexican lines. He had crossed the river and gave himself up to the Mexicans, claiming to be a deserter. Clegg discovered that the Mexican garrison consisted of thirty-eight hundred troops and that thirty-five hundred more, under General Pedro Ampudia, were expected soon. Although the Mexicans had over thirty pieces of artillery on hand, Clegg noted that many of them were old and inferior, honeycombed with rotted carriages. Clegg claimed that when the Mexicans were reinforced, they were expected to attack the Americans in the rear.

The news prompted Taylor to begin construction of a permanent fort for increased protection. Ground was selected on the riverbank about fifteen hundred yards from Matamoros on the opposite side of the river. This put the city within range of the four eighteen-pound artillery pieces that Taylor had brought with him from Point Isabel. Each brigade assigned half of its strength to labor on the building round the clock. The fort consisted of six bastions and a parapet nine feet thick, surrounded by a ditch twenty-four feet wide and twelve feet deep. Richardson thought, "If we get four or five days to work upon it, we can stand an assault of all the Mexicans who get around it."[46] War seemed inevitable, but before the first shot was fired, three officers from Taylor's army handed in their resignations. Richardson noted that General Taylor observed "if officers who had until then received their support from the government chose that time for retiring, the sooner they left, the better."[47]

On April 25, Taylor received word that a large Mexican force crossed the Rio Grande, twenty-seven miles above him, in an attempt to cut him off from his base of supplies. A cavalry patrol of sixty-five dragoons was sent to investigate and was ambushed in a narrow road, with the whole command taken prisoner at the loss of sixteen dead. "Hostilities may be considered to have commenced," Taylor wrote President Polk. "American blood has been spilled." Mexican general Mariano Arista's intention was to cut Taylor's lifeline of supplies and then finish off the American force, but he moved too slowly. Taylor quickly withdrew to protect his supplies and beef up the defenses at Point Isabel, leaving a rear guard of five hundred men of the 7th Infantry under Major Jacob Brown at the fort.

Brown was an enlisted veteran of the War of 1812 who had been promoted from the ranks for gallantry. He was a tough soldier and a good choice to command the rear guard. As Taylor mounted his horse to leave, the officers of the 7th Infantry gathered around to bid farewell. Understanding that they would be attacked soon, he promised to return as quickly as possible. "Gentlemen, this fort has no name. It will be named for the first officer who falls here."[48]

Taylor saved his ill-equipped army with a twenty-five-mile forced march to Point Isabel, but now Arista's force of almost four thousand men was between him and his rear guard, conducting an artillery attack to force the fort's surrender. Major Brown was wounded at the very beginning of the siege and died three days later. Richardson reported that at reveille at Point Isabel on May 3, he could hear a heavy cannonading from the direction of the fort, continuing until noon. He supposed the fight was going well for the Americans, as he could distinguish the sound between the heavier U.S. batteries and the Mexican guns.

As quickly as he could, Taylor strengthened the defense of Point Isabel, re-supplied his army, and marched back to the relief of his rear guard. Lieutenant Colonel Hitchcock had been ordered north on sick leave on April 13, leaving the 3rd Infantry under the command of Captain Lewis N. Morris, a West Point graduate of 1820, the senior company commander of the regiment.

General Taylor marched out of Point Isabel on May 7 and the next day, at noon, found the Mexican force deployed nine miles north of Matamoros. The ground selected by the Mexicans consisted of an extensive plain, skirted by a thick growth of mesquite bushes, called Palo Alto. Taylor deployed his force on line: the 5th Infantry, on the right; then Ringgold's battery; the 3rd Infantry; a two-gun battery of eighteen pounders; the 4th Infantry; a battalion of artillery, acting as infantry; Duncan's battery; and finally, on the left, the 8th Infantry. As the two armies were arrayed on the field within sight of each other, General Taylor could feel the tension and calmly ordered all canteens filled before commencing the attack. "After resting at the pond for half an hour, the rolling of our drums again called 'to arms,' and our march resumed."[49]

The line advanced until the puff of smoke from the Mexican guns rose, and a cannonball bounded over the infantry and wounded a teamster far in the rear. At that, Taylor ordered the infantry down and the artillery to work. It was an artillery fight more than a battle, and held that way for much of the afternoon. Richardson observed that "none of our shot was without effect, if they missed the first line of enemy, they produced great destruction among his reserve. The great superiority of the American artillery being now manifest and every shot of ours was having immense effect upon the enemy; while very few of our troops were injured, as most of the shot of the enemy passed over our heads. Our infantry was directed to sit on the ground to avoid the distant cannonade, and the battle continued with our artillery. After continuing the cannonade about an hour, the enemy, finding his masses of troops much cut up, attempted to turn our right flank with a large body of his lancers, and by that means, take us in the rear."

The Mexican cavalry made a charge against the 5th Infantry, which formed into a square and was supported by the 3rd Infantry. Richardson witnessed the Mexican lancers forming up for the charge: "The 5th Infantry being stationed at this point, formed itself into a square to repel cavalry, and the lancers fired their pistols as they came on at a charge, endeavoring to make our men fire at too great a distance, but our troops were in too good a state of discipline to be deceived by such a maneuver. The men were cautioned by their officers, and at the word to fire, given when the lancers had arrived within 16 paces of the square, most of their column rolled from their saddles and the rest retreated faster than they advanced."

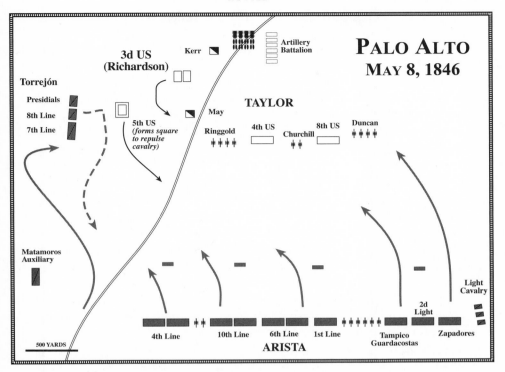

PALO ALTO
MAY 8, 1846

3d US
(Richardson)

Kerr

Artillery
Battalion

Torrejón

Presidials

8th Line

7th Line

5th US
*(forms square
to repulse
cavalry)*

May

TAYLOR

Ringgold

4th US

Churchill

8th US

Duncan

Matamoros
Auxiliary

Light
Cavalry

2d
Light

500 YARDS

4th Line

10th Line

6th Line

1st Line

Tampico
Guardacostas

Zapadores

ARISTA

After losing twenty-five lancers to the frontal attack, the cavalry repeated the same maneuver on the flank but were repulsed there also. During the artillery exchange, the grass caught fire, and the winds swept the smoke into the Mexican lines. When it cleared, it was discovered that the Mexicans had drawn back a little. Richardson recognized the danger: "The smoke having now cleared off, our artillery opened with grape and canister; a destructive fire upon the enemy's line at a distance of 250 yards. It now became evident that the enemy intended to make a general charge upon our line, and a large body of troops, consisting of some 2,000 infantry were formed in columns of attack supported by masses of cavalry on their flanks, for the purpose of carrying Duncan's artillery with the bayonet." Seeing this, Taylor advanced the right of his line, which consisted of the 3rd and 8th Infantry regiments, and the batteries of Duncan and Ringgold were put to work breaking up this enemy formation. As Richardson saw it, "Although these troops were urged on by the swords of their officers, their column could not advance a foot; three times did their columns of attack break to the rear, being cut up by the crossfire of our artillery with grape and shrapnel shell, and as often were reformed for the attack, until the last time, when they broke and fled in utter confusion.

For the last hour and a half of this battle, our artillery cut up their lines with grape and shrapnel shell, each containing seventy musket balls; while the fire of their artillery was nearly silenced; and toward the close of the action, they hardly answered us with a single solitary gun.

"The enemy now gave way at all points in confusion, leaving us entire masters of the field, and soon night put an end to the contest. If daylight had continued for half an hour longer, there is little doubt but that the destruction of the enemy's army would have been complete. Our army now encamped upon the ground the enemy had occupied, and prepared next day to pursue his retreat."[50]

At the close of the battle, the Americans were substantially in control of the ground held by the Mexicans at the beginning. Taylor's casualties were nine killed and forty-seven wounded, including Major Samuel Ringgold, whose "flying artillery" was credited for the American victory. Mexican losses were more than five hundred killed. The Mexican and American infantry were equally well armed, but the Mexican artillery fired only solid shot, while the Americans were armed with explosive shell and larger-caliber guns.

To Richardson, the results of the first encounter with Mexican forces confirmed his opinion that training and doctrine could beat raw numbers any day. He boasted, "I don't think any troops can be found in any country in a better state of discipline, or who can maneuver quicker or with more precision than our regulars. The facility and quickness with which our infantry formed from line to column and from column into line, and from column or line into squares at the battle of Palo Alto, under the enemy's fire, showed conclusively that the firmness of the courage of our troops, added to the scientific perfection in the knowledge of the movement and different positions which troops should occupy, more than counterbalanced the immense superiority of the numbers of the enemy."[51]

With the exhilarating feeling of victory, but the knowledge of a probable fight tomorrow, the army bedded down for the night on the battlefield. The dangers that had passed during the day were soon forgotten, and the whole army; except for a strong line of sentinels, were buried in slumber. Soon a distant trampling of horses was heard, the alarm was given, and the whole army stood to their arms. Still, the guards had not fired their muskets, and on further examination, the sound was discovered to come from a herd of wolves, who in large numbers were feasting on the bodies of the slain that lay surrounding the camp.[52]

Early the next morning, May 9, 1846, Taylor learned that the Mexican force had retreated to a new position straddling the road, blocking him from relieving Major Brown. Taylor parked his supply train, issued muskets to the teamsters, mustered them into the army, and marched off in pursuit of the Mexican force.

General Arista formed his second position three miles away, at a dry lake bed surrounded by thick chaparral, called Resaca de la Palma. Taylor would have preferred to repeat his easy victory of the day before by pounding the enemy with artillery, but the chaparral was so thick that long-range fire had no visible effect; even command and control of his infantry units were difficult. The fighting soon degenerated into a series of small unit actions. The key to Arista's position was the road running through the dry lake bed and on to the fort. Taylor decided to charge his way through by ramming all his infantry and artillery through the line as close to the road as possible. With the 3rd and 4th infantry regiments on the left side of the road, and the 5th and 8th infantry regiments on the right, Taylor advanced. As artillery fired down the middle of the road and the Mexican batteries answered, Taylor ordered Captain May's dragoons to charge, followed by the 8th Infantry.

Lieutenant Richardson was leading his company forward as best he could through the thorny brush. "Our officers and men rushed to the charge like perfect bloodhounds. Two of our officers fell in the first charge, they have had a lesson they will long remember."[53] The terrain broke up the regiment into small parties, with grape and canister fire whipping past their ears and small shot falling thickly among them. Small groups of Mexicans and Americans stumbled into each other, and desperate hand-to-hand fighting ensued. Lieutenant U. S. Grant, fighting in the neighboring regiment, described it as a "pell-mell affair, everybody for himself."[54] There was not enough time to reload muskets, and both sides fought with bayonets. Gradually, the Mexican troops fell back, and a battery massed in the center of the Mexican position, on the road, was captured. Once this center battery fell to the Americans, the Mexican line suddenly crumbled. The pursuit by American units, all in one mass and at a full run, was kept up for three miles to the Rio Grande.

Occasionally, the Mexicans gave indications of making a stand. Captain Phillip N. Barbour with twelve men of Company J, 3rd Infantry, rallied a detachment from the 4th Infantry. They were retreating from a large body of Mexican cavalry and together fought off the charge, emptying many saddles in the process. For his actions, the 1834 graduate of West Point was brevetted to the rank of major by General Taylor. Richardson and his company continued the pursuit all the way to the river, capturing much of the Mexican army supplies, including eight pieces of artillery, twenty wagonloads of ammunition, five hundred pack mules, and the personal baggage of General Arista, which included a large quantity of silver.

Private George Chisholm, in Richardson's Company H, 3rd Infantry, was cited for his gallant conduct. He fought with courage and tenacity, killing many of the enemy. After being wounded, Chisholm still continued firing. He died, after being hit a third time, with a cartridge in his fingers, in the act of

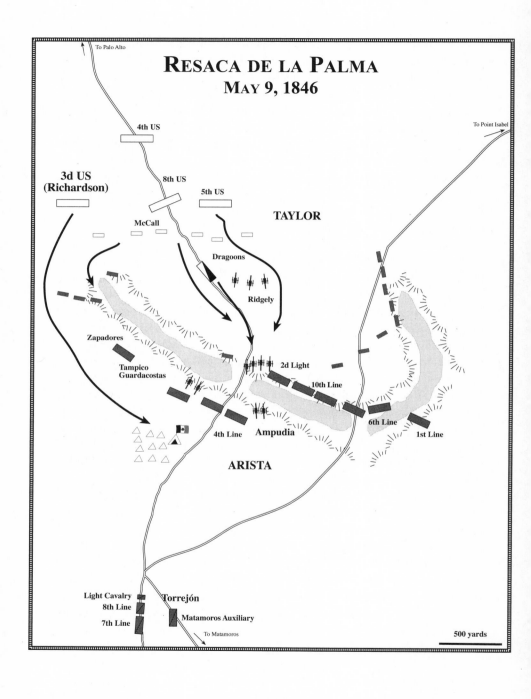

RESACA DE LA PALMA
MAY 9, 1846

To Palo Alto

To Point Isabel

4th US

3d US
(Richardson)

8th US

5th US

TAYLOR

McCall

Dragoons

Ridgely

Zapadores

Tampico
Guardacostas

2d Light

10th Line

6th Line

1st Line

4th Line

Ampudia

ARISTA

Light Cavalry
8th Line

Torrejón

Matamoros Auxiliary

7th Line

To Matamoros

500 yards

tearing it, surrounded by a pile of Mexican dead. Private Moore, in Captain Barbour's Company J, was another example of bravery and discipline. A ball passed through his cartridge box and exploded all his ammunition, tearing his box to pieces and setting his uniform on fire. At first Moore was unaware that his clothes were burning, and finding his box missing, he turned to the next man and borrowed another cartridge. While in the act of tearing the cartridge open with his teeth, his sleeve caught fire, which exploded the cartridge near his mouth, singeing off his eyebrows.[55]

Richardson proudly wrote to his father that "the best troops Mexico could produce were arrayed against us and in a strong position of their own choice, but the last general charge of our entire line with fixed bayonets, they could not withstand, and they broke and fled to the river being fired upon by our troops and also the guns in the fort. Arriving at the river, they plunged in after throwing away their arms and an immense quantity of them perished in the water. This victory may be considered as one of the greatest laurels achieved by the American army whether we consider the immense disparity of the forces engaged or the genuine and real courage and resolution of every officer and man in the army to beat the enemy at all points, and at every layer from the field."[56]

The relief of the rear guard had been achieved; the Mexicans retreated to Matamoros and were preparing to abandon the town. The fort had held out for four days under constant bombardment, with only two killed. Major Brown had been wounded early in the siege by an artillery shell that took off his leg below the knee. An amputation was done, but he died of fever as the relief column was approaching. The other fatality was Sergeant Horace Weigart, to whom the Mexicans were unusually cruel. He died immediately after being hit in the chin by a piece of shrapnel. His body was carried to the hospital tent where within minutes another shell landed and decapitated him. He was quietly buried outside the fort that night, and the next day another shell landed on his grave and disinterred the body. Fort Texas was renamed Fort Brown, in honor of its fallen commander, later becoming the city of Brownsville, Texas.

The American losses at Resaca de la Palma were thirty-three dead and eighty-nine wounded, while the Mexican losses were estimated at twelve hundred. The nation was electrified by the news of the victory, and swarms of volunteers; more than Taylor could support, began arriving in camp eager to be a part of the conquest of Mexico. General Taylor was modest in the face of news that he was now an idol at home, and politicians were proposing him for president. The low-key approach to his newly acquired fame was refreshing to his soldiers. To young admiring officers like Richardson and Grant, this was the way for a great general to act.

The character of Taylor's army began to change with the large influx of reinforcements. Resentment to the newcomers was described by Lieutenant

George Meade: "The volunteers continue to pour in, they are perfectly ignorant of discipline, and in consequence a most disorderly mass, who give us, I fear, more trouble than the enemy."[57]

Richardson also expressed doubt in the growing number of reinforcements. "The General has no sort of confidence in the volunteers, and will base none of the operations of the campaign upon them. He says his whole dependence is upon his regulars, or veterans, as he calls them. They are not in the proper discipline and I don't believe they will stand fire when they come to the scratch. The truth is also that one volunteer will waste, destroy and lose more arms, provisions and ammunition than any four regular soldiers you can pick out."[58]

More volunteers than Taylor could support now occupied camps around Matamoros as he built up his army to move against Monterrey. The crowded camps soon became disease-ridden, because the lack of discipline and leadership for troop welfare among volunteers led to many unnecessary deaths. The Louisiana regiment was sent home after three months' service without seeing any action but with a loss of 145 of their roster, twenty-five fewer than the total dead and wounded from the battles of Palo Alto and Resaca de la Palma. Rampant disease, bred from filthy camps and contaminated food and water, along with constant exposure to the elements, were the principal killers. By the war's end, 1,721 Americans would be killed in action, while 11,155 would die from disease.

On May 17, Major William W. Lear joined the badly depleted 3rd Infantry as the new regimental commander and Captain Morris returned to company command. Lear was well received by the regiment; he had begun his career fighting in the War of 1812 as an enlisted man and was commissioned as a second lieutenant in 1818. He had been promoted to major in 1842 and was a reliable leader. Due to the attrition of the regulars, General Taylor ordered a reorganization of the regiment from ten companies to six. Several of the junior officers, including second lieutenants Barnard E. Bee and Oliver L. Shepherd, were sent home on recruiting duty. The remaining companies were now only sixty-two men strong, but they were well led. Second Lieutenant Richardson was assigned as the executive officer for Company H, under command of Captain George P. Field, a West Point graduate of 1836.

The next two months were spent awaiting reinforcements and gearing up for the expected campaign to capture the principal cities in northern Mexico. Victories at Palo Alto and Resaca de la Palma had given the regulars the confidence that they could defeat any Mexican force. The Mexicans had been beaten in the open field and in dense thickets; soon the Americans would find out how they would fight behind fortified walls.

The 3rd Infantry embarked on the steamer *I. E. Roberts* for the trip up the Rio Grande, bound for Camargo, on July 28. There they were met by the 5th and

7th infantry regiments at the forward base that Taylor had selected to conduct operations against Monterrey, and waited for the remainder of the army and supplies to concentrate before moving forward. Finally, on September 5, the 1st Division of the army, commanded by General David Twiggs, moved out toward Monterrey. Captain William Henry, of the 3rd Infantry, wrote in his journal that reports of interlocking fields of fire from several batteries and the main fortress, called the Citadel, along with the rumored ten thousand Mexican soldiers in Monterrey, where stone buildings with flat roofs and straight streets made each house a strongpoint, caused "even the old regulars to open their eyes, to say nothing of the volunteers."[59]

Richardson complained that the "weather here is the hottest I ever have felt, from 9 in the morning until 4 in the afternoon, the army cannot make over 12 or 15 miles per day. I have no doubt but that we shall beat the Mexicans at Monterrey worse than we did at Matamoros, but if there is any fighting to be done, the regular troops will have it to do. I don't think any troops can be found in any country in a better state of discipline, or who can maneuver quicker or with more precision than our regulars."[60] Lieutenant Robert Hazlitt, in his last letter home, described the army's march to its objective: "I have walked all the way from Camargo to this place. All our officers walk except Generals, Colonels and Majors. When the soldiers see their officers walking by their sides, they will walk better and be ashamed to give out. I am not the least fatigued, for we only march 12 miles per day."[61]

The American advance guard, with General Taylor among them, came within sight of the fortress-city on the morning of September 19, 1846. As Taylor moved closer to inspect the defenses, guns from the Citadel, now labeled the "Black Fort" by the Americans, fired. When the third of the solid-shot cannonballs landed in front, then bounced over his head, Taylor and his staff slowly trotted back to camp and planned the attack for the next day. Richardson wrote, "The enemy are said to be in force at Monterrey and we shall probably have some hard fighting at that place."[62]

The key to the city was to capture the Bishop's Palace and the forts on the high ground on the west side of Monterrey, which would also cut off communication and reinforcements from Saltillo. But to get into attacking position, Taylor would be risking his flank and rear to fire from the Citadel. Taylor's solution was to split his already outnumbered force by sending General Worth and his 2nd Division on a turning movement to attack the west side of Monterrey. At the same time, Twiggs would provide protection from enemy attack and stage a demonstration to hold off the Mexicans in their front from reinforcing the west side of the city. A daring maneuver, considering the Americans were deep in enemy territory, greatly outnumbered, and now both wings of the army would be out of support of each other.

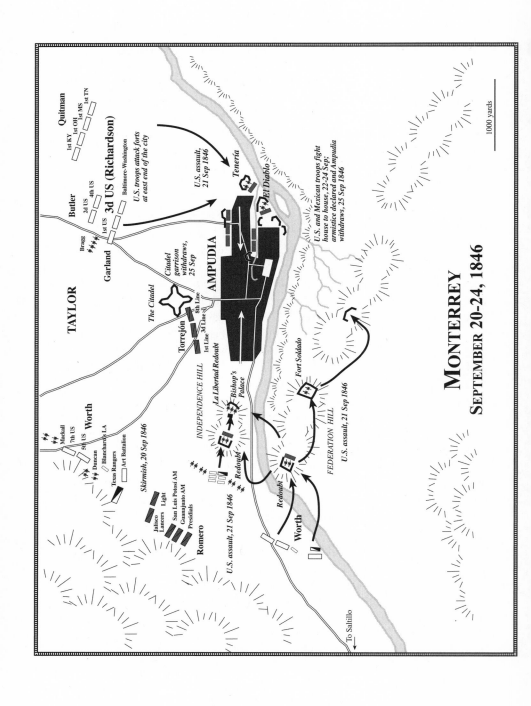

TAYLOR

Quitman
1st KY 1st OH 1st MS 1st TN

Butler
2d US 4th US

3d US (Richardson)
1st US

Baltimore-Washington

Garland

Bragg

U.S. troops attack forts at east end of the city

U.S. assault, 21 Sep 1846

Teneria

El Diablo

AMPUDIA

Citadel garrison withdraws, 25 Sep

The Citadel

U.S. and Mexican troops fight house to house, 22-24 Sep; armistice declared and Ampudia withdraws, 25 Sep 1846

Torrejón
1st Line 3d Line 8th Line

La Libertad Redoubt

Bishop's Palace

INDEPENDENCE HILL

Fort Soldado

FEDERATION HILL

U.S. assault, 21 Sep 1846

Worth
Mackall 7th US
5th US Duncan
Blanchard's LA
Texas Rangers
Art Battalion

Skirmish, 20 Sep 1846

Jalisco Lancers Light
San Luis Potosí AM
Guanajuato AM
Presidials

Romero

U.S. assault, 21 Sep 1846

Redoubt

Redoubt

Redoubt

Worth

To Saltillo

1000 yards

MONTERREY
SEPTEMBER 20-24, 1846

2

Apprenticeship

"It is almost impossible to see how any of us escaped"

At nine in the morning of September 21, 1846, a column consisting of the 1st Division of regular troops, accompanied by Major Mansfield, moved forward to begin the attack. The units conducting the demonstration were the 1st and 3rd infantry regiments and the Baltimore-Washington Battalion, each minus one company to guard the army trains at Walnut Springs. The 4th Infantry was to be in reserve, guarding the siege battery. The division, numbering about eight hundred men, was under the temporary command of Lieutenant Colonel John Garland. General Twiggs was sick; while preparing for battle the night before, he had taken an overdose of laxative on the theory that "a bullet striking the belly when the bowels are loose might pass through the intestines without cutting them!"[1]

Taylor's orders to Garland were to conduct a limited, diversionary attack with the goal of getting a foothold in the eastern suburbs. This would be accomplished by capturing the closest of the Mexican works, a fort built out of a commercial tannery known as the Teneria. This was a difficult objective because the building's flat roof and reinforced sandbagged walls held about two hundred Mexicans, who would be able to fire down on the approaching Americans. To get to the fort, Garland would have to work his way past several other smaller positions, which provided enfilading fire all along the approach. Taylor directed Garland to "lead the head of your column off to the left, keeping well out of reach of the enemy's shot, and if you think you can take any of them little forts down there with the bayonet, you'd better do it, but consult with Major Mansfield, you'll find him down there."[2]

Richardson studied the ground he was soon going to advance upon and noted, "The town was three miles in length, built of limestone. The walls of the houses are strongly constituted of masonry three to five feet thick. Immediately after the defeat last May, the Mexicans commenced the fortification of this place; and were constantly engaged at it until our attack. On the left of the city and at the ends of the streets, within musketry fire of each other, were placed four batteries and one square redoubt; having parapets of stone and ditches around them 12 feet wide and eight feet deep.

"These works were open at the rear, to secure a safe retreat of their garrisons into the city, openings to the rear were protected by parapets of stone being made across the streets within musketry range, then parapets or barricades across the streets were pierced with embrasures for artillery and loop-holed for muskets, and were again protected by other barricades of stone. In this way, three distinct systems of stone barricades in rear and within musket shot of each other were formed around the city. They evidently expected the attack at this place, and that here was to be the hard fighting."[3]

As the leading units emerged from a cornfield five hundred yards from the Teneria, the enemy began their artillery fire. Guns from the Citadel were brought to bear on Garland's right flank and rear, while the guns from El Diablo, the fort overlooking the first line of defense, and fire from the Teneria were hammering the front. The first rounds landed in front of the troops and had been bouncing over, but soon the Mexicans began to find the range.

As men fell, the officers tried to keep the advance organized. Private Barna Upton of Company C, 3rd Infantry, recalled, "We were ordered to cease firing and close to the right in to ranks. This was a trying moment; the noise of our guns had ceased and the smoke cleared away; the screams of our wounded were distinctly heard. I cast my eye along the ranks; what I expected and dreaded to see was there: the men sinking down every second all along."[4] The line steadily and rapidly advanced under this fire for five hundred yards until reaching the suburbs. Now, as Colonel Garland closed on the buildings along this ill-advised line of advance, intense small-arms fire forced the attack to veer to the right, exposing the left flank to direct fire from the Teneria.

Captain Henry, of the 3rd Infantry, recorded, "As we rushed into the streets, came suddenly upon an unknown battery which opened its deadly fire upon us. From all its embrasures, from every house, from every yard, showers of balls were hurled upon us. Being in utter ignorance of our locality, we had to stand and take it from every direction. On every side we were cut down."[5]

Under this heavy fire, in the narrow segmented streets, the attack formation quickly broke apart. Major Barbour was the first officer shot down. He was killed instantly as a bullet passed through his heart. The men carried Barbour's body and placed it in a house with the other dead and wounded. Major Mansfield, wounded in the leg, still pressed on.

Garland saw a defeat in the making and ordered the brigade to retire. In the confusion, not everybody received the word. Lieutenant Colonel William H.

Watson, commander of the Baltimore-Washington Battalion, when told of the order, took a drink from his canteen and exclaimed, "Never, boys! Never will I yield an inch! I have too much Irish blood in me to give up!"[6] More than likely, he had too much Irish whiskey in him, for he ignored the order. As he pressed forward, his horse was soon struck by a shot and fell dead. Watson continued forward on foot and shortly a ball severed his jugular vein and instantly killed him.

By this time, Taylor realized that Garland's attack was in trouble. He quickly committed the 4th Infantry to reinforce the attack and sent Major General William O. Butler's volunteer division to support it. Lieutenant U. S. Grant, detailed as quartermaster and whose place of duty was in the rear, heard the firing increase in intensity. "My curiosity got the better of my judgment, and I rode to the front to see what was going on, and lacking the moral courage to return to camp, where I had been ordered to stay, I charged with the regiment."[7] Although they advanced by a slightly different route and did not immediately join with Garland, they ran into the same buzz saw that was tearing up the 3rd Infantry. Two companies of the 4th Infantry came under such a murderous fire from the Teneria, they lost over one-third of their officers and men before falling back.

The situation now was on the verge of becoming a disaster. Reinforcements were arriving piecemeal from different routes, without coordination, and casualties were mounting by the minute. But when things looked the worst, Taylor got a break. Captain Electus Backus, of the 1st Infantry, and a party of fifty men turned left after entering the suburbs instead of right with the rest of the attacking force. This group was overlooked in the withdrawal and was left behind in a building to the rear of the Teneria. Climbing to the roof, Captain Backus found he had the perfect angle to fire down into the fort one hundred yards away. As the firing ceased, he finally received the order to retire. Backus was in the process of ordering his men out, when suddenly firing erupted again from the Teneria, signaling another uncoordinated assault, this time by the volunteer 1st Tennessee and Mississippi Rifles commanded by Colonel Jefferson Davis. On his own initiative, Backus reposted his group on the roof and supported the attack with a withering fire on the Teneria. Even with this support, the frontal attack was a bloody one for the volunteers, with the 1st Tennessee suffering twenty-five killed and seventy-five wounded, over one quarter of the day's losses, before storming over the walls and finally securing a foothold in the city.[8]

Perceptions of the fight varied with regard to different positions on the battlefield. Richardson described his company's actions later: "The attack commenced by the 3rd Infy. leading, followed by the 4th and 1st Regts. of regulars—We attacked the first three works we came to, and firing into the rear of the works, soon drove them out—Before the enemy left these works, however,

Gen. Taylor, hearing a heavy fire of musketry and artillery, immediately ordered up three Regts. of volunteers who were nearest us and charged the enemy's works, which had been left; entered them and found them empty, while we passed on to the next of the enemy's works to attack them—and the volunteers therefore say that they deserve credit of first entering these works which were deserted when we helped them.

"Capt. Backus says he entered the works after us with his Regt. and could have taken possession of them, but considered it no credit to take a work after the garrison was driven out. But Gen. Butler, commanding the Division of Volunteers, says in his report, 'that the enemy was driven out by the fire of the 3rd and 4th Infy.,' and gives us credit. Other officers in their reports, I believe, do the same.

"After moving on to the other works, we had expended nearly all of our cartridges, and it was thought not advisable to attack the next batteries until the men could get their boxes filled and take a short rest—After the fatigue of fighting all morning, they were therefore ordered into the captured batteries, slowly and in good order, and many of our troops, both regular and volunteer, were now employed in strengthening the captured works and annoying the enemy from there. Lt. Ridgely's battery and four guns taken from the enemy were worked as fast as they could be got under cover, the enemy firing into us all the time with shells, grape and musketry."[9]

With the capture of the Teneria, Davis led his regiment toward the next Mexican strongpoints, El Diablo and the Purisima Bridge. As the American forces pushed into the town, the murderous crossfire steadily took its toll. In the 3rd Infantry, Major William Lear went down with a ball entering at his nostril and coming out at the back of his ear. Lieutenant Douglas S. Irwin, regimental adjutant, was shot in the neck and killed going to his commander's aid. Soon after Lear fell, orders arrived from Garland to continue to advance, and carry the second redoubt at the point of the bayonet.

Colonel Davis moved his men near a wall that covered the front of the Purisima Bridge and encountered what remained of Company H, 3rd Infantry, with Captain Field and Lieutenant Richardson. Major Mansfield soon arrived and, together with Field and Richardson, planned an immediate attack. While the dispositions were being made, Brigadier General Hamer appeared on the scene and gave the order for everyone to retire. The junior officers tried to show the importance of their present position and argued against this order, but Hamer would not reconsider. Now the entire American force, except those holding the Teneria, were withdrawing from the city. The retreat convinced the Mexicans that they were on the verge of a great victory, and two regiments of cavalry, the 3rd and the 7th, were sent out of the Black Fort onto the plains to rout the Americans.

By the time Field, Richardson, and Davis extricated their men from these advanced positions, the remainder of the division had withdrawn a considerable distance, leaving them unsupported as the Mexican lancers charged. The lancers swung between the retreating main body and began slaughtering stragglers and wounded men.

Private Upton was among the last groups to get the word to withdraw. "We came out in a road more to the left than the others. As soon as we got out of the town we saw the Lancers coming down in great numbers at a full charge. They gained on us rapidly, firing their carbines. The slow runners were soon overtaken and killed. Captain Field was among the first victims. They killed without mercy. I turned my head and saw one of them thrusting his lance through one of our wounded men as he lay on the ground."[10]

Colonel Albert Sidney Johnston was retreating along with General Hamer and later said he felt that his hour was near. The men were beginning to panic, and he gave his sword to Hamer, who was unarmed, for them to make their last stand. Just then, he heard a familiar voice giving orders and saw the mixed command of the Mississippi Rifles and the 3rd Infantry under Colonel Davis and Richardson formed and firing at the lancers. The effect of this volley was the sudden flight of the Mexicans, leaving a number of them killed or wounded.[11]

Although the Teneria had been taken, it soon became a very dangerous place, as it was the concentration point for all the surrounding Mexican fire. General Twiggs appeared and took local command. He ordered Captain Ridgely's artillerymen to turn the captured Mexican guns on Fort Diablo in an effort to silence it. He also ordered his division to re-form and to continue the assault on El Diablo, hoping for a general collapse of the Mexican lines. As the 3rd Infantry rallied, their terrible losses became apparent: just half of the officers were present for duty, most of the senior leaders were dead, and their commander was wounded.

The regulars of the 1st, 3rd, and 4th Infantry regiments, under the cover of Ridgely's battery in the Teneria, were ordered to reenter the city and carry the second enemy battery at El Diablo. The 3rd Infantry was now under command of the man who had led them previously, Captain Morris. Lieutenant Richardson took command of Company H in the assault. As the companies moved cautiously into the city, a private from the 3rd Infantry was struck in the leg with a musket ball while dashing across the street. He clapped his hand on the spot, turned on his good leg, and exclaimed, "Boys, I've got my ticket! I'm off for camp!"[12]

Richardson remembered, "At 2 P.M., our Regt. made another attack upon the remaining batteries on the left of the town, and getting into the rear of them, kept up a continuous fire on the rear of the principal one and continued this for about two hours, our own batteries helping us as much as possible from the front. At one time we had driven them out, but getting immediately a reinforcement of over 1,000 men, they got into the work before we could leave our shelter."[13]

At this point Captain Morris, leading his men at the front of his regiment, was hit with a musket ball and killed instantly. Captain Henry Bainbridge, commanding Company F, was wounded in the hand and was put out of action. Starting the morning as the sixth senior officer in the regiment, Captain Henry now found himself commanding the 3rd Infantry. Moments later, Lieutenant Hazlitt of Company C was shot and killed while trying to retrieve the body of his company commander, Captain Morris, from the bloody street.

All of this punishment was not one-sided, however. During the fight, a Mexican regiment was spotted marching on its way to reinforce the position on the Purisima Bridge and thus was exposed to several effective volleys from the Americans. In this desperate fight, the regiment, because of the terrain, broke up into companies, each led by its own officers. In a series of separate, sharp actions, Lieutenant Richardson distinguished himself with his skill, gallantry, and perseverance.

Major William M. Graham, of the 4th Infantry, became the senior officer with this advanced command. With the enemy being strongly reinforced and his own force low on ammunition, he called for a volunteer to travel the fire-swept streets to report the situation to Twiggs. Lieutenant Grant stepped forward to take the message. Every street intersection promised death. Grant mounted his horse, with his body hanging over the sheltered side of the animal, and took off at top speed. He later recalled, "Only my horse was under fire at the street crossings, but these I crossed at such a flying rate of speed, that generally I was past and under the cover of the next block of houses before the enemy fired. I got out safely without a scratch."[14]

Colonel Garland described the end of the action in his report to Twiggs: "They entered a garden to the left and pressed forward to the street nearest the fort. These commands, though few in number, sustained themselves in the most admirable manner under the heaviest fire of the day. Here Morris fell, but they remained in their exposed position against frightful odds, until their ammunition began to fail. When hearing nothing from the battery, for which two staff officers had at different times been dispatched, I reluctantly ordered this truly Spartan band to retire."

By five o'clock, a discouraged Taylor ordered a halt to the futile attacks and sent the volunteers back to the campground at Walnut Springs. The regulars were posted in the captured Teneria. A defensive perimeter was set up, the ditch surrounding the fort was widened, and a shed was torn down to set up a barricade. When they could, the regulars flopped down on the muddy ground to sleep. No blankets, no food, and with a former distillery building in their hands, nothing to drink.

The day had not been a good one for the Americans. It ended with a casualty list of almost four hundred men, one-tenth of their army, and nothing to show for it but the possession of one small fort. Leading from the front, the officers accounted for forty-five of the casualties. Richardson recorded, "This day, our Regt. went into action with 14 officers and 201 men, and lost five officers killed and two wounded, and 53 men in killed and wounded. One third of us were constantly on guard during the night and the remainder, lying on their arms, behind the parapet, ready to repel any attacker. It rained all night, and being extremely cold, was very uncomfortable to us, as we had no blankets with us. We got no sleep that night as we had to lie down in the mud and rain without any covering."[15]

One must wonder what Israel Richardson thought about that night as he lay in the ankle-deep mud as the cold rain fell on his position in the captured fort. During his first experience in battle, at Palo Alto, he was little more than a spectator in an artillery battle. In his second battle, at Resaca de la Palma, he experienced close, small-unit combat of only a short duration, followed by the chase of a routed enemy all the way to the Rio Grande. In this, his third battle, he experienced the immediate shock of seeing his friend and mentor, Major Barbour, die before his eyes, followed by the loss of his regimental commander, Major Lear, and his company commander, Captain Field, as the Mexican lancers bore down on them. The mental and physical exhaustion of a full day of combat, followed by a cold, rainy night without food, defending an advanced outpost under constant fire, would be the hardest day in his army career. He later remarked, "The enemy ceased his fire on the closing of the day, and did not think it proper to molest us with an attack, although we should have been in far better spirits if he had attempted one."[16] If Richardson could survive a day like September 21 and keep his wits about him, he would be a man marked for future greatness, should the right circumstances fall into place.

But for all the needless sacrifice, the results of the diversionary attack had been achieved. General Worth's attack on the strategic heights at the opposite side of the city was a success. Captain Henry, who spent the night with Richardson, described it. "The first intimation we had of it was the discharge of musketry near the top of the hill. Each flash looked like an electric spark. The flashes and the white smoke ascended the hillside steadily, as if worked by machinery. The dark space between the apex of the height and the curling smoke of musketry became less and less, until the whole became enveloped in smoke, and we knew it had been gallantly carried. It was a glorious sight, and quite warmed our chilled bodies."[17]

With the dawn of September 22, Mexican artillery fire from the Black Fort continued. The hard work during the night started to pay dividends, as the men were now much better protected from the incoming fire of small arms and artillery. The trenches had been enlarged, and the artillery had been augmented with some of the pieces taken from the enemy, letting the Americans reply to Mexican bombardment. Even with the improvements, they could only work to keep down the destructive fire on their position, unable to effectively silence it. Many shells landed around the Teneria, but none burst within the works. The wounded Captain Bainbridge returned from Walnut Springs to take command of the 3rd Infantry, but for the rest of the day, the fighting switched to the western side of the city by the forces under General Worth. The only activity by Taylor on the east side of the city was to relieve the regulars who guarded the Teneria during the night with troops from General John A. Quitman's brigade late in the afternoon. Richardson and the wrecked 3rd Infantry returned to camp at Walnut Springs to care for their wounded and eat their first meal since leaving camp early on the twenty-first. Their rest was a short one, however, because with reveille on the morning of September 23, both Taylor and Worth ordered the regulars back into the city for a coordinated attack.

Mexican forces had abandoned Fort Diablo and their outer defenses to protect their position in the Central Plaza from Worth's attack. With the 3rd Infantry in support of Bragg's battery, Taylor attempted to punch his way through the city to the Central Plaza, already under bombardment by Worth. The fighting was not as severe as on the twenty-first, except in the street running directly in front of the cathedral. It could not be crossed without passing through a shower of bullets from numerous barricades and sharpshooters stationed in the top of the church building. Bragg's artillery had little effect on the buildings, but the threat of canister on the Mexican barricades helped to slow their rate of fire at the intersections. The men of the 3rd Infantry could cross without danger of being shot only when the cannons were pointed at the enemy. Then the Mexicans would fall behind their barricades, and the Americans could pass by squads. As soon as the gun was fired, the street would be impossible to cross because of fire from the enemy.

General Taylor had entered the city during the attack and was moving forward with Richardson and the most advanced companies of the 3rd Infantry. He recklessly exposed himself to enemy fire by casually walking across the streets where so many bullets were continually passing. At the end of the day, Richardson found time to write a note to his father. "Monterrey is now nearly ours, but after bloody and desperate fighting. Our Regt. suffered most in the storming. Captains Morris, Field, Barbour, Lieutenants Irwin and Hazlitt killed and Major Lear and Capt. Bainbridge wounded. It is almost impossible to see how any of us escaped. Five officers killed and two more wounded out of twelve is great destruction. Only five officers are left unhurt in the regiment."[18]

The Americans continued to advance slowly and carefully using a technique they learned from the Texans. The troops avoided fighting in the streets by advancing house to house, breaking down common walls. After creating an entry, a six-pound shell with a set fuse would be tossed in, clearing out the bottom floor; the Americans would then rush up to the roof and set up a base of fire to protect the next group, who repeated the process.[19] This tactic allowed the Americans to turn the Mexican barricades that blocked the streets. Both American detachments were now lobbing artillery into the plaza, which contained not only the Mexican headquarters but also a large number of civilian refugees and a huge, unprotected powder magazine. Faced with these circumstances, General Ampudia asked for a cease-fire to negotiate a surrender of the city. At the time of the cease-fire, Richardson noted that the 3rd Infantry was in control of all of the upper and lower parts of the town, mainly strong stone houses, like so many separate fortresses, and that the regiment had been under a cross fire of musketry and artillery for thirty-one successive hours.

Taylor agreed that in return for surrendering the city and all public property and ammunition, the Mexican army would be allowed to retain their small arms and march out of Monterrey to a line forty miles to the south. The Americans would not cross that line for a period of eight weeks, or until orders or instructions from their respective governments were received. At noon on September 25, the Mexican flag was hauled down and the Stars and Stripes were raised, with the American army marching into town to the tune of "Yankee Doodle."

In every man there is a defining moment that determines his character and influences his decision making for the rest of his life. Everyone is the sum total of their experiences and environment, which are subconsciously considered in all decisions that they make. Israel Richardson's defining moment came here at the battle of Monterrey. The impressions he came away with after this battle created an instinct that he would rely on for the rest of his life. During the prior five years of active duty and four years at West Point, Richardson had developed a reputation for sound judgment and proficiency in his duties. After this battle, his name began to be known in circles outside his regiment, to the rest of the army, and a reputation of aggressive action and bravery would begin to emerge.

When General Taylor's report arrived in Washington, the people were elated over the victory at Monterrey, with General Winfield Scott describing it as "three glorious days," but privately, President Polk and his cabinet were furious that Taylor had allowed the Mexican army to escape for a second time. The attitude represented a major lack of appreciation for the conditions Taylor was laboring under. If the Mexicans had been willing to put up more of a fight and kept attacking his supply lines, the situation might have been the complete opposite. Taylor defended his actions to the Secretary of War, arguing that "the task of fighting and beating the enemy is among the least difficult that we encounter. The great question of supplies, necessarily control all operations in a country like this."[20] Richardson noted that at the time of the capitulation of the Mexican force, the American troops were down to fewer than ten days' rations and had almost exhausted their supply of ammunition.

The importance of obtaining enough provisions to feed the army moving deeply into enemy territory was a problem that Taylor and, later, Scott wrestled with. The field commanders settled on a policy to pay the Mexican people their own asking price for beef cattle and flour instead of levying a tax of supplies to the conquered population, much to the consternation of the War Department. Richardson agreed, noting that purchasing supplies at an inflated price was still more economical then transporting them from the States, and "instead of exasperating the inhabitants, it had a conciliatory effect on them."[21]

Everyone close to the fighting thought the terms were the best the Americans could hope for under the circumstances. Captain Henry remarked, "Take it for granted that we could have forced the Mexican army into unconditional surrender, what was there to be gained by it? We would encumber ourselves with ten or twelve thousand men that we could not have fed, and would be forced to turn loose anyway."[22] Lieutenant George G. Meade thought that the casualties to the regular regiments had put those units on the verge of inefficiency, and the army was not in any condition for more heavy combat until it could be rested and refitted.

With the armistice in effect, the most pressing concern was the rebuilding of the 3rd Infantry regiment. Israel Richardson, just promoted to the rank of first lieutenant with a date of rank of September 21, was involved with responsibilities and duties much greater than his rank entailed. Of the twelve officers from his regiment on the field of battle at Monterrey, he was one of only five who had emerged unharmed. It fell on the shoulders of these junior officers to supervise and drill the regiment as it once again was built into an effective fighting unit. Richardson's personality by all accounts had been described as "unselfish and humble, a man who despised pretentiousness."[23] The current situation pushed Richardson to become a more forceful individual, and to develop a wider insight into operations above company level. Forevermore, he would be looked upon by new officers and recruits as one of the solid performers in the regiment. His bravery under fire was never questioned; now his leadership under fire; a more precious quality, was being formed.

As the armistice with the Mexicans came to a close, Taylor decided to send a force through the Sierra Madre mountain range to threaten the Mexican position at San Luis Potasi. On December 8, leaving a small garrison at Monterrey, Taylor led a brigade-size force, including Richardson's 3rd Infantry Regiment, on the march. Richardson later described the expedition as one of the most physically demanding tests he encountered during the Mexican campaign. "The army generally made but fifteen miles a day. Numerous small rivers and mountain streams crossed the road; in some places the depth was three feet, and it being the winter season, ice was sometimes met with in the current; the exposure to which brought on attacks of rheumatism to me for years later."[24] After wading streams in the winter and helping to push the heavily laden train of wagons by hand up the high hills for a distance of one hundred and fifty miles, Taylor abandoned his plan and quickly return to Monterrey after receiving a dispatch from General Worth advising that General Santa Anna was rumored to be close to Saltillo and in overwhelming strength.

On Christmas Day, 1846, a weakened Lieutenant Colonel Hitchcock arrived at Brazos Island, returning from his convalescent leave in St. Louis. His frustration was evident with his attempt to return to his regiment, and only illustrated how tenuous the lines of communications and supplies were for the Americans.

"Everybody seemed to be in motion at the front. There was scarcely any defense for Americans along the river, and the country below Matamoros was overrun by Mexicans and unsafe for any small parties. Matamoros was held by one regiment of Ohio volunteers, and the great depot of stores at Brazos was defended by only one company, without a piece of artillery. The road to Monterrey is beset by Santa Anna's men, and no small party can get through."[25]

With the arrival of 1847, the regular regiments marched out of Walnut Springs and back to Camargo, where they boarded steamers to take them back to Point Isabel. General Scott had been in Mexico for a month gathering supplies and equipment to launch his attack on Vera Cruz. This new army Richardson joined was very different from Taylor's; larger and freshly equipped but untried. Ulysses Grant, writing years later, described it in these terms:

"Taylor had a small army, but it was composed exclusively of regular troops, under the best drill and discipline. Every officer, from highest to lowest, was educated in his profession, not at West Point necessarily, but in camp, in garrison, and many of them in Indian Wars. The rank and file were probably inferior, as material out of which to make an army, to the volunteers that participated in all the later battles of the war; but they were brave men, and then drill and discipline brought out all there was in them. A better army, man for man, probably never faced an enemy than the one commanded by General Taylor in the earliest two engagements of the Mexican war. The volunteers who followed were of better material, but without drill or discipline from the start."[26]

Lost in all the success of Taylor's army was the fact that they were always operating with minimal supplies and replacements. Captain Louis S. Craig,[27] 3rd Infantry, was detailed to act as Taylor's quartermaster during the Monterrey campaign. It was an impossible, thankless duty that spared him from the bloodbath of the street fighting in the city. After the fall of Monterrey, Captain Craig returned to his regiment to help restore it to fighting condition.

The policies of the army were being hotly debated during this time, and some glaring problems with its administration became painfully obvious. The lack of a retirement system for soldiers was not efficient. An officer stayed on the regimental rolls and received pay no matter what his condition; only resignation or death could free up a slot for a replacement. In the 3rd Infantry, Lieutenant Colonel Hitchcock, although in actual daily command of the regiment for six years now, was in reality assigned as executive officer according to the regimental rolls. The official regimental commander, appointed in 1834, was Colonel James B. Many. Living in New Orleans on sick leave since October 14, 1843, he would remain commander until his death on February 23, 1852. He was replaced by Colonel Thomas Staniford, who, also on sick leave, would never actually report for duty but remain in command of the regiment until he died on March 15, 1855.

"Our regimental color is entirely riddled with musket balls and grape shot"

After two months of organization and preparation, General Scott set sail on February 15, 1847, with the rest of the army sailing in subsequent days as transportation was acquired. Scott organized his forces in three divisions, two of regulars under Worth and Twiggs, and the third of volunteers, under General Robert Patterson.

The division led by General Twiggs contained some of the most experienced units in Scott's army. It included the 2nd, 3rd, and 7th Infantry regiments, along with the regiment of Mounted Rifles. They were all under strength from the hard campaigns of northern Mexico and only recently filled back up to authorized strength with a large amount of untrained recruits. Fortunately for the 3rd Infantry, lieutenants Barnard Bee and Oliver L. Shepherd returned from recruiting duty in the United States with more than one hundred replacements just in time for the new campaign. The Mounted Rifles regiment was a newly recruited unit seeing its first action. Richardson had some personal observations about army policies in a letter to his father dated February 16:

"Gen. Scott is expected here soon—Col. Hitchcock has been chosen as Chief of Staff; and it may be of interest to you to know that Gen. Scott and he have made up their old quarrel of some years standing. I hope our Division may go to Vera Cruz, I am anxious to see the siege of a fortified place by regular approaches, and many things may be seen and learned there. I learn that the Bill for ten Regt. of Regulars in addition has passed. I hope the officers may not be taken from the citizens, as those of the Rifles were.

"The Rifle Regt. is represented as being officered by a set of loafers and fit for anything else but the army. Indeed, worse than the Volunteers—It seems the President preferred nominating citizens to those officers of the army who had already gained credit at the two first and hard fought battles of the campaign. The regular army never has before been treated as badly. I hope at least he allows us to have the names of the actions inscribed on the Colors of the Regt. which were engaged. The soldiers have fought well and nothing would excite their pride more than this. Our Regimental Color is entirely riddled with musket balls and grape shot, so is also the 4th Infy."[28]

During the Mexican campaign and afterwards, Richardson and Barnard Bee developed a special friendship that was to last for the remainder of their lives. Bee was born on February 8, 1824, in Charleston, South Carolina. His father moved to Texas in 1835, played a leading role in its creation as a republic, and later served as secretary of state. Bee spent several years there before gaining an appointment to the military academy in 1841.

Captain Edmund B. Alexander, the newly assigned commander of the 3rd Infantry, relied heavily on the experienced company commanders like Richardson and Bee to accomplish assigned missions, while at the same time training the raw recruits to function as soldiers under demanding conditions.

The siege of Vera Cruz taught Richardson and his peers about the science of warfare according to General Scott, who resisted the advice of his three division commanders to storm the city. Scott realized that he needed to conserve lives if the march to Mexico City was to remain practicable. Several young engineers in the army began to make a name for themselves in this campaign. Robert E. Lee, George B. McClellan, Gustavus W. Smith, and Pierre G. T. Beauregard seemed to be everywhere opening roads through dunes, destroying the aqueduct that supplied Vera Cruz with water, scouting and erecting entrenchments and batteries.

On March 16, McClellan returned to headquarters with his clothes ripped and torn from Mexican musket fire he and his work party had been under the greater part of the day. On March 19, Lee very narrowly escaped death. From an advanced position of one of the working parties, he started back to the American lines, accompanied by Beauregard. At a turn in the path, they suddenly saw an American soldier. The startled soldier, thinking Mexicans were upon him, fired his pistol straight at Lee. The bullet passed between his left arm and his body, singeing his uniform.

On March 24, General Scott was ready to open the bombardment that continued for the next two days. The Mexicans attempted counter-battery fire, but it was ineffective, as the American artillery was able to keep four to six shells continually in the air. Richardson, commanding his company on advanced picket duty within eight hundred yards of the Mexican works, saw the effect of the shelling from up close. "The batteries opened in the morning and continued without much interruption all day and night, with immense injury to the enemy as every shot and shell entered the city and went where it was intended. Our batteries did great execution."[29]

The bombardment was decisive, and on March 26, a flag of truce was raised by the Mexicans and the surrender document was signed the next day. Five thousand prisoners and four hundred pieces of artillery fell into American hands. General Scott's tactics had been vindicated, for the victory had cost him just sixty-eight men killed or wounded.[30] Upon the surrender and occupation of the city, Richardson was eager to visit the enemy fortifications for "the purpose of seeing their armaments, and the effects produced upon the works by our cannonade and bombardment of twelve days and nights. On examination of some of the dwelling houses, they were found to be penetrated from roof to basements by descending shells, which in some instances exploded within, blowing up whole buildings of three stories in height."[31]

Once a base of operations was secured, Scott's next priority was to move inland as quickly as possible to avoid the yearly outbreak of yellow fever that usually occurred in the beginning of the spring and was particularly deadly to the Americans, who were not acclimated to the region. As soon as limited transportation could be acquired, General Twiggs' division, containing the 3rd Infantry, led Scott's army down the road to Mexico City. General Scott had fewer than twelve thousand men in an army with a mission to march 260 miles deep into enemy territory to capture its capital, a city of more than one hundred thousand inhabitants. Any route selected by Scott led through the mountain passes that could be easily defended by the Mexicans.

Due to the lack of transportation and the limited forage, water, and provisions along the way, the army was forced to march by divisions spread one day apart. Richardson remembered that "the allowance to each company for its baggage and provisions was but one half a wagon, and no tents, except three small ones, one for the officers of the company, one for the sick, and one for the preservation of the arms. Consequently the troops had to bivouac every night, generally without fires, and the difference of temperature between the hot, sultry, coast and the table lands of the interior, was severely felt."[32]

The task seemed impossible, but the Mexican government was in chaos. Santa Anna realized his only hope in retaining control of the country lay in defeating the Americans in battle, and he quickly started to rebuild his army to accomplish this task. He had not much to work with because the cream of his forces had been decimated either by Taylor at Buena Vista or by his own subordinates with the brutal forced marches during the retreat.

The American advance began on April 2, when Colonel Harney, with a mixed command, opened the way inland by forcing a crossing of the Rio Antigua. Twiggs' division marched on April 8 and was followed the next day by Patterson's division. The division of General Worth had to remain in Vera Cruz until additional transportation could be acquired. The advance screen from the 2nd Dragoons, followed by the rest of Twiggs' division, reached Plano del Rio on April 11. The next morning, reconnaissance disclosed Santa Anna's army had heavily fortified the Cerro Gordo Pass along the National Road, eight miles from the city of Jalapa.

"Our regiment highly distinguished itself, and I myself acted in some considerable share"

General David Twiggs had been Richardson's division commander for almost one year now. His military career had begun during the War of 1812, when he served as a captain in the 8th Infantry. At the start of the Mexican War, he had been colonel of the 2nd Dragoons for almost ten years.

Twiggs was not an intellectual, and his aggressiveness was the cause for senseless casualties in battle, as at Monterrey. He was also guilty of mistakes in judgment that put his men at risk during the march. He directed his command with an iron hand. Even with these faults, he was a popular leader with his men. They took delight in his language, which was as coarse as his appearance and his habit of "swearing most vehemently on the most trifling of occasions."[33] Commanding the 2nd Dragoons at the outbreak of the war, his unit had for some time been dismounted, much to their humiliation and disgust, and when the order came for the unit to remount the regiment at Nachitoches, old Colonel Twiggs issued a verbal order that any man found *sober* in camp the next morning would be put in the guardhouse![34]

Twiggs wanted to attack as soon as possible, but preliminary reconnaissance revealed that the Mexican position was very strong. Lieutenant Beauregard, despite his modest rank, went to the general's tent to argue for a postponement of the assault. Finally, General Patterson, whose division had come up behind Twiggs, and although ill, took himself off sick report to assume command and canceled the operation until all of Scott's army assembled. When Scott arrived on April 14, he assigned Captain Robert E. Lee to make a thorough study of the Mexican position in preparation for an attack when Worth's division arrived on April 17.[35]

Going out alone on the morning of the fifteenth, Lee found that Santa Anna had chosen his ground well. The army's only hope lay in finding a practicable way through the ravines on the Mexican left. He worked his way up the ravines, ending up at a spring in the rear of the Mexican left flank. While he studied

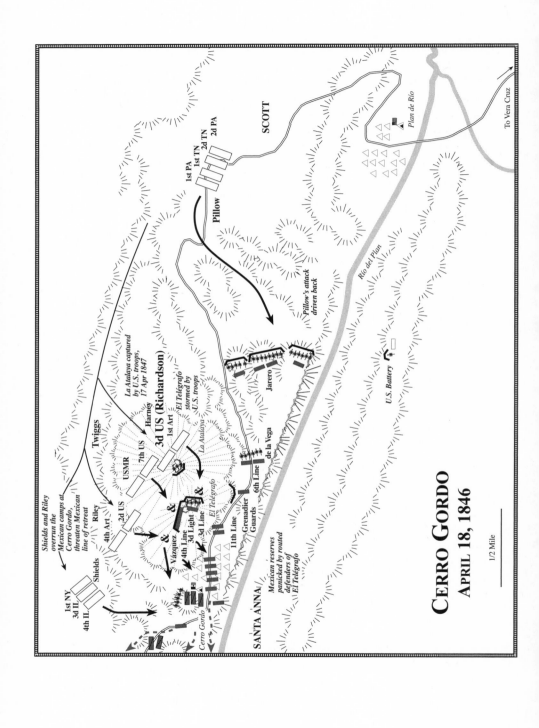

CERRO GORDO
APRIL 18, 1846

1/2 Mile

the ground, he was almost surprised by a watering detail. He barely had time to hide behind a fallen tree and was forced to lie quiet there for the rest of the day as more Mexican soldiers arrived at the spring. Finally, during the night he was able to escape and report his findings to General Scott. With this information, Scott devised a plan that called for Twiggs to follow Lee's route, come up on the Mexican left flank, break through the position, and block the enemy escape by cutting the Jalapa Road.

Richardson recalled that "Telegraph Hill, which commanded all the other works with its batteries, was the key or decision point to the whole position and could only be taken possession of by a heavy column of attack on the enemy's left, and gaining the Jalapa Road. The first object was to get possession of a hill near the extremity and by planting a battery to cripple by its cannonade the enemy's work on Telegraph Hill, so that the latter could be carried by assault. The hill first to be attacked was situated within effective range of cannon from the other; there being but a distance of six hundred yards between their summits, but both were rocky, steep and difficult to access."[36]

Twiggs' division, with Colonel William S. Harney in temporary command of Colonel Persifor F. Smith's brigade, containing the 3rd Infantry, began their march at 4:30 A.M. with Captain Lee as their guide. Although the initial portions of the route were screened from the Mexican pickets due to the rough terrain, by late morning they came under fire from the sharp-eyed outpost on the summit of Atalaya. Once the movement had been discovered, Twiggs ordered two of Harney's regiments, the 1st Artillery and the Mounted Rifles, to charge and take the hill. As the few defenders were swept aside, one of the staff members asked the logical question, "How far to conduct the pursuit?" General Twiggs, a man of few words, ordered "Charge 'em to hell!" and the two regiments rushed headlong into the teeth of the Mexican defensive position, and spent the rest of the day pinned down on the hillside, greatly outnumbered by thousands of Mexican infantry under a crossfire of artillery. Only at nightfall were they able to retreat back to American lines with severe losses, and camp on the summit of Atalaya.[37]

During the attack up the mountain, Major Edwin V. Sumner, charging at the head of the Mounted Rifles Regiment, was wounded. A spent musket ball struck his head, made a furrow, and seemingly bounced off. After witnessing this incident, Sumner's men believed he led a charmed life. For the rest of his career, he would be known as Bull Head Sumner.

Santa Anna mistakenly believed that the failed American attack on El Telégrafo had been Scott's main effort, and the Mexicans spent the night celebrating what they thought was a great victory. Prudently, he did take the precaution of adding a pair of twelve pounders along with two regiments of infantry to his defensive line.

*"I extended every effort I was capable of, and
feel that I could not have done more"*

General Scott's plan for the attack on the eighteenth called for Twiggs to continue the attack on El Telégrafo and cut the road to Jalapa beyond. At the sound
of firing, General Gideon Pillow's brigade would attack the eastern end of the
Mexican line, break through, and get into the rear of the Mexican position.

Richardson wrote, "The morning of the 18th opened fair and cloudless and
just as the first streaks of dawn aroused the troops of Twiggs' corps from their
heavy slumbers, which were soon answered by trumpets and bugles of the
enemy's line right to left, and within plain hearing. As soon as it was light
enough for our artillery men to direct their guns, the light brush which had
been left in front as a mask to the battery was now cut away, and the twenty-
four pound shot and shells opened on the enemy's palisade, and parapet to the
rear of it, if possible to make a breach for the entrance of our column of attack.
The enemy answered with grape and canister shot from all his pieces on the
Telegraph Hill and the range being short, the ground around our battery was
soon ploughed up into furrows."[38]

At first light, the battery, which was planted with so much difficulty on the
crest of the captured hill, opened fire on Cerro Gordo. The Mexicans immediately returned this fire with a plunging fire of grape and canister. Colonel
Harney was designated to lead the attack, and organized the storming party.
It consisted of the 7th Infantry, under Lieutenant Colonel J. Plympton, on the
right and six companies of the 3rd Infantry, under Captain Alexander, on the
left, supported by four companies of the 1st Artillery acting as infantry, under
Lieutenant Colonel C. F. Childs, the whole force numbering no more than
twelve hundred men.

Richardson noted, "Our fires now opened, and was returned by the enemy
with great celerity, which soon however, diminished, although its grape produced great effect upon the Rifles, 3rd and 7th Infantry and 1st Artillery which
were drawn up behind the crest of the hill, and in line of battle for a charge on
the enemy's heights. Some 70 or 80 of our men were killed or wounded during
a time of about one hour's duration.

"At this time, it was thought that sufficient effect had been produced to enable us to carry the enemy's works by assault, and accordingly, Col. Harney, of
the Dragoons, who commanded our portion of the Division, ordered bayonets
to be fixed for storming, and to sound the charge along our line. From the crest
of the hill to its foot was 200 yards, and from that point to the top of the enemy's
hill it was 400 more. The latter distance being a very steep slope, making 600
yards to overcome before the enemy would be reached, and exposing us all the
time to the enemy's grape and musketry."[39]

Colonel Harney gave his orders to the junior leaders: "As soon as you hear the word 'Charge,' rush right down the hill as fast as you can and up the other—it is rather steep, but that's all the better for us—yell like devils as soon as you reach the ravine, and then up the hill to their breastworks as soon as you can; and for God's sake don't fire unless you shoot a Mexican!"[40]

First Lieutenant Richardson's Company E was stationed near the center of the American attack and on his regiment's right flank. He was now in command of a company composed of a large contingent of raw recruits who would come under direct fire from the enemy for the first time. Not many men who had come to Texas two years ago were left in his unit, owing as much to disease as to enemy fire. Richardson would have to lead this "forlorn hope," the term given to the point of the assault and referring to their dim chances of survival, down a hill into a valley, then up a steep slope, and through three lines of defenses to reach their objective. The few veterans that Richardson had with him could only believe that this would be their most demanding mission yet.

The last time the 3rd Infantry faced an entrenched enemy, the results were disastrous. Certainly the new recruits had heard the stories, probably exaggerated, from the survivors and had to be in awe of the Mexican position and extremely nervous about making the charge. Richardson realized that to calm his company and ensure that his instructions were followed during the attack he would have to set the example and lead from the front. He could do no less than his brigade commander, Colonel Harney, who led the way, conspicuous by the wearing of his full military uniform, waving his sword and calling on his men to follow.

Like Twiggs, Harney had a reputation for an original and exhaustless vocabulary of cumulative and energizing profanity, and his men loved him for it. However, his gruff and sometimes brutal behavior outside combat situations left a bitter impression on many of his peers. During the Seminole War, he had allegedly been involved with hanging several Indian captives without any benefit of a trial. And while stationed in St. Louis, he had been involved in a severe beating of a servant girl who later died of her injuries.

Sergeant Robert Peck of the 1st Cavalry thought Colonel Harney was "the most abusive and profane officer in his ordinary conversation that I ever met in the army. He could scarcely speak a dozen words without half as many oaths or foul epithets; and when in ill humor—which seemed to be his normal condition—he would apply such language indiscriminately to any officers, soldiers or citizens who came in his way. But with all his ill nature and roughness, old Harney was a first-class Indian fighter, and this in the estimation of the soldier covers a multitude of faults; they can pardon almost anything in an officer if he is gritty."[41]

"At the signal to charge, each regiment advanced in order of battle, and at a run," Richardson wrote. "On reaching the foot, a short halt was ordered, to rest us before mounting the hill, we now being a little more secure from the heavy fire of the enemy. In a short time, the order was given to advance, and on getting within a few yards of the enemy's outer palisades, we halted, giving them a few well-directed volleys, which drove them out in great confusion, and we immediately gained the outside of the palisades ourselves. A regular line was formed, and a heavy fire was kept up by our men on the interior, the enemy firing grape and musketry, but mostly over our heads."[42]

The Americans steadily descended the hill and crossed the ravine at the bottom, all the while under a galling fire of grape, canister, and musketry from the enemy. Richardson remembered, "Until our arrival at this point, the three twenty-four pounders in our rear opened upon the works above us with grape and canister; the shot passing over our heads and in a great degree, keeping down the enemy's fire, but now they were obliged to cease firing and our infantry alone defended themselves against more than four times our own number, having the advantage of the ground as well as entrenchments."[43] As Richardson began clambering up the slope, he turned to see, on the crest of the hill where they had started from, the unmistakable figure of General Scott and his staff watching the attack. The terrain was so steep that the officers had to use their swords and many of the men their muskets for support in working their way up the slope. Leading his company, looking down along the line during his advance, Richardson could actually see his men grit their teeth, although not a single shot was returned until he halted them at the outer entrenchments within ten feet of the enemy line.

Surrounding the hill, about sixty yards from the foot, was the first Mexican position, a breastwork of stone, which was filled with troops offering a stiff resistance. When Private Barna Upton reached the wall, he stopped to catch his breath and fire several rounds. "Our whole force with a loud shout leaped the breastwork and met them at the point of the bayonet. Here for just one short minute ensued a kind of fighting which I hope never to see again. It seemed like murder to see men running bayonets into each other's breasts."[44] At this point, the Mexican commander, General Vasquez, was killed, and Lieutenant Bee fell wounded. Harney's cheering voice was heard everywhere, rallying his men and continuing up the slope.

Richardson recalled, "A Mexican gun, a six pounder, was situated exactly in front of my company. I had observed as it fired grape at us two or three times within 25 steps, which went mostly over our heads, but they continually depressed the muzzle. I was afraid the next charge of grape would be low enough to sweep off most of my company. I chose 5 or 6 of the better marksmen and ordered them to pick off every gunner and not allow a single one to work the piece.

"They did so, and the piece was not manned again. After firing about 15 minutes, our line jumped the outer palisade and I immediately ran to the piece and called out six or seven of my company to help me work this gun. I tried the inside of the piece with the rammer, and found it not loaded; the Mexicans had taken the ammunition box into the inner palisade, and I directed them to get cartridges from it while I got the gun in position to fire on the Mexicans who were retreating into the plain below in every direction. I then loaded the piece myself with round shot and a stand of canister and bringing the gun to bear upon them, primed it with a musket cartridge, and fired it. I had fired it thus three times when Col. Harney came up and ordered me to take it around to the other side of the hill and fire it on a body of Mexicans who were making a stand near a small ranch, and driving back a body of Volunteers who were endeavoring to take them."[45]

Richardson and his executive officer, Second Lieutenant Thomas R. McConnell, were recognized for their actions by Harney, who allowed them to keep and continue firing the Mexican piece, while the remaining captured guns were turned over to American artillery officers. When Richardson complained about the order that would have forced him to relinquish his prize, Harney, who was standing nearby, bellowed, "By God, Sir, You shall have the gun anyhow," and ordered Richardson to continue firing the piece until the Mexican line collapsed.

In his after-action report, the commander of the 3rd Infantry, Captain Alexander, wrote, "I trust I will be pardoned if I indulge in a slight expression of pride at the conduct of my regiment throughout this affair; and when it is considered that it was composed of at least one-half raw recruits, who only had the benefit of some eleven days of imperfect drilling, and who fired a musket for the first time, as they came into this action, I feel assured that it will speak more for the gallant manner in which the men were conducted into action by their company officers than anything I can express."[46]

Richardson was acknowledged by both Captain Alexander and Colonel Harney in their official reports for his actions during the Battle of Cerro Gordo, and it was from this moment that he became known to the army by his nickname "Fighting Dick" Richardson. In just three hours, the entire Mexican army was in retreat toward Mexico City. After the charge by Harney had unhinged the Mexican position, all of the other attacks pushed forward with light opposition. Santa Anna barely escaped, as his personal carriage was riddled with shot. The army payroll and most of his personal belongings fell into the hands of the 3rd Infantry as the Mexican leader staggered off into the hills on foot.

The captured carriage was temporarily placed at the disposal of the wounded Major Sumner, and for the moment at least, the Mexican army ceased to exist. More than three thousand prisoners had been taken, with Lieutenant Colonel

Hitchcock estimating that an additional thousand prisoners had slipped away before being processed. The American casualties were 63 killed and 368 wounded.

As the American army rested from the fight, caring for wounded and collecting prisoners and equipment, General Scott walked through the camp and spent time congratulating his commanders for their successes. While riding through the camp of the 3rd Infantry, Scott had some personal words for Lieutenant Richardson, bestowing the nickname "Fighting Dick" on him. If this was not their first personal meeting, it certainly was the most important one for Israel Richardson. In their subsequent encounters, General Scott would always refer to Richardson as Fighting Dick. The events of the day were summarized by Richardson in a letter to his father describing the battle: "As for myself, I extended every effort I was capable of, and feel that I could not have done more."[47]

The Battle of Cerro Gordo gave Scott the opportunity to immediately march on Mexico City without regard to any organized resistance from the Mexican army, but he could not take advantage of the situation because his own logistics were strained to the breaking point. Two weeks after the battle, seven volunteer regiments' one-year enlistments expired, and he was forced to escort almost two thousand men from his army to Vera Cruz for discharge. It would be at least three months before he would be resupplied with men, equipment, and funds to continue the drive toward the Mexican capital.

Finally, on August 7, 1847, Twiggs' division led Scott's army on what everyone hoped would be the final campaign of the war. For five days, the Americans advanced without encountering any Mexicans. Santa Anna could only hope to mass his army at strategic locations along the road, where the natural terrain would give him the greatest advantage to inflict crippling casualties on Scott's army. This was the Mexican hope when Twiggs came upon the prepared defenses at El Penon, twenty miles from Mexico City.

General Scott sent his engineers to search for a way around the defenses. After a thorough inspection, Captain Lee and Lieutenant Beauregard would report that the Mexican defenses were extremely strong and impossible to turn except by moving across the Pedregal, a lava field that was described as a heap of rocks, almost impassable for infantry, and totally so for artillery and cavalry. Scott chose to follow Captain Lee's recommendation and furnished him with a five-hundred-man detail to create a road through the Pedregal for his wagons. Twiggs' division was ordered to protect this force. Richardson and the 3rd Infantry found themselves supporting this action on the morning of August 19, 1847.

"We have done all the hard fighting"

At no time during the Mexican War is there a better illustration of the interaction of key players in a conflict fifteen years in the future than of the actions surrounding Israel Richardson during the next forty-eight hours. How much insight into each other's character under the pressures of stress and fatigue were they able to retain and use to their advantage when studying each other as adversaries in the Civil War? Probably the greatest example of this would be Lee's ability to anticipate the actions of his fellow engineer, George McClellan. This trait was not a fluke but rather had its root in the experiences that both men encountered while serving together and observing each other as company grade officers.

In the history of the Civil War, few things were more remarkable than the use of the knowledge acquired by key leaders in the toils of the march, in the close companionship of camp, and in the excitement of battle. The shrewder individuals probed the characters of their comrades to the quick. The clue to many upcoming campaigns, some daring to the point of foolhardiness, can be traced to a leader so intimately acquainted with the character of his opponent as to be able to predict with certainty how he would react under any given circumstance, even if the plan ran counter to every established rule of war.

In his memoirs, Ulysses S. Grant remarked on the trait: "All the older officers, who became conspicuous in the rebellion, I had served with and known in Mexico. The acquaintance thus formed was of immense service to me in the War of the Rebellion, I mean what I learned of the characters of those to whom I was afterwards opposed. I do not pretend to say that all my movements, or even many of them, were made with special reference to the characteristics of the commander against whom they were directed. But my appreciation of my enemies was certainly affected by this knowledge."[48]

Early afternoon, as the road-cutting expedition was nearly completed, the sharp sound of musket fire was heard ahead. Lieutenants Foster and McClellan returned from scouting to report a strong picket of Mexican soldiers to the front. McClellan had his horse shot out from under him in a hail of Mexican bullets. Pillow ordered up the 3rd Infantry, and Captain Lee sent for Captain John B. Magruder's artillery battery. McClellan placed this unit into position and stayed with it during the cannonading, helping the unit wherever he could. As the 3rd Infantry came up, Pillow ordered Captain Alexander to support the artillery. Three companies were detached: Company A under Captain Louis Craig, Company E under Richardson, and Company I under Captain Daniel T. Chandler, altogether numbering five officers and approximately one hundred men, all under the overall command of Captain Craig.

Magruder instructed Craig to make what dispositions he thought best to support his battery. Craig had his men take up positions under what little cover was available a short distance in front. The battery was set up in the open within grapeshot range from the enemy works near the village of Contreras, and Magruder complained his position was dangerously extended. Other soldiers witnessing the scene agreed with his assessment. Lieutenant D. H. Hill, never at a loss for words, commented, "Certainly, of all the absurd things that ass Pillow has ever done, this was the most silly. Human stupidity can go no further than this."[49]

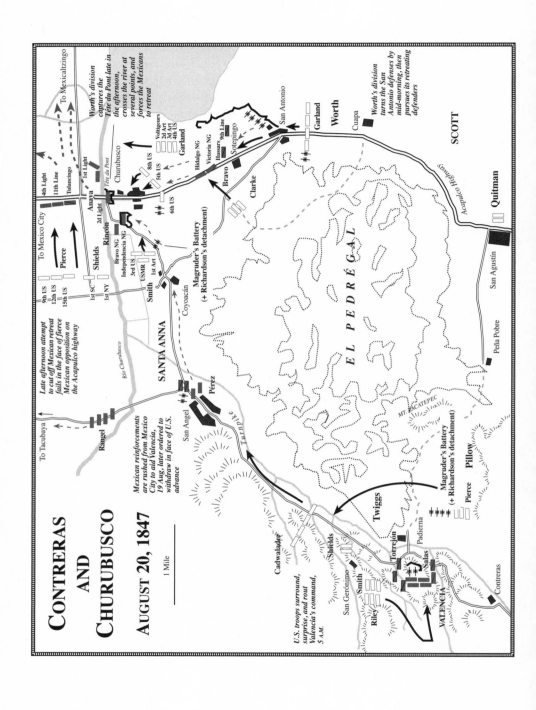

CONTRERAS AND CHURUBUSCO

AUGUST 20, 1847

1 Mile

U.S. troops surround, surprise, and rout Valencia's command, 5 A.M.

Mexican reinforcements are rushed from Mexico City to aid Valencia, 19 Aug, later ordered to withdraw in face of U.S. advance

Late afternoon attempt to cut off Mexican retreat fails in the face of fierce Mexican opposition on the Acapulco highway

Worth's division captures the Tête du Pont late in the afternoon, crosses the river at several points, and forces the Mexicans to retreat

Worth's division turns the San Antonio defenses by mid-morning, then pursues its retreating defenders

To Tacubaya

To Mexico City

To Mexicaltzingo

Rangel

Río Churubusco

SANTA ANNA

San Angel

Pérez

TURNPIKE

Coyoacán

USMR
3rd Art
1st Art

Smith

Independencia NG
Bravo NG

Shields
Rincón

1st SC
1st NY

9th US
12th US
15th US

4th Light
11th Line
Tulancingo

1st Light
2d Light

Amaya

Pierce

Churubusco

Tête du Pont

8th US
5th US
6th US

Voltigeurs
2d Art
3d Art
4th US

Garland

Hidalgo NG
Victoria NG
Hussars
Sotepingo
Bravo
Clarke

San Antonio

Garland
Worth

Cuapa

SCOTT

Acapulco Highway

Quitman

San Agustín

Peña Pobre

EL PEDRÉGAL

MT ZACATEPEC

Magruder's Battery (+ Richardson's detachment)

Pierce
Pillow

Twiggs

Cadwalader

Shields

Smith

Riley

San Gerónimo

Torrejón

Padierna

Salas

VALENCIA

Contreras

Magruder's Battery (+ Richardson's detachment)

From two o'clock in the afternoon until eleven at night, Magruder's battery of six pounders held their position in a continuous exchange with twenty-nine pieces of Mexican artillery, including several eighteen pounders and three eight-inch howitzers. The battery took a pounding from the enemy shelling, and its executive officer, Lieutenant John P. Johnston, was mortally wounded. Immediately, Second Lieutenant Thomas J. Jackson took command of his section of guns and continued to fire without a letup.

Magruder's battery was ordered to maintain a rapid fire to draw the attention of the enemy as American units moved toward their attack positions. The resulting damage so crippled the battery they could not withdraw under their own power and had to rely on Richardson's men when they were ordered to fall back out of range.

After dark, Lieutenant Fitzgerald, aide-de-camp to General Franklin Pierce, reported to Craig that a portion of his volunteers, about fifty men, were surrounded in the ruins of an old house a short distance from their front, by a Mexican force exceeding 250 men who had made a raid from their entrenchments. He spoke with Magruder as to the chance of taking a portion of his command to their relief. Informed that one company would be sufficient to protect the battery, Craig left the slightly wounded Captain Chandler with Company I in position, and took Company A and Richardson's Company E to the relief of the surrounded unit.

Craig and Richardson, with their force of approximately sixty men, approached the house under the cover of darkness and steady rain, and discovered that the American force had left the house, now occupied by Mexicans. The small force worked their way close to the house without being seen and, with one surprise volley and charge, drove the Mexicans out of the house and back to their entrenchments "in a most gallant manner," according to Magruder. During this exchange of fire, one Mexican soldier was killed and one American was wounded. Searching the ruins, three wounded American soldiers were found and carried back to the battery.

Returning to the battery, Magruder informed Craig and Richardson that he had received orders to retire his battery out of range of the enemy's shot and wished that the 3rd Infantry would accompany him. Together, they moved out at a late hour and, because of the darkness of the night, the rain, and the terrible condition of the road, progressed only a short distance before daylight broke. They soon met the 9th Infantry, advancing for the general attack on the Mexican positions. Craig was ordered to return and take up a position near the enemy's works, in order to make a diversion for the assaulting party.

The three companies of the 3rd Infantry returned to their original positions. Now that the rain had stopped, an exhausted Richardson had his men wipe out their muskets and reload them while he and Craig went out to reconnoiter the ground to their front. They found a large number of Mexicans reoccupying the same house they attacked the night before. Together they formulated a plan. As the 9th Infantry approached the Mexican works, Craig gave the order to open fire on the occupied house, and after firing several volleys, the men succeeded in drawing a heavy fire from the Mexican batteries away from the American main effort. The detachment from the 3rd Infantry charged on the house and again drove the enemy from the ruins, pursuing them down a ravine that ran below the main Mexican entrenchments, killing many and capturing thirty, with a loss of two men killed and nine wounded.[50] Within seventeen minutes of the start of the American attack, the Mexican defense began caving in. Craig crossed the ravine with his command and rejoined Captain Alexander and the rest of the 3rd Infantry. After a short halt in the village of San Angel to regroup, the regiment was back on the road after participating in the routing of Santa Anna at Contreras.

The Mexican line had crumbled quickly, and Scott could sense a decisive victory at hand. He ordered an aggressive pursuit down the National Highway to crush any organized resistance remaining. But the Mexican army was relatively intact, and Santa Anna ordered his men to "hold at all costs" the critical bridge across the Churubusco and turned the convent in the village into a fortified position. Considering the ease with which the Mexican army had been defeated so far, Scott thought he could brush aside this defense as well. However, the unit detailed to hold the convent was the elite San Patricio Battalion, commanded by Colonel Francisco Moreno. Among the soldiers of this battalion were many American deserters who had left the army before hostilities started at Matamoros.

To say that Mexican resolve to defend this strongpoint was strengthened by the presence of the American deserters would be an understatement. There would be no surrender for them; they were well aware that capture would probably mean a death sentence. The 3rd Infantry rushed into action at Churubusco as the battle escalated. Around noon, Scott's pursuit had crashed into this strongpoint, and he allocated most of his strength to overcoming it. Two brigades under Worth were trying to fight their way across the fortified bridge when Twiggs committed the 3rd Infantry into action against the supporting strongpoint in the convent.

Captain Alexander advanced his regiment along a line of mud huts within sixty yards of the convent, while they poured a brisk and effective fire on the Mexicans. This continued for about an hour and a half, and while trying to flank a body of Mexicans in the cornfields, Captain Craig fell, severely wounded. Gradually, portions of Worth's command worked their way eastward, outflanking the Mexican left, crossing the river, and moving up the Mexican side of the works. At the same time the 5th and 8th infantry regiments carried the bridge in hand-to-hand combat, capturing 192 prisoners and three pieces of artillery.

Now all weapons were brought to bear on the convent, including Duncan's and Taylor's batteries and those of the captured Mexican pieces from the bridge. The fire was concentrated on the tower of the church, which throughout the battle was continually refilled with some of the best sharpshooters of the enemy. The barricades of the convent were greatly thinned when the Mexicans moved a cannon from the south side of the convent to reply to Worth's artillery. Captain Alexander saw this weakness and ordered the 3rd Infantry to charge and scale the parapet. Climbing over the wall, Lieutenant Don Carlos Buell was severely wounded.

Led by Alexander, two companies of the 3rd, commanded by Captain James M. Smith and Lieutenant Oliver L. Shepherd, entered the work and cleared the way by fire and bayonet. The defenders, fighting hand to hand, retired inside the convent building. Resistance was hopeless, but three times as a Mexican attempted to raise the white flag, the San Patricios would shoot him down. Finally, Captain Smith, commander of Company B, 3rd Infantry, stopped the slaughter by putting up a white handkerchief himself. The Mexicans, given the opportunity, quickly laid down their arms.

Richardson noted, "The assault on Churubusco would have ended much sooner had it not been for about 200 deserters from our army on the Rio Grande and other places who had joined the Mexican Army and were now fighting under its colors—These deserters stood by their guns long after the Mexican troops had given up all hope, and raised the colors three times after they had been hauled down by our enemies—About eighty of them were taken prisoners; among them several from our Regiment. Three General Courts are now in session for their trial and without doubt they will all be shot in front of the Army.

"In the battles of the Rio Grande, our regiment—the 3rd, was second to none, it is well known, in those battles; but in those of Cerro Gordo, Contreras, and Churubusco, it stood prominent among all others. Before leaving Puebla it had been reinforced by three companies from the States, and other recruits had been added to it, so that at Contreras, we went into action with nearly 600 officers and men. We escaped on the 19th and 20th with but little loss, not withstanding the hard fighting which we did and our exposed situation especially at Churubusco—Two officers belonging to it (Capt. Craig and Lt. Buell) only were wounded, and the killed and wounded of officers and men amounted to 40, almost the smallest loss we sustained in any battle in the war in proportion to our numbers.

"By perusing the different battle reports of the 19th and 20th, you will see that *I was there*. Little was done generally by the new 'levies,' although no doubt, the papers will be full of what the volunteers did, etc. But little attention ought to be paid to them; and in truth, with the exception of one or two regiments, they were hardly brought into action. But of course, *we* who do and have done all the hard fighting will get no credit; while they who have done nothing in fact, but look on, run off with the laurels."[51]

Once again a Mexican rout was on, but except for Harney's dragoons, the exhausted Americans did not pursue. General Scott thought it better to consolidate his force again and move on the capital in a calculated method. He had achieved a great victory, but at the cost of 1,053 killed or wounded. Mexican losses were estimated at approximately four thousand.

The 3rd Infantry was posted to the convent at Churubusco as Scott halted the advance to tend to the wounded and reconstitute his force. Lieutenant Richardson had again lived up to his nickname of Fighting Dick, as his men fought a nonstop thirty-six-hour battle. Facing continual fire while supporting Magruder's battery and conducting the rescue sortie in the darkness and the rain; the manhandling withdrawal of the crippled battery and the diversionary attack at dawn; joining in the general assault at Contreras and finally storming the convent at Churubusco: all of these actions came on top of each other with no time to rest and little time to plan. The success of these missions gave strong evidence of Richardson's strength, determination, and competence as a company commander. Captain Craig, in his report to the regimental commander, spoke highly of the conduct of Lieutenant Richardson. General P. F. Smith, the brigade commander in his report to General Scott, also praised his manner under fire. On the skirmish line, on the tip of the bayonet, no officers did more to beat the Mexicans at Contreras and Churubusco than Craig and Richardson.

Three hundred miles away from their base of supply, the American army was without hope of reinforcement, short of rations and ammunition, and facing an army several times its own size behind a fortified position. On September 6, Scott terminated the armistice when he learned that the Mexicans reportedly had a stockpile of powder and were melting down church bells and casting them into cannon at Molino del Rey, a flour mill and former foundry near the fortress of Chapultepec. Since the main assault would not be launched for several days, he assigned Worth's division the task of carrying the foundry and blowing up its stores.

The Mexican position was very strong. Worth reasoned that a hand-picked assaulting party, the "forlorn hope," chosen from different regiments, could punch their way through the center and, when followed by Colonel John Garland's brigade, could storm their way in and take possession of the objective.

The attack was launched, and the handpicked assault party was cut to pieces, with eleven out of fourteen officers killed or wounded. The battle became a replay of Monterrey, with units attacking, breaking up under fire, rallying, and moving forward in small groups. Lieutenant Colonel William Montrose Graham, wounded four times, kept fighting until his men captured an enemy strongpoint; he died after he was hit a fifth time. (His son would command an artillery battery and witness Richardson's mortal wounding, fifteen years later.) In the face of the American advance and their willingness to take heavy casualties, the Mexicans conducted a fighting withdrawal back to Mexico City and the fortress of Chapultepec.

Lieutenant Colonel Hitchcock, the inspector general of Scott's army, witnessed the attack and wrote privately later that he considered General Worth's assault to have been made blindly and could not help regretting the events of the day: "a few more such victories and this army will be destroyed!"[52]

"I never saw a braver set of men"

On September 13, Scott completed his preparations and the long-awaited attack on Mexico City began. The first phase would address the fortress of Chapultepec, high on a hilltop overlooking the city. General Quitman's division was to attack the fortress from the southeast, while Pillow was to attack from the west. The assault was to be reinforced by a select group of 250 men from each of the divisions of Twiggs and Worth to act as the lead storming party. The 3rd Infantry contribution to the assault party was to be two officers, seven noncommissioned officers, and forty-five soldiers. So many volunteered for the mission that lots had to be drawn to determine who would go. The remaining part of the regiment was assigned the position of following up the main assault behind Quitman's division.

For the first time in his career, Lieutenant Richardson would not accompany his company in the attack. He and Lieutenant Bee were chosen to be part of the "forlorn hope" that was to storm the fortress of Chapultepec, knowing that the Mexican army was now backed into a corner and the appalling losses from the attack on Molino del Rey were evidence that this next attack would be bloody. As the elite company marched up to its assigned positions, Richardson remembered, "As our storming party passed the camp of the Rifle Regt., the officers and men of the regiment simultaneously and without orders gave three hardy cheers, and certainly I never saw a braver set of men in one body; the pick and selection of Twiggs' whole division."[53]

The volunteer company was placed under the command of Captain Silas Casey. Armed with scaling ladders, axes, and crowbars, they planned to scale the southeast wall of the fortress. During the night, the storming party was placed in a ditch on the left side of the Tacubaya causeway and in the rear of an American battery, which protected them from the plunging fire from Chapultepec. At dawn, the Americans opened up with artillery fire to soften up the Mexican defenses. At eight o'clock, the advance order arrived from

General Scott, and Casey got his men up and formed in a matter of seconds. On the command of "Forward!" Richardson moved down the road at the "double quick," and for six hundred yards, the group was exposed to a raking fire from the castle. Grape shot from Mexican batteries, and musket fire knocked over several men, including Lieutenant Tower. Stopped by a large water-filled ditch, the stormers veered off the road to the left and charged through an opening visible in the surrounding wall. A West Point classmate of Richardson, Lieutenant Levi Gantt, was shot dead while receiving an order from Captain Casey, who was wounded at the same time. Richardson struggled to cross the low, wet ground intersected with ditches between the road and surrounding wall. A section of Duncan's battery under the command of Lieutenant Hunt was pushed forward to support the storming operation, firing and continually elevating its guns as Richardson began to climb up the slope.

The lower works were carried without much trouble; in fact, the quickly advancing infantry and the retreating Mexicans became so intermingled that the Mexican engineer officer in charge of firing the land mines for the defense hesitated to detonate the powder trains. He was captured, and the expected explosion never came. Halfway up the slope, however, the advance was stopped in front of a wide ditch at the base of the palace's retaining wall. On the other side of the castle, the attack bogged down with riflemen content with keeping a steady fire on the fortress roof and windows, waiting for the scaling ladders to come up. General Pillow, who was wounded, feared the attack was stalling and sent a message to Worth to move forward quickly.

General Quitman's attack on the eastern side was also encountering difficulties. Quitman was forced to send his men down the road in the face of an enemy strongpoint containing a five-gun battery, defended by a battalion of infantry straddling the causeway.

The only chance for success was to get down the straight causeway quickly. Four pieces of artillery trailed the assault, firing at targets of opportunity. When the Americans reached the battery, the Mexicans stood firm. Now, some of the problems that Lieutenant Colonel Hitchcock described at Molino del Rey began to repeat themselves. As the advance slowed, Colonel P F. Smith moved his brigade, including the 3rd Infantry, off the road and into the marshy ground on the right as he attempted to flank the Mexican positions.

On the western side the scaling ladders had been lifted and the final assault was under way. Men of all commands were intermingled as the struggle to raise the ladders commenced. Lieutenant Lewis A. Armistead, the first man into the ditch, was wounded. Lieutenant James Longstreet, who was also shot down while carrying the regimental colors, followed him. Lieutenant George Pickett stopped long enough to retrieve the colors before he continued with

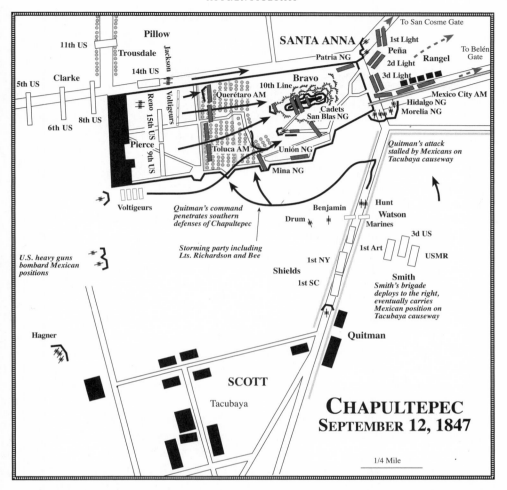

CHAPULTEPEC
SEPTEMBER 12, 1847

1/4 Mile

the charge. As the men climbed the walls, some ladders fell, but many were successful, and soon an overwhelming American force was within the walls of the fortress.

The Mexican guns fell silent and the American flag was raised above Chapultepec. The battery on the Tacubaya causeway also surrendered under the attack from the front and the flanking movement by P. F. Smith's brigade. General Scott, who once again observed the attack of Richardson and his fellow soldiers, hastened to the castle and was mobbed by the ecstatic Americans. The whole operation had taken two hours.

Richardson described his participation in the assault in a letter to his parents: "A heavy cannonade from all our batteries was commenced at daybreak, which the enemy hardly answered and which was continued until 8 o'clock in the morning when the assault commenced. Our party, being in advance of Tacubaya, followed the road under a terrible fire from 4,000 infantry and five pieces charged with grape, and although losing three officers and 70 men in killed and wounded, nothing could stop us. Halting a few minutes as we came to a good cover for the troops to take a breath and give them a few volleys of musketry, we marched into the lower works with the bayonet and routed them in short order. After carrying the lower works, we soon led up the hill and assisted Worth's Division in taking the main work.

"I hope you will see that I am mentioned with some credit, although it is considered sufficient in itself to be selected on a 'forlorn hope.' The Storming Party of our Division were promised rewards, if it proved successful; every officer upon it was to be brevetted one grade higher, every noncommissioned officer who distinguished himself would be made an officer and every soldier to receive two dollars extra per month during the service.

"Congress, I suppose, will attend to it next winter, if now the danger is passed, they forget our service—I have picked up several trophies and curiosities, which I intend to carry home. Among others is a helmet of brass belonging to the Cuvassiers, which I intend to give the State House at Montpelier."[54]

With the road now open to Mexico City, the American army began its advance. With Worth designated the main effort, Scott let Quitman attack first along the shorter route, hoping Santa Anna would focus his attention on the Belen Gate. The fight here was a stalemate and caused extensive casualties on both sides.

Worth's attack also was successful in breaking through the San Cosme gate with the help of tremendous individual efforts by artillery lieutenants Thomas J. Jackson, Henry J. Hunt, and Jesse Reno. With both entrances to the city now open, Santa Anna realized his position was hopeless and withdrew his army outside the city. The next morning, General Scott and his staff, in full military uniform, arrived at the National Palace to close the fighting of the Mexico City campaign.

For the next nine months, until the Treaty of Guadalupe Hidalgo was ratified on May 30, 1848, Richardson and the 3rd Infantry were garrisoned in Mexico City, enjoying the hospitality of the capital. With the campaign over, the army found time to honor its soldiers for their achievements. Richardson thought his prospects of promotion were good, writing his father early in 1848, "Several vacancies have lately occurred in our regiment. Capt. Dobbins has been dismissed, Capt. Smith is dead, Lt. Johnson resigned, Lt. Jordan is now a Capt. In the Quartermaster Dept., and will probably stay there. Those vacancies make me second for promotion to Captain, Lt. Buell being first. Lt. O'Sullivan, who never was fit for an officer and who the President appointed against the recommendation of the commanding officer of the regiment, we have run out and obliged to resign. It is understood that he has joined the Mexicans.

"I have been recommended for a brevet for Cerro Gordo to the government in Washington, although I am not at liberty to say what officer recommended me to be a brevet captain, he thinks there is no doubt but I shall get it. Although I care more for it on account of my friends than myself. If I live, I shall soon be a full captain anyhow."[55]

Richardson started the hostilities as a second lieutenant in his regiment with three years' time in grade. His promotion to first lieutenant after Monterrey came as much for his bravery as for the fact of the many vacant positions caused by casualties. Now as a reward for past services, First Lieutenant Richardson received a brevet promotion to captain, dated August 20, 1847, for gallant and meritorious conduct in the battles of Contreras and Churubusco, followed by a brevet promotion to major, dated September 13, 1847, for gallant and meritorious conduct acting as a member of the storming party in the Battle of Chapultepec. During a regimental review by General Scott, the 3rd Infantry was given its distinctive nickname when Scott remarked to his staff, "Gentlemen, take off your hats to the Old Guard of the Army."[56]

In the relative quiet of garrison duty in Mexico City, egos and army politics began to emerge. A sharp difference between General Pillow and Winfield Scott led to Pillow's court-martial for insubordination, of which he was later cleared. During the first week of April 1848, Israel Richardson sent a letter to his father, describing his duties and the army gossip during the occupation: "I attend the Court of Inquiry regularly. . . . Gen. Pillow's case is getting a good deal under the weather. . . . I was invited to dine with Gen. Scott today. . . . I shall send proceedings of the court every time the mail goes. . . . I send you also a full list of the officers who entered the valley of Mexico, showing when and where engaged. . . . If the retired list should pass Congress this Winter, all three of us would be promoted. . . . Although I am in doubt if we shall have peace soon, still I think our fighting is about over."[57]

The confidence gained by Richardson in the Mexican campaign was due to his good fortune to be mentored by a mix of leaders such as the intellectual, open-minded Hitchcock; brave and disciplined leaders like Field, Lear, and Morris; and the companionship of loyal and dedicated friends like Craig, Henry, and Bee. The loss of so many officers and friends, not only within his regiment but also throughout the army (nine deaths from his West Point class of fifty-two, a rate of almost 20 percent), would always motivate him to set and enforce high standards.

3

Adversity

"On the whole, it is a most dreary and disagreeable place"

With the conclusion of the war and the signing of the Treaty of Guadalupe Hidalgo, Mexico gave up its claim to Texas and California and lost its northern outpost in New Mexico. The 3rd Infantry returned by sea from Vera Cruz to Pascagoula, Mississippi. Richardson wrote, "We are encamped here in a pine forest on the sea beach, halfway from New Orleans and Mobile, distance from each about 90 miles. Two steamboats from each land at the wharf of the Hotel Pascagoula every day. No people reside here except a hundred or so of the ladies and gentlemen who come here a few months in the summer time for their health. On the whole, it is a most dreary and disagreeable place for a military post that I have the bad luck to be stationed at for some time. Fortune might possibly favor us once and take our regiment to the north, it has been in the southern country for the past twenty-one years." An added note to his sister reminded her to not fail and pass on his greetings to "Ellen," ending with "tell Ellen I am going to make a dead set at her, when I come home."[1]

Orders arrived dividing the regiment in two, with four companies remaining in New Orleans and six others sent to the frontier to garrison San Antonio, Texas. As the government began taking steps to occupy its newly acquired territory in the southwest, Richardson's duty would be to protect frontier settlements and to contain the hostile Indians.

The veterans of the 3rd Infantry settled into their new duties with the observation that while at times dangerous, life in the territories meant adjusting back to the bureaucracy of army life. With the discovery of gold in California, the tremendous influx of settlers renewed the urgency to develop the southwest. One of the better routes to the Pacific lay through the settlement of El Paso. Generally speaking, it lay level all the way from Independence, Kansas, to California. It also connected with roads coming from the southern areas such as Memphis and New Orleans, and at El Paso, it intersected another important road, the old Spanish route from Mexico City to Santa Fe.

The trails from Texas to the West were known to few people, and past the outpost of San Antonio lay a stretch of inhospitable Indian country that extended to the Rio Grande in New Mexico. The nearest locations of outposts to the west were Taos, Santa Fe, and Albuquerque, almost nine hundred miles away. The land between was so unknown that the border between Texas and New Mexico had not yet been fixed.

Late in the spring of 1849, the column for El Paso got under way. Being the senior company commander in the 3rd Infantry, Captain Jefferson Van Horne was chosen to lead the expedition; this left his Company E under the command of his executive officer, Lieutenant Richardson. A wagon road had to be constructed to permit resupply of the established posts along the route, and the fact that no friendly outposts would be encountered until they reached their destination forced the party to carry supplies consisting of a year's clothing and sixty days' rations for the march, along with six months' provisions to carry over the garrison until it could be resupplied again.

As executive officer, Richardson was deeply involved with all logistical aspects of the expedition. In preparation, he worked closely with the chief of commissariat of the Department of Texas, his old friend Lieutenant James Longstreet. It was an enjoyable time, for they had last seen each other a year and a half earlier when both men served on the storming teams during the Battle of Chapultepec, in which Longstreet had been wounded. While convalescing back east, he had married his regimental commander's daughter, Louisa Garland, and together they returned back west to take up duty in San Antonio. The Longstreets entertained Richardson often, and their old friendship was renewed during the busy days of gathering equipment for the journey to El Paso.

On June 3, 1849, six companies of the 3rd Infantry and the Regimental Howitzer Battery, a total of 257 officers and men, left San Antonio. Also included were 275 wagons loaded with supplies, 2,500 head of livestock, and a group of immigrants taking advantage of the protection offered for their travels westward.

After victory in Mexico, symptoms that confront all demobilizing armies caused serious difficulties as Richardson worked to organize the expedition. He made note that in the rush to downsize, a fine train of some four hundred wagons, which had supplied the army on its march from Vera Cruz just a year before, had been sold at auction. Wagons worth seventy five dollars were dealt away for five dollars, and mules worth eighty dollars changed hands for ten dollars. "The government must have known at the time the army left Vera Cruz that the whole of the train would be wanted on the frontier of Texas. The treaty having been established, and military forts on any distant frontier always requiring more or less a large train of wagons to transport provisions and military supplies.

"Sometime last spring it was determined to outfit the expedition to El Paso, and Gen. Worth was ordered to San Antonio. Wagons had to be brought from Philadelphia and Pittsburgh at great expense, and poor, unbroken mules were bought at 30 dollars each instead of giving 50 dollars each for good, serviceable mules. The ox train is in good condition, but the mule train, besides having some 130 mules condemned as totally unfit for service, was in the worst condition I ever saw a train in the army. For the want of good mules, we have been delayed over a month, which is not a small matter when we consider that the command of over 700 men have to be fed." Although disgusted with the army policy and bungled logistics, Richardson at least had the presence of mind to remind his family that army regulations prohibited the publishing of news articles relating to marches and military operations. "I hope no editor of a paper will see this," he concluded.[2]

Richardson spent a busy summer on the plains of Texas, helping to manage the plodding convoy along its journey. Along the route they traveled, the army would later build the outposts of Fort Clark, Fort Davis, and Fort Quitman. One hundred days and 675 miles later, the expedition arrived at its destination. The command was surprised to discover that the "town" of El Paso, which they had been ordered to occupy, consisted of only three widely scattered ranch houses on the U.S. side of the Rio Grande. The long established and thriving town of El Paso del Norte, later called Juarez, was on the Mexican side of the river. The garrison's arrival was welcomed by both settlements, because for many years, they had lived under constant fear of the Indians; the Apaches had been known to raid ranches and houses in broad daylight and within sight of the town. Before the completion of the transcontinental railroad, this route would be used regularly by troops, government and commercial trains, the Overland Mail and Stage, Texas cattle drovers, and settlers migrating westward.

With the lack of facilities on the American side of the river, Van Horne was forced to improvise shelter for his men as he set up camp at Billy Smith's ranch, the closest of the settlements to El Paso. The other two ranch houses in the area were Hart's Mill and the Stephenson ranch. Soon the usual adobe post was constructed on leased property, and an American military presence was established in the newly created Department of New Mexico. During the fall of 1849, Companies A and C were engaged in escorting supplies from the Pecos River, while Van Horne and Richardson, with the thirty-nine men of Company E, conducted an expedition against the Apaches at the Copper Mines near the present-day town of Santa Rita. In his report to the regimental commander, Van Horne stated this movement was in response to the situation caused by "citizens (Americans) who were selling powder, lead and guns to the

Apaches in exchange for animals and other property which the Indians had stolen from the Mexicans."[3]

"The major told them to vamoose . . ."

Establishing the post at El Paso stimulated considerable fort-building activity over the next several years, with posts being erected along the trail blazed from San Antonio and northward to Santa Fe. Isolation was ending for the few residents of El Paso. The presence of a garrison of soldiers to protect the region caused a greater influx of settlers and the start of prosperity for area residents.

Once the post at El Paso was established, a sense of routine garrison life started to settle in on the soldiers stationed there. Shortly after his arrival, Richardson became acquainted with Mr. Hugh Stephenson, a wealthy American merchant who had been trading with the Mexicans since 1824. A former Kentuckian, he had settled in the El Paso, and the Stephenson ranch was one of the few American settlements established before the arrival of the 3rd Infantry. In due course, Richardson was introduced to the Stephenson family: Mrs. Stephenson, Mexican by birth, who did not speak English, and their daughter, Rita. Over the course of the next few months an attachment between Israel and Rita developed, culminating with their marriage on August 3, 1850.

The territory of New Mexico was more or less under control of the Indians and a few bold traders and cattlemen. Reports of periodic attacks on scattered settlements brought many complaints to the government. The Mexican government also complained and filed huge claims against the United States for attacks committed by Indians coming across our border. To remedy this state of affairs, the War Department decided to strengthen its forces and expand the number of posts along the Rio Grande.

Infantry units, which made up the bulk of the army, were just not mobile enough to counter the raiding style of Indian warfare. Despite uniform agreement that infantry units were at a great disadvantage in fighting mounted Indian warriors of the plains, the 3rd Infantry was made responsible for the main burden of frontier defense. The difficulty of securing horses and the exorbitant cost of maintaining mounted units in the Indian country were undoubtedly the deciding factors for this dubious policy.

After his wedding, it was time for Richardson to ponder his future. Including time spent at West Point, he had served the army almost fifteen years now and was arguably one of the most combat experienced officers in the best infantry regiment in the nation, though he had nothing to show for it but a first lieutenant's commission. His new father-in-law, a successful businessman and trader, must have had discussions with him concerning his future, and on October 10, 1850, Richardson took a six-month furlough. With this long overdue leave, he journeyed east, traveling through Pontiac and on to Burlington with his new bride, to whom he introduced his family.

While spending time with family affairs in Vermont, his promotion to captain was announced on March 5, 1851. Along with the promotion, Richardson was ordered to report to New York City to take command of 230 new recruits bound for New Mexico. It was sad to note that his promotion was the result of the death of his friend, Captain William S. Henry, caused by illness while he served on recruiting duty in New York City. The promotion and accompanying increase in pay were a welcomed event for the couple just starting a family. Also pleasant was that he would be accompanied on the trip by his wife and his sister Marcella. The party left New York harbor bound for New Orleans on April 5 aboard the cutter *Juliet*.

Arriving in New Orleans, they boarded a paddle wheeler up the Mississippi to St. Louis and traveled across country to Fort Leavenworth, the army's logistics staging point for all outposts in the Southwest. The Richardson family waited until supplies and replacements were gathered before heading out West in a huge wagon train. Soon after they started, Marcella began to record in her journal the trials and tribulations new recruits experienced as they learned their profession. On May 25, 1851, she wrote, "We rose at 4 o'clock, everything in sad confusion from last night's storm, which was the most terrific I ever witnessed. The soldiers were all recruits and knew nothing of striking tents or packing wagons, so after two hours hard work, we were ready to break camp."[4] Her narrative related the pleasures and miseries of the journey. Accompanied by Major Buell and Colonel Sumner, the large party took almost a month to cross the plains before reaching their final destination. Along the way Marcella wrote of immense herds of buffalo, a cholera epidemic, tarantula spiders, and the chasing of deserters; it was an exciting adventure for two women crossing the country for the first time.

Upon arriving at Las Vegas, seventy-five miles from Santa Fe, on July 26, Colonel Sumner granted Richardson a twenty-day leave of absence to escort his wife and sister down to the home of Rita's parents in El Paso. Upon arriving at the Stevenson ranch on August 6, Rita went into a difficult labor and died as a result of giving birth to a son, named Theodore Virginius Richardson. Israel was forced to leave his son in the caring hands of his in-laws and sister as he returned for duty on August 16, 1851.

Over time, Richardson's old circle of mentors and friends began to fade away. Colonel Hitchcock received a transfer to California. Captain Craig was murdered in California on June 6, 1852, while tracking down a pair of deserters. Finally, Richardson's wartime regimental commander under Scott, Captain Alexander, was reassigned when he was promoted to major in the 8th Infantry on August 1, 1852.

Frontier duty became more burdensome with the arrival of a new regimental commander on September 16, 1851: Lieutenant Colonel Dixon S. Miles, who had graduated from West Point in 1824 and had seen extensive service in Florida, Texas, and New Mexico. In the Mexican War he had proven his bravery at the siege at Fort Brown and the Battle of Monterrey; he spent the remainder of the war as commander of the garrison at Vera Cruz. His only experience in a combat command occurred in January 1848, when he was put in charge of twelve hundred troops escorting five hundred wagons from Vera Cruz to Mexico City. This proved a failure when Mexican bandits drove off more than half of the wagons in his overextended convoy. Only after being reinforced with four hundred infantry plus artillery was he able to reach his destination. Comparison of this incident with Miles' conduct at Monterrey suggests that he was stronger on personal courage than on military management.[5]

Lieutenant William W. Averill served with Miles in New Mexico during the late 1850s and described him as "a great talker who gave his vivid imagination a loose rein. Colonel Miles had the energy and willingness to assume any responsibility, but needed near him a man like Lane [Lieutenant William B. Lane, adjutant] with sound judgment and who enjoyed the confidence of everyone, in order that misdirection and eccentricity might be prevented."[6]

It is fair to say that the command style of Lieutenant Colonel Miles was a little unsettling to the officers of the 3rd Infantry. Within one month of the change of command, Lieutenant Andrew J. Williamson resigned his commission and Lieutenant Charles B. Brower was arrested and dismissed from the service. One has to wonder how the pressures of such an erratic commander affected Richardson's outlook on his career in the army. As an isolated company commander in charge of Fort Webster and later Fort Thorn in southern New Mexico, he had some sense of autonomy and his command group was extraordinary. His company command consisted of approximately fifty infantrymen and fifty mounted dragoons. For a time, his executive officer was Lieutenant Barnard E. Bee and his training officer was Lieutenant Junius Daniel; later Lieutenant Henry H. Walker[7] would be assigned to Richardson's company. All of these men would rise to become general officers in the Confederate army during the Civil War, and they all became known as quality infantry leaders who excelled in combat. The fact that Richardson was their principal source of leadership during this period of isolated duty speaks for his ability as a motivator, instructor, and role model.

With the death of his wife and the need to provide for a very young child, Richardson returned to active duty with his regiment. He was given command of Company K and from September to December 1851 was on patrol duty throughout southern New Mexico. In the spring of 1851, the United States–Mexico Boundary Commission, under the protection of Captain Craig, arrived at the

Santa Rita copper mines in the heart of Chiricahua Apache territory. They occupied the old fort, which had been built in 1804 to protect the mines. The camp was renamed Fort Webster in honor of Secretary of State Daniel Webster. When the commission moved on to continue its work, Craig recommended that "since Santa Rita del Cobre was in the heart of Apache country, a permanent garrison be established there. If not, the Apaches would force the fifteen or twenty citizens engaged in mining to leave the area."[8] Soon after the report was filed, Captain Richardson, along with his Company K, received orders from Sumner to occupy the post and thus establish a presence within Apache territory.

Though now deserted, the copper mines had once been the leading source of copper for Mexico. Indian raids had stopped all travel to Chihuahua in 1833. The mines had been abandoned, leaving a desolate cluster of adobe huts and an imposing three-sided presidio. The Chiricahua Apaches in the area were led by Chief Mangas Coloradas. This active band caused the army many problems with their continuing attacks on settlers in the area.

On December 29, 1851, Richardson and his Company K marched out of Fort Fillmore with the mission to occupy copper mines at Santa Rita del Cobre. During the next two weeks, the command marched along the Rio Grande, stopping at Las Cruces, Dona Ana, and San Diego. Noting that his unit was being closely followed by a growing band of Apaches, Richardson had his men bring out the old brass howitzer and fire several rounds into the mountains for target practice near where the Apaches could be seen gathering. This act caused a great excitement among the Indians but did them no harm.

As the march continued, it became evident that the Apache presence was increasing. On January 16, Richardson's men reached the settlement of Mule Springs only to find that the Apaches had been there less than half an hour earlier, killing a young Mexican boy and stealing four horses from Spanish owners. Witnesses vividly described the incident to Richardson: "the Apaches enticed the boy to leave the protection of their camp while under cover of a white flag and then brutally murdered him."[9] Richardson's mounts were so jaded at the end of the day and the Rio Grande border was so close that any pursuit of the Indians was considered useless.

On January 21, Richardson reached his objective, the abandoned Spanish fort. The outpost was in a state of disrepair, but the walls were good protection from musket balls. Rich quantities of copper ore found dumped in front of the entrance to the mine gave evidence the place had been quickly abandoned by the miners, who had feared attack.

The next morning, approximately one hundred Apaches were spotted approaching the fort. Richardson ordered his entire command to arms and manned the walls of the fort. Private Sylvester W. Matson, of Company K, later described the action in his diary:

"An old squaw walked out alone in front of them with a white shirt attached to a pole as a truce flag. When she got up to the front of the fort an interpreter and a party of officers went out and spoke to her. She was sent to tell the white soldiers that the Apaches wanted to make peace with them. Our Major told her to go back and tell her people to all come in and he would treat with them. The squaw returned to her band, they held a long pow-wow, then only two of the chiefs came forward. They said they wanted to 'smoke peace with the soldiers.' The Major told them he would not smoke until they returned the mules and horses taken from our train at Fort Fillmore last month. The two chiefs replied the mules and horses were not taken by their band, but by one on the other side of the mountains over in Mexico led by Mangas Coloradas. The name of the chief of the present party was Ponce. The Major told them to vamoose and informed them if he caught any of them prowling around the vicinity, he and his soldiers would send them to the happy hunting grounds. They scampered back to their band and soon showed signs of preparing for a fight, so we opened fire on the Apaches first with our muskets and after with our old brass howitzer. Several of them fell beneath our fire and their companions picked them up and carried them off. They fled leaving two wounded squaws, which we captured."[10]

Richardson's official report gives more detail to the affair. In his opinion, the Apaches had come to the copper mines intending to kill three miners who had recently preceded Richardson to the area. Upon finding the fort fully manned, the Indians attempted to lure the command group outside the protection of their men and murder them in the same fashion as the incident at Mule Springs, a few days before.

"On finding us here, the main party kept at a distance of 400 yards from the fort while one or more of them came nearer for the purpose of speaking with us. I had the company formed about 130 yards outside the fort. Lt. O'Bannon, Dr. Hammond and myself preceded the company about 100 yards further to get near the Indians who came up to speak with us. In a short time, their Chief, Delgadito also came up and said he wished to live in peace with us. We told him we wished to live in peace also, but were not satisfied with the affair of the Mexican boy (at Mule Springs). That if he wished peace he might bring in his Indians and we would talk the matter over with them.

"He said he would come in if we would send off our soldiers and come out ourselves further toward the Indians. We told him we never went out in this country without our men. He said in that case, he could not come in. We told him there was no alternative; that he must either make peace or fight us, upon which he began to run off with his other men. We called on him to stop. Lt. O'Bannon and the doctor discharged their pistols and I ordered our men to fire.

"It is thought that from four to six Indians were killed or badly wounded. The horse of their chief, Delgadito, was killed and it is thought the chief also was killed, he being lashed upon another horse. We pursued them for a mile but could not overtake them."[11]

Delgadito, a trusted lieutenant of Mangas Coloradas, was seriously wounded during this skirmish. Richardson planned his first encounter with the Apaches to be a show of force, which would intimidate them into a peace treaty. For that reason, he displayed the entire garrison outside the fort during their first meeting. The Apache tactic at Mule Springs was still fresh in the minds of the negotiators and caused the nervousness, creating a disastrous conclusion to the parley.

After this brush with the Apaches, Richardson immediately set to work to strengthen the Fort Webster defenses from attack, which everyone expected would come shortly. A platform was erected, and the brass howitzer was mounted to be able to fire over the wall. Work details were sent out to gather wood. On January 26, the Apaches struck again. Private Matson described the skirmish:

"At 11 o'clock this morning we were suddenly summoned by the beating of the 'Long Roll' which in haste called us to arms. We had a sizable herd of cattle, principally oxen used for draft purposes. The cattle were permitted to graze outside of the enclosure and herders tended them. This morning the herders fled into the fort and announced that a band of Apaches had suddenly attacked them while driving off the cattle. As quickly as we could form and start after them we gave pursuit to the Indians.

"The squaws and very young bucks drove off the cattle while the older warriors guarded their retreat and decoyed us off in a different direction. We had a lively skirmish with them. The attack was so sudden there was no time to get the old brass howitzer into action.

"About fifty Apache warriors engaged us. They took advantage of some stunted brush growing in the valley and circled about us. Their arrows swished very close to our ears and one grazed my cheek. They also had some guns and pistols which they fired at us and the bullets came very close.

"In the heat of the skirmish our Major who was leading us got separated from the balance of the command. I was detailed with a corporal's guard to search for him. We took off in the direction we had last seen him going. We could not find him and returned to our party. In the meantime, the Indians had concluded correctly that the squaws and youths had gotten the oxen safely away and the warriors themselves skipped. They got away with their dead and wounded. We saw several of their numbers fall and were sure of killing and wounding more of them than they did of us."[12]

The Apaches had been successful in avenging Richardson's preemptive attack. Although much work had been completed to strengthen the fort, Richardson was forced to keep his livestock a half mile away, at the closest grazing area available. The Apaches surprised the guard, killing Private John Croty and driving the rest into the fort to sound the alarm. Richardson, along with the majority of his company, made their way to the grazing area at a run, but the Apaches already had a two-mile head start on the soldiers. Men on foot started a pursuit of the mounted enemy as best as possible, and some thirty head of cattle were soon recovered. Over the next five miles, the Indians stopped several times, splitting into three groups, then moving on, as if luring Richardson farther away from his base, all the while taking care to remain just outside the range of the soldier's weapons.

Richardson's pursuit is described in his report: "By this time, five horses, which had escaped being taken, were saddled and brought to the front. Myself mounting one, and four men, among who were Sergeants Bernard O'Dougherty and Nicholas Wade, mounted the others. Myself and the four others then went ahead for the purpose of keeping the Indians in sight; Lt. O'Bannon was directed to follow with the remainder of the men as fast as possible. After getting about a mile ahead, we came within a short distance of the herd protected by a strong guard of Indians in the rear and on the flanks. I halted for the company to come up having first ordered my men to stick close to their horses and follow me if anything should happen. We had not halted five minutes when eighty Indians made their appearance in a ravine on our rear and flank not more than 130 yards from us. The Indians immediately charged, and we took a circuitous route across the ravine for the purpose of forming with Lt. O'Bannon and his party. In coming within fifty yards of the nearest Indians; notwithstanding the many cautions which I had given them to keep close to me and stick to their horses; I became aware that Sergeants O'Dougherty and Wade had separated from me and had taken another route. After crossing many hills and ravines and being headed off by the Indians, I at length found Lt. O'Bannon with my two remaining men."[13]

While Richardson was circling around the Apaches, O'Bannon was closing in on the main band, who had taken a defensive position on top of a large hill. As O'Bannon formed up his men for an attack, the Apaches abruptly mounted their horses and retreated. The Indians had been using this time to stall any pursuit and to let the stolen herd of cattle escape. Richardson now joined O'Bannon and moved the company forward in search of the two missing sergeants. After a short time, the body of Sergeant O'Dougherty was recovered. Richardson and O'Bannon agreed that nothing more could be accomplished. The pursuit of a mounted enemy by foot soldiers was an impossible mission, and the command returned to Fort Webster. The next day, Richardson and his entire company returned to the area, and following the circling vultures, the men found Sergeant Wade. His body had been scalped and mutilated. The

Apaches had evidently captured Wade and tortured him to death, to avenge the killings of their band on the previous day.

As the pressure on Fort Webster eased and communication became more regular, one of the first visitors came from El Paso with tragic news. Richardson received word that his six-month-old son, Theodore, had died. He wrote his sister, "I have just received your letter together with several others but I have not opened them; the melancholy contents have been given to me by the old Mexican, Alejo. Major Morris has promised to order me down on duty as soon as more troops come up."[14] It was a devastating personal loss to add to his professional failure in his first independent command. Sumner wanted a presence established in the heart of Apache territory to suppress their marauding, but he deserved some of the blame for the failure of Richardson by not resourcing him properly enough to allow any measure of success. The small detachment, without a dependable line of communication, was unable to take any offensive action and could only look to its own protection.

When Colonel Sumner forwarded Richardson's report to General Twiggs, he added his own comments which criticized Richardson's actions: "1) I disapprove decidedly of Bvt. Maj. Richardson's firing upon the Indians while in parley with them. If he had reason to suspect them of treachery, he should have been cautious, but until they committed some overt act of perfidy, he was not justified in firing on them. 2) . . . it was extremely imprudent to allow his cattle to graze without a sufficient guard to protect them, even if it had taken the whole company, with the exception of a few to hold the fort. 3) . . . there was no reason to leave his command for the purpose of keeping the Indians in sight, when the company could, certainly, have followed the trail of a herd of cattle and two hundred Indians. Under all the circumstances of this case I think it proper to refer it to the Comdg. General of the Division."[15]

When Richardson heard of Sumner's remarks to General Twiggs, he was not pleased. He submitted a letter to the division commander, Twiggs: "In consequence of certain accusations made against me by Colonel Sumner, I request the opinion of a Court of Inquiry, knowing that I am abundantly able to prove myself clear, by good and sufficient evidence of any error committed by me at this premises."[16] Colonel William Bliss responded, explaining that a Court of Inquiry could not be ordered on such a vague charge that Richardson had put before it. Any specific accusation would still be premature as Twiggs had taken no action, but Bliss acknowledged that Richardson had the right to demand a Court of Inquiry if any censure came from the division commander. The matter was dropped soon after when Twiggs declined to take any further action or investigation.

With his crushing personal and professional difficulties, it appears that Richardson suffered in a depressed state. For almost a year, there is no record of any letters sent to family members. In November of 1853, because of continuing difficulties supplying the post, Richardson and the garrison of Fort Webster were transferred to a location one mile from the Rio Grande, halfway between El Paso to the south and Fort Craig to the north. Richardson was ordered to construct a new fort with a mission to protect the Camino Real against Apache raids. He built an adobe fort near the principle wagon trail that ran between El Paso and Santa Fe and named the post Fort Thorn, in honor of Captain Herman Thorn, who had drowned in the Colorado River on October 16, 1849.

He made his apologies to his family in a letter dated March 7, 1854: "I put off writing a letter until I should hear from you at Fort Webster; when some four months ago we were ordered to break that post and move to establish a new one, and what with my responsibility in building up to this place, being Comdg. Officer of the post, and quartermaster and commissary and command-ing the company, and there being no officer at the post able to do duty except one subaltern, the Doct. And myself, I assure you a person of my sedentary habits has had his hands full.

"I have had some small troubles with some of those officers under my com-mand which have amounted to nothing in the end, but which, at the time were extremely vexatious—We will begin soon to build another set of quarters of adobe, for a permanent fort—So that my time has been much occupied that I could hardly find time sit down, but I should have written if I had not been waiting to get a letter from home—The last mail but one; was burnt up on the Plains, and I suppose at the time that your letters were burnt up in it—I am waiting with much anxiety for your next letter. I hope you will forgive me for not writing, I shall make an effort with Gen. Garland to get out and go home to visit in August or September, I have a considerable stock of cattle and hogs on hand which I hope to dispose of before that time."[17]

By 1855 the boredom of frontier garrison duty on the outlying parts of civi-lization had probably worn heavily on Richardson. The peacetime army of the 1850s had greatly deteriorated due to budget cuts in Washington. In fact, the base pay for company-grade officers had not been increased since 1798, although added allowances had increased their income. Those who felt this the most were junior officers stationed in the West, due to the economics of the California gold rush.

Captain William T. Sherman was depressed by the contrast between the seventy dollars he received each month and the three hundred dollars any servant he hired expected to be paid monthly. As Ulysses S. Grant pointed out, a cook earned more than a captain.[18] Several officers took leave and tried their hand at speculating in the boom economy of California and became rich. Two captains, Joseph L. Folsom and Henry W. Halleck, both made fortunes on land and business deals before resigning their commissions in 1854.

"They set us off from the States badly sup-plied, we must however, do the best we can"

With each passing year, the wear of missions not properly resourced on the lonely frontier was beginning to take its toll. In time of war, commanders were put in charge of units based on their ability to get the job done. In the peacetime army, command reverted to the seniority system that was jealously guarded by those whose only qualification for command was years of service. In 1855 Colonel Thomas T. Fauntleroy[19] became post commander of Fort Union. A Virginian, he was commissioned during the War of 1812 and served a long and unspectacular forty-three years in the army. This was exactly the type of officer that Richardson had difficulties dealing with throughout his career. If a commander could not lead by example, Richardson's lack of respect immediately became apparent.

In June of 1855, Major Richardson traveled to Fort Leavenworth to command a detachment of new replacements for the frontier. His route followed the Santa Fe Trail to their new posts in New Mexico. Not only did these green troops have to march across the Great Plains to their destination, but the task of teaching them the rudiments of discipline and drill while on the march also fell to Richardson.

The expedition started out from Fort Leavenworth on June 28 with some five hundred men, along with one hundred thousand dollars in government funds and a large supply train. The party consisted of 350 brand new infantrymen who were issued muskets without any training, and 150 dragoon recruits, unarmed and having a spare mount to take care of during the course of the journey. In typical fashion, the new infantry soldiers constantly straggled under the unaccustomed demands of their new profession. Richardson complained in letters home about the conditions he was forced to deal with: "I, being the senior officer of the line present for duty, have command and am obliged to attend to everything here, and having a set of very raw recruits to command, I am completely tired out and have but little time to write. To tell the truth, I live worse on this trip than I ever did in my life before, having plenty of men but can't get cooking fit to eat—I hope to quit the army by next spring."[20]

He found time to write a short note to his sister during the march: "We have marched away from the cholera after losing some 30 men at Fort Leavenworth and afterwards. All of the officers and families are well. The Indians have told us that 600 Comanches are waiting to attack us on the Arkansas. We don't entertain any fears for our safety unless we should be attacked by immense numbers. They sent us off from the States badly supplied, only 200 muskets and 4000 cartridges for the Inf; the 100 Dragoons have no arms at all. We must however do the best we can."[21]

Approximately halfway into their journey, while camped at Big Cow Creek, disaster struck Richardson's command. A servant dropped a hot coal in the dry grass while cooking, and a rapid prairie fire sprang up and burned out the camp. As the fire reached the tent containing the muskets and powder, many went off, wounding five men and consuming the ammunition. A routine mission was now transformed into a hardship operation. There was no alternative other than to continue on to New Mexico through dangerous Indian territory without critical equipment destroyed by fire. Almost all of the tents and shelters were lost along with clothes and much of the food.

Richardson described the incident in a letter: "We had most of our camp consumed by fire, lost nearly all our tents, some 30 muskets and most of the men's cartridge boxes, canteens and knapsacks burnt up and some provisions also; two men shot by burning muskets; one of these has since died; and most of the clothing and blankets also lost. The fire spread so rapidly that although we fought the fire for nearly an hour with 500 men it was impossible to keep it out of camp, and we had difficulty saving the horses and mules. However, we still have 180 muskets in firing condition. I only dreaded an attack of the Indians while the fire was going on; but they fortunately left us alone. That is the time they generally select, and I had the guard stand to their arms during the continuance of the fire."

On several occasions during the remainder of the journey, bands of Indians would trail the party. Once, a huge party of Comanche, led by their chief, Shave Head, fell in alongside the column and followed for twelve miles. Richardson put up a brave front, for all he had to work with was bluff. He later recalled, "I must confess I felt not altogether safe; and took the precaution to march the wagons in close file with a space of 40 feet between files so that we might take to the wagons and fight it out. The Dragoons were formed in columns of fours in rear of the Inf. and a guard of 40 Inf. were put at the rear of the wagons. We marched in this manner for a distance of some ten miles; the Indians being massed in front, on one side and in rear, sometimes coming within 40 or 50 yards of the wagons. I think from our determined front more than any other cause they decided to leave us alone; although we looked like a mere speck in front of a mountain, compared to them in number."[22]

Had the Comanche known that Richardson's green troops were unarmed and would probably run at the first sign of attack, the Indians would surely have wiped out the command. Richardson's party escaped the confrontation and limped along for almost a month before reaching their destination in very rough shape.

On August 17, 1855, the detachment reached Fort Union. Richardson decided not to conduct them within the fort, in order to keep his detachment out of the control of the post commander, Colonel Fauntleroy. While retaining jurisdiction over his command, Richardson entered Fort Union to make "the usual call of respects to the commanding officer"; during his meeting he stated verbally the purport of his orders. Miffed at his aloofness, Fauntleroy asked "if the purport of his orders was his exact orders." Richardson replied that he gave them "verbally and from recollection." Fauntleroy countered, "That is not sufficient," and that his orders "were required." Faced with a positive demand, Richardson left, promising to comply. But he did not return, and thereafter "positively refused to show Fauntleroy the rolls of the Dragoon recruits."[23]

Fauntleroy's first reaction was to place Richardson under arrest for his disrespect, which had taken place in the presence of General Garland. But he considered "the nature of the Command, and his having in his possession a very large amount of public money . . . and it would have subjected the command to a delay that might have proved injurious," so he waited until Richardson's command moved on, then filed his charges and specifications over the incident with General Garland. The end result of this ugly scene was that Colonel Fauntleroy was nursing a grievance at Major Richardson for disrespect and at General Garland, who considered Fauntleroy guilty of meddling with Richardson's command and chose not to receive the "charges and specifications" over the incident.[24]

General Garland, knowing Richardson well from their Mexican War days, wisely decided that this was nothing more than an argument that had gotten out of control, caused by the pride of both men, and wasn't worth the trouble of a formal hearing. In fact, he sided with Richardson, writing that he "did not recognize the right of a junior officer (Fauntleroy) to demand and examine the papers with which an officer (Richardson) passing his post may be charged to deliver to a superior (Garland), nor does he deem it proper for Col. Fauntleroy to have meddled with Maj. Richardson's command."[25]

The stress of completing what might be argued as his most dangerous assignment to date, only to be accused of a lack of propriety by a pompous senior officer, was the last straw. The steady decline in the quality of life in the army stationed in New Mexico, evidenced by the poor quality of recruits being accepted and the heavier mission requirements, finally forced Israel Richardson into making a decision.

The future outlook on his career was a bleak one at best. For all the sacrifices that he had made in his army career, which included the deaths of his wife and son, the reward of continued service in the army had become tarnished. Now, reality told him that it would be a long weary wait until the end of his career.

Richardson's cousin Origen D. Richardson, who partnered with his father in their law firm in Vermont, had moved to Michigan and settled in Pontiac in 1826. By 1841 he had been elected as a Democrat to the office of lieutenant governor, serving under Governor John S. Barry. Richardson's sister Susan had moved to Michigan from Vermont and married a farmer, Joseph A. Peck, in Pontiac on March 18, 1844. Through the years, the rest of the Richardson family came to reside in Pontiac, including his aged mother and his father, who was gradually going blind. Current leaders like Fauntleroy and Miles made his choice an easy one.

Effective September 30, 1855, after nearly twenty years of service to his country, Brevet Major Israel B. Richardson resigned his commission in the U.S. Army.[26]He left the frontier of New Mexico, which had claimed his wife and child, and traveled to Pontiac, Michigan, to start a new life. Interestingly, on the same day Richardson was submitting his resignation, General Garland also forwarded some correspondence:

"At the request of Colonel Fauntleroy, 1st Dragoons, I have the honor to forward charges preferred by him against Bvt. Major I. B. Richardson, 3d Inf; I will hereby remark that there was no intention, on my part, of accusing Colonel Fauntleroy of having given an illegal order, but having given an unreasonable one. It is my opinion that the Colonel's conduct was capricious, and tyrannical."[27]

Although vindicated by the commander of the New Mexico District, Richardson had enough. Duty on the frontier was getting progressively harder with the lack of funding and a peacetime mentality where commanders were more interested in maintaining an army bureaucracy than looking out for the soldiers in their commands. His decision probably was the right one at the time, because there would be no improvement to conditions until the start of the Civil War.

4

Tutor

"Load at will, and be careful none of you get the ball down first!"

For almost the next five years, Israel Richardson adjusted to civilian life and his new career as a farmer. The young city of Pontiac, where the Richardson family had come to reside, held many opportunities. In 1854 the senior Israel P. Richardson and his wife Sarah, both over sixty years old, decided to relocate to Michigan. The eldest daughter, Susan, and son-in-law Joseph A. Peck had worked a farm there since their marriage in 1844. In this thriving town north of Detroit, Richardson settled into a successful life of a gentleman farmer, looking after his parents and enjoying the social life of the area. In his spare time he began work on an autobiography that he titled "Twelve Years Service in the U.S. Army." It was an in-depth look at his military experiences at West Point and in Florida and Mexico. His history project ends abruptly after the battle of Monterrey, probably put on hold due to his being called back to service.

The political atmosphere in Michigan was one of intense passion against secession. Austin Blair, one of the founders of the Republican Party, served as state governor. Blair was a vigorous advocate of Lincoln's measures and became a distinguished member of the notable group of Northern "war governors."

After the firing on Fort Sumter on April 12, Richardson was among the first to offer his services to the state of Michigan. Because he was a West Point graduate, his experience was badly needed. The 2nd Michigan Infantry regiment was mobilized from militia companies around the state. They were the Scott Guard (from Detroit), Hudson Artillery, Battle Creek Artillery, Adrian Guard, Niles Color Company, Flint Union Greys, Constantine Union Guard, East Saginaw Guard, Kalamazoo Light Guard, and Kalamazoo Blair Guard. Initially, these companies were called into service as a three-month regiment, but as soon as the men were gathered at the state fairgrounds in Detroit, instructions were received from the War Department to reorganize the unit as a three-year regiment. This was accomplished without much turnover of personnel, and on May 25, 1861, the 2nd Michigan Infantry regiment was formed under the command of Colonel Israel B. Richardson, with Henry L. Chipman appointed as lieutenant colonel. The regiment had the distinction of being the first three-year unit raised for service, with a total of 1,013 officers and men on its rolls.

Originally, Governor Blair had selected Chipman to command the regiment, with Richardson as the major. Chipman, a political appointee, lacked any army experience and preferred that a graduate of West Point should command the regiment. Governor Blair brought the question up to Colonel Orlando B. Wilcox, West Point class of 1847 and commander of the 1st Michigan.

"A man by the name of Israel B. Richardson, of Pontiac, has applied for a commission in the Second. But," the governor added, "the people of Pontiac think he is crazy. Do you know of him?" Wilcox responded, "I know something of him as a West Point graduate. He has seen service in Mexico." "Well," the governor said, "he is modest anyway. He says he had resigned a captaincy in the regular army and thinks he might fill the office of major in the volunteers. Will you please see him?" Wilcox related, "I soon found that Richardson was so far from being insane that he was as sound as a nut, but he was slouchy and slovenly, something of the style of cadet that Stonewall Jackson was, and also quite absentminded. He went about Pontiac looking queer perhaps and certainly unsociable. But in talking over old times, the Mexican war and the coming strife, I found him clear and alert and up to the occasion. It did not take me fifteen minutes to 'size him up,' and returning to the governor, I reported most emphatically: 'That is your man, not for major, but for colonel, the man to drill your Second regiment.'[1]

When he was informed by the adjutant general of the governor's decision, Richardson became agitated to some extent, his face coloring up, his head dropping a little, and casting his eyes on the ground, he was silent for a short time; then, without raising his head, he said, "I did not expect anything higher in the regiment than the majority. I think it is all that I am capable of. I do not think I am fit to command a regiment of men, and would rather decline the colonelcy."[2] He was promptly overruled by the governor, and the change in command was affirmed.

Suddenly, West Point graduates became a source of instant credibility. All over the country, these individuals were called on to lead their state's soldiers into battle. It gave renewed opportunities to ex-soldiers like Ulysses S. Grant, who was scratching out a living as a clerk at his family's store, and William T. Sherman, who was struggling to make a living as a teacher. After accepting command of the 2nd Michigan Infantry, Richardson, all at once being in high demand, received an offer from the state of Vermont to command the 2nd

Vermont Infantry regiment. "I feel greatly obliged for the high honor conferred upon me; and would gladly accept if I were not the head of the 2nd Regt. of Infantry from this state, and have been engaged some 3 weeks in preparing it for service. I would gladly join you, but under the circumstances; could not do so with honor," he replied.[3] Instead Governor Underwood of Vermont chose another West Pointer, George J. Stannard, who went on to great success in the war.[4]

The task of preparing a regiment of inexperienced men into a disciplined fighting unit was a daunting effort. It wasn't a novel task, as Richardson had some experience conducting and drilling new recruits to their stations in New Mexico. He quickly recognized the differences between regular army recruits and volunteer recruits and had to react accordingly. In the first few days of mustering, both the leader and recruits struggled to find a common ground.

Tough training proceeded during the coming weeks in an attempt to change novice volunteers into soldiers as quickly as possible. Drill sometimes was amusing. One company commander, painfully inept at giving orders, told his company, "Boys, why in hell don't you come out? You know where to go just as well as I; don't wait to be told every time!" Yet officers who knew their duty were not universally respected throughout the regiment. On June 4, an altercation between Captain Gustav R. Brethschneider and a sergeant led to the sergeant being arrested. The prevailing opinion within the regiment was that "the sergeant was undoubtedly wrong in a military view. The old German officer, who had served several years in the Prussian army, however needs to learn there is a wide difference between American and German soldiers. He is a good officer in many respects, one of the best in the regiment, but holds military rules stricter than we are yet accustom to."[5]

Richardson earned the respect of his regiment for his tough, no-nonsense approach to training. Sergeant Charles B. Haydon was questioned and sharply berated by Richardson for not knowing his duties completely. He recorded in his journal his chagrin at earning the wrath of his regimental commander and vowed it would never happen again. Haydon would later earn a commission and rise to become lieutenant colonel and executive officer of the 2nd Michigan before his death of pneumonia on March 14, 1864. Because of his confidence, Richardson's command philosophy was successful in building a competent fighting force in quicker time than most. He was remembered by an old veteran of the regiment many years later, "'Old Dick' Richardson was our brigade commander. We remember him as a man who understood volunteers and appreciated the difference between them and regulars. He generally went around camp wearing an old straw hat and citizen's coat, his slouchy appearance anything but military, but he would stay in a fight as long as any one, and looked after the comfort of his men with a fatherly solicitude."[6]

Captain Edmund B. Alexander took command of the 3rd U.S. Infantry Regiment after the unit was decimated in the fighting at Monterrey. A fine commander, he led Richardson and his men on General Winfield Scott's campaign to Mexico City. During the Civil War, Alexander served on the western frontier. He retired in 1868 as a brevet brigadier general. (Courtesy of Barry and Jane Hazzard)

Ethan Allen Hitchcock led the 3rd U. S. Infantry in Florida. The grandson of Revolutionary War hero Ethan Allen, Hitchcock was an enlightened leader who mentored Second Lieutenant Richardson and diligently trained his regiment to the point of earning a reputation as one of the best units in the army. (Library of Congress)

Colonel John Garland, an excellent regimental and brigade commander, led the Twiggs' division attack on the first day of fighting at Monterrey. After the Mexican War, he was placed in charge of the Department of New Mexico. On the same day that Richardson resigned his commission, Garland wrote a report to Washington defending Richardson's actions in a confrontation with the pompous Colonel Thomas T. Fauntleroy. Although a native Virginian whose daughter married James Longstreet, Garland remained loyal to the Union. He died on active duty in New York on June 5, 1861. (Library of Congress)

Richardson (*seated, left*) posed with his officers of the 2nd Michigan Regiment for a formal picture in Detroit on May 31, 1861, one month after the regiment organized and only seven days before it departed for Washington. The age and condition of some of these company officers suggests that not all would be up to the task of full-time training and the hard campaigns ahead. (Courtesy of the Burton Historical Collection, Detroit Public Library)

Lieutenant General Winfield Scott, hero of the War of 1812 and the Mexican War, met Richardson soon after the battle of Cerro Gordo and bestowed on him his army nickname of "Fighting Dick." When they met again in Washington, D.C., in 1861, Scott quickly elevated Richardson to brigade command. (Library of Congress)

Colonel Dixon S. Miles, Richardson's eccentric commander on the New Mexican frontier and at Bull Run. The rigid army seniority practice and the lack of a retirement system left the Union Army with incapable commanders such as Miles in key leadership positions at the start of the Civil War. (Massachusetts Commandery Military Order of the Loyal Legion and the U.S. Army Military History Institute)

Brigadier General Israel B. Richardson is shown here as his soldiers rarely saw him, dressed in a formal uniform and wearing the sword presented to him by the officers of the 2nd Michigan. (Library of Congress)

In this seated pose, taken after the First Battle of Bull Run, Richardson wears a standard-issue cavalry sword, possibly a replacement for the one he left leaning against a tree during the battle. (Massachusetts Commandery Military Order of the Loyal Legion and the U.S. Army History Institute)

General Richardson, dressed in the casual style he preferred, is shown here at his field headquarters on the Peninsula. (Massachusetts Commandery Military Order of the Loyal Legion and the U.S. Army History Institute)

General Israel Richardson with the staff of the 1st Division of the II Corps of the Army of the Potomac. Top row (*left to right*): First Lieutenant Herbert, Second Lieutenant Charles S. Draper, Captain Newell. Bottom row (*left to right*): Surgeon William O'Meagher, Richardson, Captain John M. Norvell. (Massachusetts Commandery Military Order of the Loyal Legion and the U.S. Army Military History Institute)

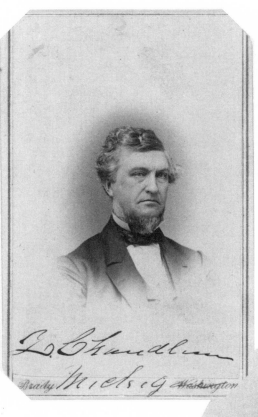

Zachariah Chandler, U.S. senator from Michigan and a powerful leader of the Radical Republicans. Chandler's displeasure with General George B. McClellan strengthened his already close ties to Richardson, whom he held up as an example of an aggressive, fighting general. (Library of Congress)

Colonel Edward E. Cross, the hard-fighting regimental commander of the 5th New Hampshire Volunteers. Part of Richardson's success can be attributed to the number of high-quality regimental commanders within his division. Most of them, however, would not survive the war. Cross would be killed at Gettysburg. (U.S. Army Military History Institute)

General Francis Barlow and General Nelson Miles both received their baptisms of fire under Richardson on the Peninsula and stood tall at the battle of Antietam. Each man led from the front, and both were lucky enough to survive wounds as the division fought through some of the toughest actions of the war. Both men would rise in rank to command the division that Richardson first led in battle.

(Both images from the Library of Congress)

Just as Barlow and Miles, young lieutenants, rose to command divisions, two enlist-ed men, Thomas Livermore (*left*)of the 5th New Hampshire and Charles B. Haydon (*right*) of the 2nd Michigan became officers and went on to command regiments. Both men credit Richardson as an inspirational leader who took time to address their concerns. Livermore survived the war as a colonel, and Haydon died of pneu-monia in 1864 as a lieutenant colonel. (Livermore, U.S. Army Military History Institute; Haydon, Charles B. Haydon Papers, box 851446 Aa2 mf99c, Bentley Historical Library, University of Michigan)

The whirlwind of the excitement of these days seemed without end. Richardson, after serving fifteen years of selfless duty with only little reward and much hardship, now became the center of attention from politicians and powerful businessmen. A pleasant reunion occurred, as the mustering and disbursing officer stationed at Detroit was none other than Lieutenant Colonel Electus Backus, one of the heroes of the Battle of Monterrey and now executive officer of the 3rd Infantry Regiment. The two had spent many years together in Mexico and on the frontier, and the endorsement of Richardson by Colonel Backus, who represented the regular army in this region, helped bolster Richardson's reputation among the already adoring public. This popularity reached its peak when most of the city turned out for his wedding to Frances A. Travor in Detroit on May 29, 1861.

The legend of how Israel Richardson and Fannie Travor became married was told around campfires throughout the 2nd Michigan. When the regiment first went to Detroit, Richardson had been engaged to an acquaintance during his days as a farmer living in Pontiac. With the announcement that only three-year regiments would be accepted into service, his girlfriend objected. She was willing to marry him and go on a three-month campaign but thought three years in camp was too much, and she refused to consent to it. "Very well, Madam, there are others who will. Good Day!" Richardson called for his hat, crossed the street, and offered himself in less than ten minutes to a girl whom he had never seen but twice before. She accepted, and Israel and Frances were married within two weeks.[7]

The men of the regiment were glad to see their colonel so pleased. "The effect of the colonel's wedding is excellent," wrote a member of the unit. "Colonel Richardson was never so pleasant before as at drill yesterday. He said no less than three times that we did well—a thing he has never done before. He begins to be pretty pleased with his regiment and was no doubt modified in his manner by the resolution of the captains not to serve under him unless he behaved better."[8]

As part of his duties, Richardson attended a large recruiting rally hosted by the citizens of Detroit. Impassioned, patriotic speeches were given by local politicians. The main speaker, Senator Zachariah Chandler proposed that everyone present take the oath of allegiance to the United States. A regular army captain, assigned to mapping the Upper Peninsula coastline at the time, and now returning east for assignment with the Army of the Potomac, joined the rally but caused a commotion when he refused to take the oath. The Captain felt it was an insult to his integrity of an officer to be asked to do such a thing and refused. Senator Chandler would always remember this episode and consider the officer unreliable. His name was George G. Meade.[9]

Because the situation in Washington called for rushing the regiment to the defense of the nation's capital, the 2nd Michigan was given fewer than sixty days of drill and training. On June 8, Colonel Richardson put his men and new bride on trains eastbound to protect Washington from the growing rebel threat. Private Perry Mayo recalled the scene as the regiment traveled east. "We left Detroit on Thursday afternoon after being greeted with the utmost enthusiasm. The girls were stationed at the windows waving flags and firing revolvers to cheer the men on to the great duty they had to perform. We were nearly fed to death on the road through Ohio with pies, cakes, and lemonade. Flowers showered us at every station."[10]

The 2nd Michigan arrived on the outskirts of Baltimore near sundown of June 9. A strong secessionist movement prevailed in the town, and a riot caused by Southern sympathizers had killed or wounded several members of the 6th Massachusetts as it marched through the city on April 19.

Once the men were off the trains and into formation, Richardson addressed them. "Second Michigan, we may now meet our first engagement. You will at the command, load at will; and be careful none of you get the ball down first! Let every man keep his head. Don't get excited, and do not fire unless you receive orders. As you march, let the first four men on the right and left flanks watch the roofs and windows, and if attacked, see that you bring down the assailant, be it man or woman." The chief of police arrived with a large squad of men and said he would escort the regiment through the city. Richardson responded, "You can march ahead if you want to, but my men came here prepared to take care of themselves. Now, let them attack us and we will show them what a ball and three buckshot will do!"[11]

The march through the city went without incident, but as the 2nd Michigan was boarding the train to Washington, the crowd threw several stones through the car windows, hitting a few soldiers. A sergeant who spotted a stone thrower fired his musket from the train window and dropped the man in the street. A loud cry for revenge rose from the crowd. Just as it appeared that a riot would break out, Richardson stepped out on the platform, with saber drawn, and commanded the crowd, in resolute tones, to disperse at once or he would charge them with a thousand bayonets. His quick action quieted the crowd and proved to the men of the 2nd Michigan that they had not only a good drill master but also one who could be relied on in a tight situation.[12] As was starting to be typical with him, Richardson took the time to credit the sergeant for preventing what could have been a serious attack on the regiment.

Without further difficulties, the regiment arrived on June 13, 1861, and marched to Camp Winfield Scott, five miles from the White House. There Richardson had a warm reunion with old friends from his happier days in the army. "I was invited to dine with General Scott, which I did, and spent a most pleasant afternoon. Found my old friend and classmate, Schyler Hamilton on his staff. He said he had seen nothing to make him so glad as to see me back again. I found many other friends here also. Marched the regiment by Gen. Scott's quarters to salute him. Gen. S. appeared in full uniform; a great compliment. He says he shall do all he can."[13]

When Richardson was reintroduced to his old commander, Scott exclaimed, "I am glad to have my 'Fighting Dick' with me again, and have plenty of work for him to do!"[14] General Scott had assembled a force of some thirty-five thousand men under General Irvin McDowell around Centreville, Virginia, and a force of about twelve thousand under General Robert Patterson at Harpers Ferry. Although he had no intention of launching an offensive with his three-month militia, politics and public opinion were calling loudly for action.

As the army started to take shape, Colonel Richardson became noticed for his professionalism and discipline in drilling his regiment. Many times, during the conduct of regimental drill, his men would hear him remark, "I shall make good soldiers of you before I get through."[15] It was a refreshing sight to see a regimental commander who knew his duty, as opposed to the many politically appointed colonels. Because Richardson was a veteran, his orders took on a practical aspect. When surrounding farmers complained that their cows, who had wandered into camp, were being milked, Richardson announced in formation that if this was so, it must be stopped, as much as *possible*. His regiment was proud of the fact that Richardson, while maybe not as polished in manners as some of the other regimental commanders, was recognized as a fighter.

The men of his regiment were fond of his command style and took pride in his fighting reputation throughout the army. Private Mayo heard that "the Colonel was offered an honorable position (in the regular army), but he says he will never leave the regiment unless he goes to the next world."[16] Many stories were being told in camp of his exploits in the old army. "I heard an officer of the regulars say that he saw him kill four Indians in Texas with his sword in less than a minute. He was attacked by about one hundred Indians while reconnoitering. The Colonel knocked the first one off his horse by a stroke on the head with the back of his sword, immediately mounted his horse and slashed the other three in quick time. I believe there is not a better fighting man in the U.S. than Colonel Richardson."[17]

The 3rd Michigan heard of Colonel Richardson's reputation as a drillmaster and asked him to come to their camp and put them through drill. On June 21, at nine o'clock in the morning, he called them out and drilled them until noon— more than half the time at the double quick. They swore they never wanted to see him again. When they saw Richardson tramping up and down the field on foot, his great iron sword sheath hung at his side with chains rattling like a log chain on a pole bridge, giving orders loud enough to be heard a mile, reprimanding the officers in a manner that fairly raised them off their feet, and keeping them on the jump by the hour, they thought the devil had surely come![18]

On July 8, 1861, Scott rewarded Richardson's hard work with a promotion to brigade command. He was assigned the 4th Brigade of Brigadier General Daniel Tyler's 1st Division, consisting of the 2nd and 3rd Michigan, 12th New York, and 1st Massachusetts. Tyler was a West Point graduate of 1819 and served in the army until his resignation in 1833. He was typical of the top leadership being assembled by the Lincoln administration, politically powerful but with no combat experience, and twenty-seven years out of date with current military thinking.

In these frenzied early days of the war, both sides were building armies at an equal pace, but the Confederate government had the advantage in selecting leaders to manage the growth. President Lincoln had no experience as a chief executive officer, and he lacked knowledge about military affairs or his present leaders in the military. Dated personnel regulations and the seniority traditions of the entrenched bureaucracy hindered him. On the other hand, Jefferson Davis, at the head of the Confederacy, was a graduate of the military academy, had commanded a regiment in the Mexican War, and had been secretary of war under President Franklin Pierce. Before he left Congress, Davis served as chairman of the Military Committee in the U.S. Senate. He not only was professionally trained in the art of war but also knew the character and capacity of promising officers of the army. There was nothing experimental in his choice of high military commanders.

Another advantage enjoyed by the South was a quickly growing intelligence apparatus. Three weeks before Richardson arrived with his men in Washington, his first company commander and mentor in the old regular army, Captain Thomas Jordan, resigned his commission and traveled a few miles south to the Alexandria line to take up duty as adjutant to General Pierre G. T. Beauregard, with the rank of colonel. Before he left the Washington area, he set up a crude spy ring of Southern sympathizers and arranged for the delivery of several Northern newspapers, which due to the lack of censorship, provided Beauregard with a great deal of information. Northern forces were mostly in the dark as to the size and intentions of the Confederate army.

On the Fourth of July, the noncommissioned officers led the regiment in drill, with Sergeant William B. McCreery acting as colonel. Colonel Richardson watched the maneuvers with much pleasure. Turning to the regimental surgeon, he said in his particular drawl, "Dr. Lyster, these noncommissioned officers drill the regiment better than the commissioned officers can do it." In less than a month, Richardson promoted Sergeant McCreery to first lieutenant and quartermaster.[19]

As newly minted general officers continued to stream into Washington, Richardson sought assurances from General Scott as to his position: "I called on Gen. Scott the other day and inquired of him if in the event of other Brigadier Genls being appointed by Congress, if I should be superceded [*sic*] in command.

The Genl. was very emphatic and said I never should be superceded if ever so many appointed; that he gave me the command himself, and he should take particular care of his West Point friends."[20]

On July 12, 1861, Richardson's brigade moved to a new location on the Maryland side of the Chain Bridge. On the eve of the first great battle of the war, a few amusing vignettes reveal the inexperience of newly formed regiments in everything from field craft to drill. A letter to home from the 2nd Michigan complained that the camp "had been reduced to the point of starvation." When a polite inquiry would be made as to whether dinner was ready: "'Well, it aint, you know!' would be the somewhat unmilitary reply. Any ordinary cook would have been dismissed, or sent to the guardhouse, but coming from the nephew of the major, it had to be condoned."[21]

The strong-willed Fannie Richardson had accompanied her husband to Washington and regularly busied herself by meddling into all aspects of the 2nd Michigan's operations. It was generally believed by the men that Mrs. Richardson was the "power behind the throne," as Dr. Henry F. Lyster, the assistant surgeon of the 2nd Michigan, recalled, and that it was not until the colonel had become a general in command of a division that he outgrew his better half and supervised things generally himself.

Even the rank and file commented on Fannie's ability to influence her husband's decisions. A rumor spread through the camp of the 2nd Michigan that they were being considered for assignment within the city of Washington to act as home guards. "It is a post of honor and in many respects a very desirable assignment. There will be no knapsacks to carry. . . . If we go there, we shall be made a fancy regiment, well drilled, clothed, and equipped. Colonel Richardson may go on his wife's account. He would never do it if it were not for her. He would push us into Virginia as far as orders would allow."[22]

"Go in again, on the double-quick! On the double-quick, I say!"

"I wanted very much a little time," recalled General McDowell, "All of us wanted it. We did not have a bit of it." The answer was, "You are green, it is true; but they are green also; you are all green alike."[23] And so with the cry of "On to Richmond!," General Irvin McDowell's army of five divisions began to move southward on July 16, 1861. Brigadier General Daniel Tyler's 1st Division started in the lead, with its four brigades commanded by Erasmus D. Keyes, Robert C. Schenck, William T. Sherman, and in the van, Israel B. Richardson. Most were unused to the fatigue and hardship of the march of that hot July day, which ended with the men dust-grimed, footsore, broken down, hungry, and without food,—they had wasted the rations that they had been issued, and the supply trains had not yet come up. Progress of the march was constantly slowed by the straggling and the general disregard for discipline.

At every creek, the men fell out to fill their canteens. An entry from a 1st Massachusetts's diary described the general feeling of the day: "Went blackberrying after eating a piece of salt meat."[24] Jerome Robbins, from Richardson's 2nd Michigan, wrote, "After a march of ten miles, partly performed in the night, we were glad to lie down and receive a short repose after the heat and labor of the day."[25] Colonel Richardson was put in the same position he had faced fourteen years before, when as a young lieutenant commanding a company, he set his green recruits' fears at ease at the start of Scott's Mexican campaign. Now he did the same thing with his brigade, going from regiment to regiment, cheering up the men and telling them generally what they could expect tomorrow.

In a conversation with an officer who had just arrived from Washington, Richardson was told of an Ohio regiment that had been driven back from an enemy battery they were ordered to take. As the men crowded around, trying to get a piece of the news, Richardson asked, "How many men were killed?" "Fifteen," replied the officer. "Oh! Was that all—humph—and they did not take the battery?" responded Fighting Dick. It was well understood by all who heard the remark, and quickly spread through the rest of the brigade, that had they been there, the battery would have been taken or many more than fifteen would have fallen.[26]

Israel Richardson's personal style of leadership was one calculated to get the most out of a volunteer force. His own reputation of walking through camp in a straw hat, dressed more like a farmer than a brigade commander, made the men feel as though he were like themselves. Other brigade and regimental commanders conducted their units under more stringent conditions. Experience had taught Richardson the difference between discipline for the sake of discipline and caring for people. The inexperienced commanders were more preoccupied with the techniques, as opposed to mission accomplishment that was so focused in Richardson's leadership philosophy. Unconsciously, he imitated the style of the leader from his past he most respected, General Zachary Taylor.

At seven o'clock on the morning of Thursday, July 18, Tyler's division, with Richardson's brigade in the lead, advanced down the Warrenton Pike to Centreville. As the brigade moved into rebel territory, Richardson made sure that his unit would not be surprised. He kept a light battalion of infantry a quarter mile in advance of the brigade, and threw out pickets even farther.

The light battalion of skirmishers was another innovation born of Richardson's long combat experience. He organized the 160-man unit from the best men in his brigade, under the command of Captain Brethschneider. The men turned in their standard buck and ball cartridge muskets for Harpers Ferry rifles and went into a separate camp to receive intensive training in skirmish tactics.

Behind the light battalion followed two twenty-pounder rifled field guns and the rest of the brigade. On the march to Centreville, Tyler received instructions to observe the roads to Bull Run and Warrenton, and not bring on an engagement. This advance was intended solely as a demonstration to mask the movement by McDowell's army to cross Bull Run at Wolf Run Shoals.

The march to Centreville was quiet, and at nine o'clock Richardson's brigade entered the small village, which showed signs of abandonment by the rebels the night before. Tyler allowed the troops to halt and rest, while he reported to McDowell and awaited instructions. During this lull, Richardson's brigade was sent out beyond the town in search of water, as there was none in Centreville itself. After waiting for an hour and a half without receiving orders, Tyler determined that he should move forward and continue the reconnaissance toward Manassas Junction.

Richardson, believing that the rebels would not have camped in the area without a source of water, searched the recently abandoned camp of the enemy, found water, and rested there. Fannie Richardson had decided to accompany her husband on the campaign. During this pause in the march, she saw to it that the regimental quartermaster of the 2nd Michigan was sent on his way back home for the inexcusable offense of tampering with honey in the beehive she had brought as part of the headquarters baggage.[27] One can only wonder whether Richardson himself was not greatly relieved to get away when General Tyler proposed that they reconnoiter the road leading to Bull Run.[28]

Richardson ordered four companies of infantry, one company of cavalry, and a section of artillery to probe Blackburn's Ford. As Tyler and Richardson crested a hill, they could see several rebel batteries emplaced but no large body of infantry near. General Tyler directed Richardson to bring up the rest of his brigade and make a movement with the purpose of finding the position and strength of the enemy forces. Soon the two pieces of artillery (rifled twelve pounders) were firing from the top of the hill as Richardson detached 160 skirmishers into the skirt of timber on the edge of the run, in front of the enemy position, where they began to encounter enemy fire.

Sergeant C. W. Greene, 12th New York, serving with skirmishers, recalled, "When we were ordered down to the timber, the enemy's guns, which had been silent, commenced firing over our heads. When we reached the pine scrubs, we passed over the still burning fires of the enemy's camp and drew their fire on the bank of the stream. Our bugler sounded the call to 'advance,' but we could not go further, as we were confronting the enemy in their rifle pits. After we were withdrawn; which was done in response to the 'recall' sounded by the bugler, we rallied and lay down for our brigade to pass over us and attack."[29]

In the distance, Richardson saw a house flying a rebel flag. As Captain George W. Ayres' howitzers arrived, Richardson called out to the battery commander, "Capt. Ayres, can you see that flag on that building?" "Yes, Sir," was the reply. "Well, can you bring it down?" "I think so."[30] Richardson directed the two twelve pounders to be placed at the top of the hill for support, then personally moved two six pounders down to the tree line in close support of the skirmish line. As he moved down toward the timber, he found General Tyler and suggested that he form his four regiments in line of battle on the outside of the timber and assault the rebel position on the other side of the run. He also requested Sherman's brigade to come forward quickly to support the attack. Richardson's description of how he personally directed the action as it unfolded was told in testimony before Congress later in the fall of 1861:

"I formed the New York Twelfth on the left of the battery, and directed Colonel Walrath to make a charge into the woods. I spoke a few words of encouragement to the regiment before they went on. I told them that it was a good regiment, and I expected they would do well. As soon as I had given this direction, I ordered up the Massachusetts First. I formed them in line of battle on the right of the battery, then the 3rd Michigan on the right of them, then the 2nd Michigan still to the right—all in line of battle.

"When I finished putting the 2nd Michigan on the line at the right, I moved back to see what had become of the New York Twelfth on the left. It had probably taken me as much as twenty minutes to go through with this formation. I found, on arriving at the left, parts of two companies of the New York Twelfth, about sixty men altogether, retreating outside the woods, carrying along a few wounded. I asked them what the matter was, and where they were going. They said the regiment was all killed, and they were falling back—those who had not been killed. Says I, 'What are you running for? There is no enemy here; I cannot see anybody at all. Where is your Colonel?' They knew nothing about it. They knew nothing about any of their officers. I could not find any officers with the men at all, I believe.

"The other three regiments, at the same time, were standing firm and ready to advance; and the skirmishers, at the same time, held their ground in the woods in front. I sent an aide to General Tyler to acquaint him on the retreat of the New York Twelfth, and to come down to see me. I proposed to him to rally the New York Twelfth in the woods as a support, and move on with the other three regiments against the batteries; and I asked him at the same time, where Sherman's brigade of his division was. He said that brigade had not yet arrived. General Tyler then said that it was not part of the plan of battle to do anything more at that point than a mere demonstration—to make a reconnaissance to find the force of the enemy; and, as I understood him, it was against orders to bring on a general engagement at that place. He then ordered me to fall back with the three regiments in the rear of the batteries—and not to undertake to rally the New York Twelfth. 'Let them go,' he said."[31]

A half mile to the rear of Bull Run, on the porch of the McLean House, Confederate Captain Alexander was talking with Colonel Thomas Jordan.

With his spyglass, Alexander had seen a group of Union officers and a battery crest the hill on the other side of the run. After a consultation, the guns on the hill were unlimbered and fired in his direction. The first shot fired sailed high, landing in the cornfield in the rear; the second shot was short a hundred yards, landing in the peach orchard. The next volley was right on target, going through McLean's kitchen without causing any casualties but destroying the Confederate commander's dinner.[32] It came "very near destroying some of us," Beauregard's aide, Captain John L. Manning, wrote later that day.[33] (A disgusted Wilmer McLean soon sold his farm and, wishing to never see a soldier again, moved two hundred miles away, to the quiet safety of a town called Appomattox.) The first opposing shots of this engagement literally were

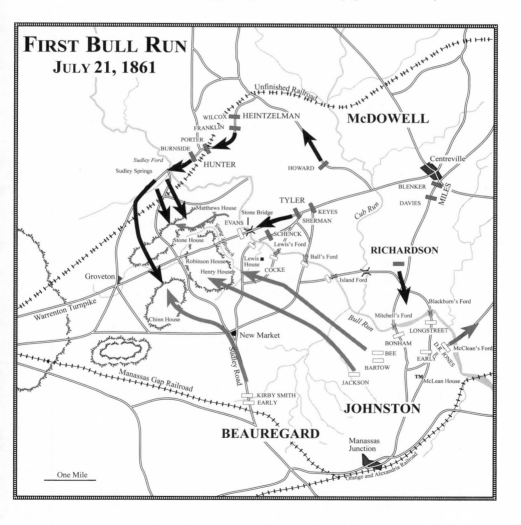

FIRST BULL RUN
JULY 21, 1861

One Mile

of brother officer against brother officer, as Richardson directed the fire of his artillery on his former company commander during the Seminole campaign, Colonel Thomas Jordan.

Return fire from the Washington Light Artillery took off the leg of a sergeant in Ayres' battery. A 2nd Michigan soldier remembered that "watching near by, Colonel Richardson rode up to the battery, and as he was engaged in giving orders, a solid shot came whizzing by in such close proximity to his head that he was stunned for [a] moment. After a brief instant, he turned up the side of his head and shrugged his shoulders, a peculiarity of his, and in his usual nasal twang said, "Rather close quarters," and rode away apparently as unconcerned as if it was a hummingbird which crossed his path."[34]

A Virginia brigade defended the rebel position that Richardson was probing. The commander of the Confederates was Richardson's old friend James Longstreet. On June 17, 1861, Longstreet was promoted to brigadier general and had been assigned to command his brigade only since July 2, giving him just over two weeks to make his mark on their training.

The terrain at Blackburn's Ford was favorable to Richardson attacking from the north. The hilltop where Tyler posted the artillery commanded the whole position. Longstreet had posted, in a line along the southern bank of Bull Run, his three regiments, the 1st, 11th, and 17th Virginia, totaling about twelve hundred men altogether. Four companies of the 1st Virginia were in the rear as the brigade reserve, and one company of the 11th Virginia was deployed forward on the north bank.

The skirmishers and three companies of support from the 1st Massachusetts, under Lieutenant Colonel George D. Wells, worked their way down the wooded slope toward Bull Run. From across the creek bank, the Confederates fired a volley that went high over the heads of the Federals. Wells ordered his men to advance, and they came on steadily, firing as they moved forward. "The first pouring-down of volleys were most startling to the new troops. Part of my line broke and started at a run," Longstreet reported.[35] As the Confederate line began to show signs of panic, Longstreet moved among them quickly, with his saber drawn in an effort to head off the confusion of his troops. Order was reestablished quickly, and heavy fire was traded for about ten or fifteen minutes before the Federals withdrew. After about twenty minutes, a furious volley marked the start of another Federal advance. Longstreet called for the reserve brigade, commanded by Colonel Jubal Early, and started his own regiments forward to meet the attack.

In this first skirmish of the war, the confusion and uncertainty of combat began to take its toll on leaders and units of both sides. The initial advantage seemed to be with the Federals, but when they were stopped, the Confederates gained momentum until they received friendly fire from their rear, causing their own movement forward to stall. The engagement never became one of regiment against regiment, but rather individual company combat. On each side of the battlefield, companies disintegrated due to inexperienced leadership, and small groups of men found their way to the rear, figuring they had enough fighting for one day. Moving everywhere among his three other regiments, Richardson steadied them by his personal example.

Sergeant Greene, of the light battalion of skirmishers, recounted, "Our brigade attack was soon driven back in confusion, and it was then that General Richardson, seeing that two guns of Captain Ayres' which had been brought down into the scrub, were in danger, himself gave the order to the skirmishers; 'Go in again, on the double-quick! On the double-quick, I say!' And we went in again, and gathered around those two guns, without any attempt at formation, taking advantage of every possible cover, fighting in real skirmishing style taught by our drill officer, we poured our hottest fire into the ranks of the enemy, who were advancing up the slope. Joe Labeff, of Company A, 12th New York, received a pistol ball in his shoulder, from a rebel officer, and called out to one of our men, known as 'Dutch Pete' to 'Shoot the damned rebel quick!' Says Pete, 'Me shoot him once,' and literally put a hole through the officer, who was not twenty feet away. The two pieces of artillery were doing great execution with grape and canister, and while our loss was slight, the enemy must have suffered considerably. An officer, whom I suppose to be Captain Ayres, rode among us and shouted: 'Charge them, you damned cowards; charge them, or I will lose my guns!' And Corporal Eugene Rawson, of my company, shouted back, 'Charge them yourself, if you want them charged!' After we were withdrawn, this same officer had the grace to ride up to us and say: 'Boys, you did well; you saved my guns.'"[36]

According to Dr. Lyster, Richardson seemed to be everywhere; the doctor had already administered to his first wounded casualties and was in the process of helping a "quite white and limp" lieutenant into his ambulance when his Colonel appeared, ordering the lieutenant out of the wagon, and back to his company, with "some very harsh words." After Richardson rode off, Dr. Lyster told the lieutenant to get back in the wagon and was carried to the rear, never to be seen again.

Richardson wanted to continue the attack even after the 12th New York broke, knowing that Sherman's brigade was on its way. By that time he had already lost about sixty men, but some of his skirmishers, led by Captain Brethschneider, were already across the run and were taking the Confederate battery under musket fire. Richardson thought that at the cost of another sixty men, his brigade, supported by Sherman, could have taken the Confederate positions.[37] His analysis was probably correct. In this first skirmish, the troops from both sides were nervous, and any strong movement led by a dynamic leader would have had an excellent chance to succeed. Longstreet thought his own lines were being stretched to the breaking point. In maneuvering to bring his green units across the run to confront the Federals, the Confederate positions had become vulnerable to attack. However, a nervous General Tyler put this thinking to an end by ordering a withdrawal, just as Sherman was arriving at the scene at the head of his brigade.

Tyler described how the withdrawal was decided upon: "Having satisfied myself that the enemy was in force, and also as to the position of his batteries, I ordered Colonel Richardson to withdraw his brigade, which was skillfully but unwillingly accomplished, as he requested permission with the 1st Massachusetts and 2nd and 3rd Michigan regiments to charge the enemy and drive him out. It is but justice to these regiments to say that they stood firm, maneuvered well, and I have no doubt would have backed up manfully the proposition of their gallant commander."

Personal incidents concerning the three brigade commanders involved in the battle give some insight as to how exasperating it was for career officers to lead barely trained volunteers into battle. As Sherman hurried his brigade forward to the sounds of fighting, he became annoyed as his men began leaving formation, ducking and dodging shells meant for Richardson, but fired high and long into the woods through which he was marching. "Keep cool," he told them. "There is no use ducking shells that they could hear, for, by the time the missile was audible, it had already passed." Just then a large shell crashed through the trees directly over the colonel's head. Amid the terrible noise of the passing projectile, Sherman instinctively ducked down close to his horse's mane. When he raised his head again, it was to see a line of grinning faces from his 79th New York Highlanders. He broke his usually stern face into a broad smile. "Well, boys," he said, "you may dodge the big ones!"[38] While trying to repel the initial Federal probes, Longstreet called for reinforcements from Colonel Early's brigade. The 7th Virginia came forward to support Longstreet's regiments as they crossed Bull Run to attack the Federals. In the midst of this maneuver, Richardson's men let loose a volley from the bluffs. The 7th Virginia responded by returning fire without orders, putting Longstreet's men in the middle of crossfire. General Longstreet thought he could stop the 7th Virginia's fire by riding along the front of its line, but before he could get their attention, he was forced to dive off his horse as another volley screamed over his head. Longstreet's horse got away from him and ran riderless down the line afterward, causing some to think he had been killed.

Finally, as a thoroughly disgusted Richardson was carrying out General Tyler's orders to withdraw, he came upon the 2nd Michigan. In a scornful manner, he suggested to the regiment that it had better be getting back or the enemy's cavalry would cut them off. Upon hearing his sarcastic remarks, and moving the regiment well into the woods, the acting regimental commander, Major Adolphus W. Williams,[39] formed them into a hollow square, a maneuver used in Napoleonic times to resist an expected charge of cavalry. Dr. Lyster recalled, "How well I can remember the beautiful appearance the regiment presented in the timber, with fixed bayonets. In the movement, I was left outside, and tried in vain, to get into the place where the adjutant and major seemed so safely protected. Colonel Richardson's remarks to the Major, when he discovered our position and proceeded to unravel us, were not of a character to be repeated, even at this late date."[40]

With Sherman's brigade on the scene, the battle turned into an artillery duel, each side being content to exchange long-range shelling. General McDowell appeared on the battlefield around four o'clock and appeared upset with General Tyler's decision to bring on an engagement. Before returning to his headquarters in Centreville, he ordered Tyler to use Richardson's and Sherman's brigades to occupy the high ground from where the attack had started. Tyler disregarded this order as soon as McDowell left, because rations had not come up and a source of water for the troops could not be found. Early that evening, both brigades marched back to spend the night camped just south of Centreville.

The day's work had cost the Federals nineteen killed, thirty-eight wounded, and twenty-six missing. The rebel losses were fifteen killed and fifty-three wounded. The troops were sullen on the march back to camp, with the men of the 12th New York blaming Richardson, not Tyler, for their losses, believing that he had picked on their regiment to lead the attack because Colonel Walrath had been paying too much attention to Mrs. Richardson. Meanwhile, Colonel Richardson was still fuming for not being allowed to continue the attack. The fact that enemy fire had cut his horse's crouper strap, making it difficult to control his horse, did nothing to ease his irritability.[41]

Upon their arrival in camp, his character changed with the greeting he received from Frances Richardson. "His pretty young wife embraced him in a most distracting manner,"[42] wrote Sergeant Haydon, as the brigade marched into camp. After dinner, while making the rounds that evening, Richardson had calmed down enough to tell some of his men that he was very pleased with their performance in the fight that afternoon.[43] The next morning, at daylight, the brigade again moved out to its former positions on the hilltop and started work on improving their defenses, and a source of water was obtained by the digging of a well.[44]

As a result of the Battle at Blackburn's Ford, McDowell's entire army had come up and concentrated at Centreville by the evening of July 18. In hindsight, the biggest aftermath of the fighting was not the blow to Union morale or the uplifting of Confederate spirits as some of the participants commented on; but rather the stalling of McDowell's timetable. While his logistics came up, he pondered his next move. His intelligence had told him that he outnumbered Beauregard, and a prompt follow-on attack might have crushed the rebel force. His careful maneuvering gave Beauregard the extra hours he needed, allowing General Joseph E. Johnston's forces to link up with his army. Richardson's brigade remained in their position for the next two days, while the final touches were put on the offensive plan by McDowell, who feared Blackburn's Ford would be too heavily reinforced now to be the object of his main effort.

"A great battle will be fought here tomorrow"

One week before the Union army moved, Colonel Richardson had been summoned to McDowell's headquarters for a mission. His experienced reputation earned him command of a reconnaissance of possible routes south. This assignment, accomplished with only a dozen men, only increased the pride that his regiment felt for him. The story told about camp was that upon his return, General Joseph K. F. Mansfield, an old comrade from his Mexican days, criticized Richardson for moving farther south than his orders had allowed. Richardson replied that he did not read his orders, and that if he had been able to take his brigade with him, he would have captured Fairfax. General Mansfield informed him that if he had done such a thing he would have been court-martialed. Everyone nodded in agreement that Richardson would have been higher in command now if he had not fought two or three times in Mexico without orders.[45]

When Richardson reported to the commanding general, McDowell confided his campaign plan and asked for his opinions. Richardson later related the conversation in his testimony to the joint committee on the conduct of the war:

"About a week before we moved toward Bull Run, I was ordered to make a reconnaissance from the Chain Bridge, on the road to Vienna, with a squadron of United States cavalry, to see whether it was a practicable road for artillery and wagons. Vienna is about eleven miles from Chain Bridge. I made the reconnaissance, and went a mile beyond Vienna, and found nothing but an abatis across the road where the enemy had been at work. I came back and reported to General McDowell. He told me that there was a meeting of the officers, to which he read his instructions for carrying on the campaign, and wished to read me the plan which had been submitted to General Scott, and which had not been disagreed to so far.

"He read me this plan, and stated the brigades and divisions which were to move on such and such roads. He stated that each division was from 10,000 to 12,000 men strong, and our division—Tyler's—would be the strongest, as it looked toward Johnston on the right. Johnston, he said, was in that direction. But General Scott thought that if Johnston moved toward Manassas, Patterson 'should be on his heels,' as he expressed it.

"Says I, 'General, are there any cross-roads to communicate from the right of the line to the left, so that if one of these columns is attacked by two or three times its number, it can concentrate on any of the other columns, or any other columns can concentrate on it?' He said it was not known whether there were any cross-roads or not on which any troops could concentrate; but that our columns were heavy and able to protect themselves."[46]

Richardson described his reconnaissance, noting, "I passed the point at which Gen. Schenck tried to run a Regt of troops in a railroad train into a battery of cannon. He was repulsed, because he failed in the first duty of a commander, viz: that of throwing out a line of skirmishers in advance—and finally letting his men be slaughtered in the cars by cannon shot, instead of ordering them to leave the cars and storm the battery. I examined the site particularly and could easily have taken the battery with 50 good men. So much as to Brigadier Generals of the modern appointments; who were good country lawyers at home, but make indifferent warriors in the field. Fortunately, the Govt. puts little confidence in them and the Comdg. Gen. keeps their command as low as possible."[47]

Colonel Richardson, along with all of the division and brigade commanders, was summoned to General McDowell's tent for a council of war on the night of Saturday, July 20. As the officers assembled for the briefing, Richardson, a brigade commander, had a better grasp of the proposed operation than some of the division commanders. The concept had changed slightly because of Tyler's encounter at Blackburn's Ford. Now the main attack would follow the Warrenton Pike and cross Bull Run, while a division would remain in reserve, conducting a feint at Blackburn's Ford and protecting the army's rear.

In the cramped tent, McDowell gave instructions to his commanders, talking from an ill-defined map he spread on the dirt floor. The attack was to commence at daylight with reveille for the troops at two o'clock in the morning. At this notion, Richardson spoke up to his superior, General Tyler, and in the presence of other brigade commanders, commented, "It is impossible, General, to move an army of regular troops under two hours, and you will take at least that time to move volunteers; and if reveille is not beaten before two o'clock in the morning you cannot get into action at daylight; it is impossible. If you beat reveille at midnight, with volunteer troops, you may get into action at daylight, but not before; that is the best you can do."[48]

His point was well taken, but McDowell did nothing to change the jump-off times of the operation. At eleven o'clock the meeting was adjourned, and as the officers returned to their units, they could hear faint train sounds marking the arrival of close to fifty carloads at Manassas. Richardson had heard the same sounds throughout the night before and, comparing notes with Sherman, concluded that McDowell had lost his numerical advantage by allowing

General Johnston to link up with General Beauregard during his two days of relative inactivity.

Twenty-four hours earlier, fifty miles to the west, in the Shenandoah Valley, another staff meeting had taken place. An old comrade of Richardson, Barnard Bee, received his orders from General Johnston to concentrate the Confederate army at Manassas.

Since Bee and Richardson had parted company in New Mexico, six years ago, Bee continued to show talent in his army career. Leaving the 3rd Infantry for a posting as captain in the 10th Infantry on March 3, 1855, he was stationed at the Cavalry School at Carlisle Barracks, Pennsylvania, and performed frontier duty at Fort Snelling, Minnesota, in 1856. He spent the next·several years as a senior captain on frontier duty in the Dakotas, at Fort Laramie.

Strong ties to his native state of South Carolina and the events of the day encouraged his resignation from the U.S. Army on March 3, 1861. President Jefferson Davis promoted Bee to brigadier general on June 17, 1861, and sent him to General Johnston's army in the Shenandoah Valley. Here he was given command of the Third Brigade, consisting of the 2nd and 11th Mississippi, the 4th Alabama, and the 1st Tennessee regiments. Bee's brigade, along with the remainder of Johnston's army, left their defenses and headed east to join Beauregard, leaving behind a screen of cavalry commanded by Colonel J. E. B. Stuart to mask the movement from the Union forces of General Patterson.

With the dawning of July 21, 1861, the Federal troops were still moving out from their bivouacs and not yet in position to launch the attack. Richardson's prediction of the night before had come true. The confusion of the men and the lack of experience of the officers spread throughout the regiments, causing long delays before they could be sorted out. In McDowell's plan, Richardson's brigade had been detached from Tyler's division and placed in reserve under the command of Colonel Dixon S. Miles. The mission of this reserve division was to make a demonstration on Blackburn's Ford. The result would be to hold the Confederate forces in the area from reinforcing the defenders near the Warrenton Turnpike and prevent Beauregard from swinging around the left flank by means of the many crossing fords on Bull Run and cutting communications with Washington. In any event, McDowell strictly forbade any movement across Bull Run.

The fact that Richardson was placed under the tactical command of his old eccentric commander from his New Mexico days was not a pleasant development. Yet his orders were precise, and the likelihood for a decisive fight was slight. Any action to their front would only be a sideshow to the main assault on the right.

When Richardson returned to his headquarters following McDowell's staff meeting, his nervous energy was recognized by his headquarters guard.

Private Allen R. Foote, from Co. B, 3rd Michigan, remembered the occasion afterward:

"On the night before the battle, I was detailed to do guard duty before Colonel Dick Richardson's headquarters. He was occupying a small house. About 11 o'clock, he came and asked me if I would be on duty there at 3 o'clock in the morning. I answered, 'Yes.' Then he said, pointing in the direction of the Stone Bridge, 'About 3 o'clock in the morning a cannon will be fired over there. When you hear it, call me at once. A great battle will be fought here tomorrow.' I needed nothing more to keep me awake that night, nor did the Colonel. He was out two or three times before the alarm gun was fired."[49]

The first light of dawn on July 21 brought a nervous anticipation to the men of Richardson's command on the hills overlooking Blackburn's Ford. He later described the events of the morning in testimony before Congress:

"I waited until eight o'clock in the morning before I heard a gun fired on the right, and then I commenced a cannonade on the enemy's line with my artillery. About this time, Colonel Thomas A. Davies came up with his brigade, and inquired the date of my commission as colonel, and told me his, and found that he ranked me by eleven days. He took command of the two brigades. At the same time I showed him my position in front of Blackburn's Ford. He wished a good position for his artillery to play. I took him to a hill some 600 hundred yards on our left, with a ravine between, and showed him a good position for his battery to operate on a stone house, which was said to be the enemy's headquarters, in front of us about a mile, which our rifled ten-pounder guns could easily reach.

"He immediately took up that position, which was at a log house on this hill to our left, which was fully as high, and a little higher, than the hill we were on. 'We kept up a fire from two batteries of artillery until eleven or twelve o'clock—perhaps until noon.'"[50]

The feint that McDowell hoped would freeze the enemy in their positions was being carried out strictly by artillery, directed by Richardson, which fired on suspected rebel positions hidden in the woods across Bull Run. Major Henry Hunt noted in his report that this tactic "produced little or no effect, as there was no definite object, except when the enemy's moving columns came from time to time into our range."[51] Colonel Davies sent word to Miles that the artillery ammunition was running low and requested to slacken his fire. Miles sent back a message to fire on, which Davies complied with, although at a much slower pace.

At noon, Colonel Miles made his way from his headquarters in Centreville toward the front. He was not feeling well, suffering from a case of diarrhea, for which his doctor had prescribed a small amount of brandy. On his way to Blackburn's Ford he came across two regiments that Colonel Davies had detached from his brigade to protect a road that could threaten his left flank from McLean's Ford. When Miles found Davies, he angrily gave him a "very severe dressing down in no very measured language"[52] and ordered the two regiments forward, without regard to the purpose they had been placed there for. Davies complied with the order but quietly sent his pioneers back to cut down trees, blocking the road for a quarter of a mile, and posted a picket on the intersection.

From Davies' position, Miles now moved in search of Richardson and found him at a log house on top of a hill that Richardson was using for his head-quarters. Richardson had already observed a Confederate brigade under the command of Colonel Jubal A. Early moving into the entrenchments on the far side of Bull Run. He estimated the total reinforcing units to be at least four regiments in strength. With field glasses, Richardson pointed out the positions to Miles just as the last rebel regiment entered the entrenchments to their front. Seemingly unconcerned, Miles left Richardson's position. At the same time, the battle was in full progress to the west and rebel forces could be seen moving toward the stone bridge in large numbers. Richardson took these targets under fire whenever they came within the range of his ten-pounder rifled gun.

Richardson's estimate had been correct; he was facing four regiments: the 7th Louisiana, the 13th Mississippi, and the 7th and 24th Virginia. The Confederates crossed the run and concentrated in the lowland, which was dead space to the Federal artillery. Early had been trying to organize an attack on Richardson's position for most of the morning, but poor staff work had held up the brigade from taking up a position to support the attack. Longstreet used two of Early's regiments to strengthen his line and then ordered Early to attack Green's battery, which was shelling the rebel line. Early, using a pair of field glasses, surveyed the defensive works laid out by Richardson and was not enthusiastic about his assignment. In the midst of preparation for the assault, a courier arrived with orders from Beauregard to move north and reinforce the units engaged in the fight for the Stone Bridge. "I felt this as a reprieve from almost certain destruction," Early recalled.[53]

Miles interpreted Early's movement as a general retreat toward Manassas. He wanted Richardson to attack the enemy position to their front in order to "drive them out."[54] Perhaps still smarting from the rumored criticism by his commander of exceeding his orders at the Battle of Blackburn's Ford, Richardson provided Miles with his written instructions. "Colonel Miles, I have a positive order for this brigade not to attack at all." Reading the order, Miles responded with, "Yes, that is positive,"[55] and said no more of conducting an assault. He then proposed throwing out a few skirmishers to test the enemy's works. Although Richardson was leery, he detached 160 skirmishers, along with three companies to support them. A volley of small arms fire stopped the advance in its tracks and satisfied Richardson and Miles that the enemy was still across the run in strength. Lieutenant Prime had accompanied the skirmish party and, returning to Richardson, made the observation that before nightfall, Centreville would be our front instead of our rear, suggesting that the Federal forces at Bull Run were being beaten. This was Richardson's first indication that things were not going according to plan by McDowell.

Late in the afternoon, at his headquarters in Centreville, Miles received news of McDowell's defeat from a frantic staff officer, Captain Chauncey McKeever, sent by Colonel Heintzelman in search of reinforcements to protect the retreat. Captain Thomas M. Vincent, of Miles' staff, also appealed to the colonel to give some orders to his division. Miles put his hand on McKeever's shoulder and pushed him aside, saying curtly, "I know all about the fight. You can't give me any information. I have something else to attend to."[56] Apparently having composed himself after McKeever left, Miles finally took some action by sending the brigade of Colonel Blenker forward to aid McDowell, and sending separate orders to Richardson and Davies to withdraw their brigades from their now very exposed positions near Blackburn's Ford.

At about five o'clock, the news of the Union defeat was confirmed to Richardson by his receipt of orders from Miles to withdraw to Centreville. In spite of Richardson having been ordered by General McDowell to hold his position at all costs, he was under Colonel Miles' direct authority, and made preparations to put his brigade on the march.

Of all the mistakes made on this day by Miles, this had the greatest potential to lead to disaster. Instead of directing the withdrawal to Davies, the senior officer and commander on that portion of the field, he sent orders to each unit separately, so that each unit moved independently of one another and without coordination. The firing that Richardson heard from Davies' position was a repulse of a Confederate brigade under D. R. Jones that had crossed Bull Run and was attempting to cut off the main Union force before it got to Centreville. Luckily, Davies was able to deal with the threat with the force he had at hand, because at the very time he was becoming engaged, Miles was ordering his supports off the field.

The Confederate advance was beat off with nothing more than artillery fire planned by Davies and executed by Major Hunt. Davies reported, "I knew very well that if they got into that basin, the first fire would cut them all to pieces; and it did. We continued to fire for thirty minutes, when there was nothing more to fire at, and no more shots were returned."[57]

The Confederate advance was halted with a loss of thirteen killed and sixty-two wounded, a fortunate occurrence for Davies, who was facing an enemy brigade with just one artillery battery and two regiments of infantry. The speed with which the Union artillery almost single-handedly wrecked Jones' advance forced the Confederates to quickly retreat from the field at the same time their opponents were hastily withdrawing at the opposite end.

Members of the 2nd Michigan, who had not seen any action yet, were preparing for supper as the bugle sounded. The unit fell into line of battle and lazily moved across the road under the command of Major Williams. "Just then, Colonel Richardson came up and shouted, 'Battalion!, Left face, double quick, march!' The brigade marched down the road toward Centreville. After a great deal of double quick, a line of battle was formed, behind a stone wall waiting for the approach of a victorious enemy. We could have inflicted a great loss on them here but were after a few minutes ordered to fall back on another position by Colonel Miles."[58]

Dr. Lyster gave another perspective of the withdrawal: "I had just made my first amputation, and was examining the bones of the amputated arm, when Colonel Richardson rode up and reiterated his warning of three days before, that 'you had better be getting out of here or the enemy's cavalry will cut you off.' Complying with this apparently well founded order, loading up my solitary patient, I was about to mount my horse, when Colonel Richardson asked me if I would be obliging enough to let Mrs. Richardson have my horse, as she could not find hers, and he was about to send her back to Alexandria under the escort of Captain Brethschneider and his two companies of flankers. Of course, however much I felt I needed a horse at the moment, to avoid the charge of black horse cavalry, momentarily expected from the left, I acceded to the Colonel's request, assuring him that I considered it a privilege to render any service to either the male or female commander of our brigade!

"Reasoning that if I was obliged to walk, I had better go at once, and started off at a brisk pace. I had not proceeded more than one hundred yards, when I looked back and spied old Dan eating clover, and Mrs. Richardson mounted upon another horse and starting off under Captain Brethschneider's escort. I turned back, mounted old Dan, and rode down to Centreville, where I witnessed a retreating, uniformed, unorganized, unarmed crowd, pour down towards Washington at a steady unhalting pace.

"It was at Blackburn's Ford, that Colonel Richardson lost his sword and wife's horse and sidesaddle. The sword he left standing against a tree, and forgetting it there when he moved on. He borrowed mine, greatly to my relief. It was a heavy cavalry saber, which had been issued to me by the State—for ornamental purposes, I presume—and was the counterpart to the one lost by the Colonel. He later applied for permission to send a flag of truce, hoping to have the horse and sidesaddle returned, but was refused by General Tyler, very curtly. Richardson had known General Bee, and he told me he knew that if Bee was able to do so, he was sure that he would send them back."[59]

Lyster was not the only one put off by Richardson's personal request. Captain Brethschneider privately complained, "The brigade commander thinks there is no one besides me! So he has even trusted me with his young wife to take her safely from the field to Washington."[60]

Davies pushed his two regiments and artillery battery harder when he realized that his little force was all by itself. As he caught up to Richardson, the two brigade commanders tried to make sense of what was happening. Why was the retreat ordered? Didn't Miles know that Jones' advance had been stopped cold? Wasn't abandoning the Blackburn's Ford position contrary to the specific orders of McDowell? Neither man had any idea of what was happening or the reasons behind it. The closer the units marched to Centreville, the more confusing the situation became.

Major William F. Barry, McDowell's chief of artillery, arrived on the scene to collect and post the artillery in a defensive position. After placing one battery and while in the act of moving another, Barry was approached by Miles, who demanded that he not interfere with his arrangements. Replying that he was only carrying out McDowell's orders, Barry heard Miles reply in an angry tone that he would not have his arrangements interfered with by anybody. Another of McDowell's staff officers, Captain James B. Fry, was alarmed enough after witnessing the antics of Miles to ride and report the situation to McDowell personally.

The time was now about seven o'clock on the heights outside Centreville, and as Miles' men became entangled with the retreating forces of McDowell, problems with command and control increased. Captain B. S. Alexander, of General McDowell's staff, reached Richardson and Davies as they were nearing the village and ordered a defensive line set up immediately to block the road running to Blackburn's Ford.

Richardson quickly began to arrange his brigade into a defensive position. After placing the 3rd Michigan and the 12th New York, he moved further down the line to attend to the rest of the brigade. Private Lyman E. Stowe of the 2nd Michigan remembered Richardson, hatless and without coat and sword, riding up to the regiment and shouting, "Major Williams, where are you taking the regiment? About Face!"[61] Soon Lieutenant Colonel Ambrose A. Stevens approached Richardson with word that Colonel Miles had ordered the 3rd Michigan out of the position in which Richardson had left it.

"How is that?" demanded Richardson. "I do not know. But we have no confidence in Colonel Miles," responded Stevens. "Why?" Richardson inquired sharply. "Because Colonel Miles is drunk!" was the answer. As Captain Alexander rode up, Richardson turned to him and complained bitterly of the difficulties being caused by Colonel Miles. "I can not effect any arrangements of the line of battle as long as I am interfered with by a drunken man!" explained Richardson. "Never mind," said Alexander, "McDowell will be here in half an hour and it is his order that you take the general disposition of troops into your own hands. Take command of this part of the field."[62]

The defensive line created by Miles was unmanageably long and too thin. Richardson set out at once to restore the regiments to their original positions, emplaced to protect against enemy cavalry, which he considered to be the main threat coming from Blackburn's Ford. Soon, Miles appeared on the scene. "Colonel Richardson, I don't understand this. You should march that regiment more to the left." Richardson responded, "Colonel Miles, I will do as I please; I am in command of these troops." "I don't understand this, Colonel Richardson."

"Colonel Miles, you are drunk!" was Richardson's reply, as he turned away to supervise the movement.

"I will put you in arrest!" fired back Miles, reacting to the disrespect he was receiving from a subordinate.

"Colonel Miles, you may try that on if you have a mind to," snapped Richardson, who realized that Miles had lost all his authority to issue any such order, as he led the regiment away. As Miles tried to absorb what had just taken place, General McDowell rode on to the scene; as he approached Miles, it was Miles who spoke first.

"My plan of battle has been interfered with!" Miles tried to point out to his commander.

McDowell, who did not know Miles personally, made several observations that confirmed what he had been told by his staff officers. Miles sat on his horse in a stupefied manner, and his language and tone of voice were not in the manner of proper respect normally given to the commander of the army.

"Colonel Miles, your troops are all in confusion, or you have no plan of battle! You are relieved from command!" Miles started to protest, but it was of no use; McDowell was already riding away in search of Richardson.

When McDowell found Richardson, he asked, "Great God, Colonel Richardson, why didn't you hold on to the position at Blackburn's Ford?" Richardson replied, "Colonel Miles ordered me to retreat to Centreville, and I obeyed the order." While they were still together, Richardson told him, "Colonel Miles is continually interfering with me, and he is drunk, and is not fit to command." McDowell replied that Miles had already been relieved and that he wanted Richardson to continue making defensive preparations in the area. With this McDowell left for Centreville to sort out his army and conduct a defense of Washington.[63]

The new line was established about half an hour before sunset. At that moment, the head of the enemy's cavalry made its appearance through the woods on the road from Blackburn's Ford. Richardson was the first to spot the rebels and raised the warning. Turning to Lieutenant Benjamin, commander of one of the Union batteries, he said, "There is the head of the enemy's cavalry; you may open on them with your two guns immediately, and as fast as you can." After four shots were fired at the horsemen, they fell back and were not spotted again.

After dark, Richardson's brigade became the only Federal unit remaining on the battlefield, acting as the army's rear guard in its blocking position outside Centreville. At ten o'clock that evening, Richardson received a message from General McDowell that a retreat of the army had been decided upon and that the troops must be started on the road to Fairfax as soon as possible. Richardson's brigade was to move last and cover the withdrawal of the army. At two in the morning, he began to pull his unit back to the new defensive position around Arlington Heights. The 2nd Michigan stayed behind in position until the rest of the brigade made good their escape before pulling out to rejoin their comrades. On reaching Fairfax, he found it abandoned. The brigade was left alone by the rebels for the remainder of the march and returned to Arlington at two o'clock Monday afternoon, sullen and disappointed.

The next day, the 2nd Michigan took up camp on the flats below General Robert E. Lee's residence, now serving as General McDowell's headquarters. In the afternoon, the regiment was called out by Richardson, and after forming battalion line, they were greeted by President Lincoln, Secretary Seward, and Senator Chandler. Chandler addressed the regiment, praising the men for their valor and discipline during the recent unfortunate campaign, and complimenting Richardson for his abilities as a leader.[64]

Although the army was defeated, they could take pride in the fact they were one of the few intact and disciplined units left in the Union army, and although few realized it at the time, Richardson's brigade was instrumental in keeping a quarter of the rebel force, about ten thousand men, stationed near Blackburn's Ford from becoming involved in the main fight. Less than a week before, Richardson and his brigade had ventured out of Washington as the vanguard of the largest army ever assembled in the nation's history. Still proud and determined, they now acted as the army rear guard and were the last brigade to enter the defensive works. The romance of war began to fade as the reality of fighting set in. A 2nd Michigan soldier wrote in his diary, "It was a terrible sight to see the wagons coming in last night loaded with dead. Six days of marching and sleeping on our arms and living on bread and water has used us up pretty much and we need a few days to recruit before we can move again."[65]

"The Colonel is both celebrated and bullet proof; that is what my men believe"

The defeat of McDowell at Bull Run was a shock to the Lincoln administration and the country. Political circumstances would soon call for a change in leadership. Both sides were guilty of blunders during the engagement, which could only be corrected with intense and long-term training. For the short term however, on the battlefield, the commander's intent could only be demonstrated to the troops with leadership by example, a truly deadly mission for any leader.

By necessity, Richardson had to lead his command from the front. Fortunately, he had survived and his reputation within the ranks grew quickly. "The Colonel is both celebrated and bullet proof, that is what my men believe," wrote Captain Robert Brethschneider of the 2nd Michigan to his wife on July 26.[66]

The pressure that commanders of raw soldiers were under was illustrated by the actions of Richardson's close friend General Bee. At the sound of firing on the morning of July 21, the aggressive Bee was already marching his units toward the fight in the absence of any orders from the confused Confederate command staff. His action put his brigade squarely in the middle of the advancing Union units, and with the help of the brigades of Nathan Evans and Francis S. Bartow, they held their own against a much larger number of Federals. When two brigades of Heintzelman's division extended the Federal right, and Sherman's and Keyes' brigades arrived to extend the Federal left, the Confederates were forced to retire. But they had held up the Union advance for over two precious hours, enough time for other Confederate reinforcements to appear.

As the weak Confederate forces started to give way, Bee saw the brigade of General Thomas J. Jackson on the crest of the hill behind him. Legend states that Bee's speech to the remnants of the 4th Alabama ended with the statement, "There is Jackson standing like a stone wall. Let us determine to die here, and we will conquer. Follow me." Bee, at the head of the regiment, led his men back into a charge toward the Union batteries of Charles F. Griffin and James B. Ricketts. The effect of the Federal fire was terrible, and the company that Bee was leading personally was separated from the rest of the regiment. The unit began to break up under the murderous fire, and Bee was seen riding all around and through the men trying to rally them, but it was no use. The inexperienced soldiers were disorganized beyond help. Finally, witnesses claim they saw General Bee turn his horse toward the enemy and deliberately ride alone into Federal fire. Soon he was mortally wounded and carried from the battlefield to a nearby cabin where he survived a painful night before dying on the morning of July 22, 1861.[67] At the beginning of the war, this was the only type of leadership that appeared to get results. Until soldiers were taught discipline and junior leaders could be taught to develop the situation, the pressure on senior leaders to lead from the front would be tremendous.

Disciplined army regulars became a valuable commodity in the race to establish superior fighting units. Both sides were able to recognize the leadership problem, but the solution would take time until each army gained experience.

Richardson described his frustrations to his family in a letter. "Genl.

McClellan has just arrived here, after being ordered to this front, being second in rank to Gen. Scott only. With that, we have now only two heads instead of a dozen. I feel that we shall be beaten every time we shall fight unless we get a new set of regimental officers through out the army. . . . The enemy suffered greatly from the loss of officers. Among the killed was Capt. Bee, a particular friend of mine, and a general at the time of his death."[68]

One of McClellan's first orders was to establish a basic training course for the new volunteer regiments that were arriving in Washington. General Silas Casey, a veteran officer who had written the drill regulations many years before in the regular army, commanded this camp. In addition, he organized additional schools of instruction for the regimental and company grade officers in the art of warfare.

Regular officers were encouraged to accept volunteer commissions in order to put qualified commanders at the head of regiments instead of political leaders. McClellan put his regulars to the best use in the artillery. His goal was to attach four batteries to each division; one would be a regular army battery in order to furnish experience and to speed the unit training of the other three. By the middle of October, the nine poorly equipped batteries he had inherited from McDowell had increased to twenty-seven. He saw artillery superiority offsetting his supposed disparity of infantry strength.[69]

A new sense of professionalism rejuvenated the army, as training became more intense in the camps surrounding the capital. Soldiers were seldom seen in the city as before, the provost marshal required passes of all who entered, and commanders made sure passes were hard to come by. The politicians were all pleased with the improvements they witnessed and gave McClellan the support an incoming commander needed to more efficiently build the army.

Richardson's brigade was assigned positions around General Lee's estate of Arlington. The already tough training was increased with Richardson, who applied his personal guidance to exercises. On July 27, the same day General McClellan took command, Colonel Richardson confronted a group of sutlers from the De Kalb Guards who were selling beer in front of his camp. In his usual style of abrupt and colorful language, he ordered the men off the grounds. Feeling that they didn't have to answer to Richardson for their actions and taking exception to his offensive words, three Dutchmen charged on him with their bayonets drawn. In a blink, Richardson knocked down two and the third ran away. The provost marshals arrived shortly and arrested about a dozen men, and the establishment was immediately shut down.

"I have no wish to crowd Colonel Miles"

On July 25, 1861, Colonel Richardson's official report of his brigade operations publicly accused Miles of drunkenness during the battle. Miles had no choice but to ask General McDowell for a court of inquiry in the hopes of clearing his reputation.

Miles' request was granted by McDowell, who detailed General William B. Franklin as president of the board, along with Colonel John Sedgwick and Captain Charles Griffin as board members. Miles retained the services of Reverdy Johnson, one of the most famous lawyers of the day. Johnson's resumé included being a U.S. senator from Maryland, attorney general for President Zachary Taylor, and prevailing counsel in the Dred Scott case before the Supreme Court. Against this high-powered legal representation, Colonel Richardson would act as the accuser with the help of his counsel, Lieutenant Colonel Sylvester Larned, a private attorney in Detroit before the war. Writing his family, Richardson indicated, "I only wish to prove my report; I don't care to push matters further than that."[70]

The proceedings consisted of thirteen days of testimony over a two-month period. It was immensely difficult to schedule more than fifty witnesses and assemble the court while the reorganization of the army was occurring. The theme Richardson continually hammered away at was that because Miles was drunk, he made bad or, what is worse, no decisions during July 21, 1861, and the witnesses Richardson called all supported that argument with their testimony. For his part, Miles admitted he had taken drinks of brandy, but not in excess and only as a prescription by his physician. He brought forth witnesses who testified in his behalf, and argued that Richardson had used this occasion to repay his former commander for past disagreements during the time they served together in New Mexico.

On the second day of the proceedings, Colonel Richardson was called to testify. "I went on to place my brigade in line of battle, as directed. I formed one regiment, the Michigan 3rd, in close column, by division, near the Blackburn Ford road, and left it a short time to look after another regiment, and upon returning found it formed in line of battle. On inquiring of the commanding officer, Lieutenant Colonel Stephens, how that change came to be made, he informed me that it was done by order of Colonel Miles, and he wanted to know whether he was to obey my orders or those of Colonel Miles; that he had been sent to me to find out by Colonel McConnell, of the 3rd Michigan. I asked Lieutenant Colonel Stephens what the matter was. He replied, we have no confidence in Colonel Miles. I asked him why. He answered, because Colonel Miles is drunk. Captain Alexander came up about that time, and I told him that I could not effect any arrangements of line of battle as long as I was interfered with by a drunken man. Captain Alexander told me that it was General McDowell's order for me to take the general disposition of the troops in my own hands; that I was in command, I understood him, of the troops in that part of the field.

"I went on forming line of battle, as I could best, of whatever troops I came to. I was conducting another regiment into line when Colonel Miles proposed that I ought to take it in another direction different from the one I was going, and I told him that I had no more orders to receive from him; and he replied, Colonel Richardson, I shall place you under arrest; and I told him that I would not obey his arrest. He answered that he did not understand this, and I left him and went on. From the time that Lieutenant Colonel Stephens had been speaking to me up to this time, I noticed more particularly the actions and conduct of Colonel Miles, and I came to the decided opinion that he was intoxicated, so much so as to be unfit for duty. I came to that conclusion from observing his actions and his manner of talking, more particularly. His voice was guttural and his language was incoherent, and he had difficulty in maintaining his seat in his saddle. This was between half an hour before sunset and dark."[71]

With Richardson on the stand, Miles attempted to guide the court's opinion from his conduct to second-guessing Richardson's actions on the day of the battle. His line of questioning tried to show that interfering with Richardson's command was done not only by the fact that he was the overall commander but also because of bad tactical decisions made by Richardson.

Question: When the accused visited the first time your position at Blackburn's Ford, did you not report that you had not seen any of the enemy at Blackburn's Ford after the first few fires by the artillery, and it was your opinion there were no troops of the enemy there? *Answer:* I did report so; nothing but the enemy's pickets in the woods, and what we could see of the enemy with the glass in the batteries, but no advance; that was about 10 o'clock in the morning; the enemy seemed to remain in the same position that they occupied the day before. *Question:* Did you not suggest, as it was a waste of ammunition to fire at nothing, that the artillery should cease firing? *Answer:* I think I did, because the ammunition was getting short, not because there was no enemy.

Finally, Miles tried to show that Richardson's accusations were not based entirely on current events, but that he had an ax to grind with his former commander from New Mexico.

Question: Did not the accused give you an order twice to halt your regiment, when you were placing them in position, before using the word arrest? *Answer:* I don't know that he did, or he didn't. There was something said about the regiment. *Question:* Have you not entertained a prejudice and unfriendly disposition towards the accused ever since you served in the same regiment with him in New Mexico? *Answer:* I don't think I have entertained a prejudice or unfriendly feeling. *Question:* Did you not more than once while in New Mexico utter threats against the accused; you would do him an injury on the first occasion that offered; and was not this in the presence of Lieutenant

O'Bannon, Lieutenant (now Captain) Alley, and Mr. Duvall, the sutler of Fort Thorn? *Answer:* I can't remember of ever having done so.

With the conclusion of Richardson's testimony, many witnesses were called by both the prosecution and the defense to buttress their cases. On October 26, 1861, Miles stated that although he had many more witnesses he would like to put on record, he would not delay the proceedings any longer. He closed his case with a written summary.

"On arriving where I had left Hunt's battery, I found the troops moving apparently in all directions and in the greatest confusion. On asking Colonel Richardson, who passed me leading a regiment by the flank, by whose order the change was made, he replied, by a superior one to yours, etc., etc., and passed on. If, gentlemen, you had been placed as I was then, and had not been filled with indignation and intense excitement, you would have been more than mortal. The testimony of General Richardson is manifestly actuated by malicious feelings, engendered in former years in New Mexico, when he was a captain of the 3rd Infantry, of which regiment I had the command."

Richardson also submitted a written summary of the prosecution. It is interesting that while reminding the court to focus their attention strictly to the charge at hand and not his alleged ill feelings toward a former commander; Richardson was able to get one last dig in by bringing up Miles' reputation in the old army.

"The case itself is narrowed to a small compass, and if we confine ourselves strictly to the charge and the testimony, it would seem that there is no difficulty in disposing of it. . . . The only question to be determined is whether this charge is probably true, and this question must be determined by the evidence on the record, and that alone. The consequences to Colonel Miles, the motives of the accuser, the supposed enmity of a witness cannot alter the facts; as *they are,* so must the matter be determined.

"Was Colonel Miles intoxicated at the time and place alleged? Twenty-eight witnesses have sworn plainly, unhesitatingly, and explicitly that he was. Most of them have described his conduct and manner not only, but his language and tone, all totally inconsistent with the idea of his being sober. Many of these witnesses are army officers, and have known Colonel Miles long and well."[72]

Writing home, Richardson predicted, "Col. Miles, having his defense some forty witnesses, will try the old dodge, that of extreme debility and sickness, and of taking opium. With the mass of evidence that I have introduced, I entertain no fears respecting myself. I wish merely to prove my own report, and beyond that, have no wish to crowd Col. Miles."[73]

On October 29, 1861, the Court of Inquiry issued their verdict: That Colonel I. B. Richardson was justified in applying the term *drunkenness* to Colonel D. S. Miles' condition, about 7 o'clock P.M., on the 21st of July last. Dixon S. Miles, under normal circumstances, would be subjected to a court-martial for his actions on July 21. But these were not normal times, and several factors came into play allowing him to keep his commission. First was the political decision of having a high-seniority regular army officer, from a wavering border state of Maryland, involved in a scandalous trial. Second was the impracticability of conducting such a spectacle. The leadership of the army had more pressing business to deal with. It was convenient for all parties involved to put Colonel Miles on leave of absence and awaiting orders. Although officially not reprimanded for his conduct, the fact that Miles remained a colonel while most of his peers in the seniority-conscious army were being promoted to general, including his chief accuser, Richardson, was not lost on anybody.

Clearly, Miles was not only incompetent but a drunk as well. Captain Sigmund Elble, of Hamilton, Ohio, served in the army on the frontier and during the Civil War, collecting nine arrow wounds and two gunshot wounds during his fourteen years of service. His remarkable combat record as a soldier allows his personal assessment of Miles' ability to be pondered. "I served under Miles when he commanded the 3rd Infantry in New Mexico. I was personally acquainted with him and knew his character as a soldier; also as to his sobriety and loyalty. At Fort Thorn, Col. Miles was so beastly drunk that he fell from his horse. J. H. Eaton, Captain of Co. F, brought charges against him for drunkenness on duty, and kept him under arrest during the whole campaign. He was tried by court-martial at Fort Fillmore, but was acquitted because the prosecuting witness did not drink out of the same bottle that the Colonel did, and therefore could not prove that the contents were intoxicating. Miles' son-in-law, Lieutenant L. W. O'Bannon, who was quartermaster of the regiment and a southern man, went to the rebel army. In my opinion, Colonel Miles was a drunkard, a coward and a traitor, and if I had had the power I would have had the United States buttons taken from his coat."[74]

For all that could be said against Colonel Dixon S. Miles, with his idiosyncrasies and lack of abilities, it is clear that he loved his country and the army in which he served. The only reason he was placed in such a position of responsibility during July of 1861, was the fact that he had more service seniority than anyone else. In an army with a pension system, he would have been retired long ago. On a personal level, the court of inquiry was deeply humbling to the old soldier, and from this point until his death, he would never drink another drop of liquor again.

5

Opportunity

"He is bullheaded, brave, and a good disciplinarian"

After the battle at Bull Run, Colonel Richardson received what had to be a very gratifying reward, both personally and professionally: a brigadier general's commission in the U.S. Volunteers. His strengths were just the type that McClellan needed as a general officer in the rapidly expanding army. The commanding general was pleased with Richardson's work, describing him as "an officer of the old army; bull headed, brave and a good disciplinarian."[1] Announced in orders published August 9, 1861, the commission was backdated to May 17, 1861. This was important in giving him seniority over many of the newly created political generals surfacing in the expanding army. With this promotion, a turning point in his military career could be detected. For the past twenty years of his military profession, Israel Richardson was concerned only with the tactical aspects of units under his command. His knowledge was based on hard lessons learned during two prior campaigns and years of cutting-edge missions with the 3rd Infantry regiment. Within the Army of the Potomac, no other brigadier general could boast of more infantry fighting experience than Richardson.

Now a general himself, Israel Richardson automatically became the expert in all things military to the many questioning civilian leaders in the government. Just five months before, he had been a simple farmer in Pontiac, Michigan. It would be a difficult situation for anyone to cope with, and Richardson had the added distraction of a newlywed wife, who didn't understand her role within his military profession. The challenge facing him in these heady days was to maintain a clear perspective based on his experience and to guard against acting pompous or arrogant to his civilian superiors.

Half a mile from the campground of Richardson's brigade was a large and beautiful peach orchard owned by a farmer with strong Southern sympathies. At the farmer's written request, Richardson placed a guard over the orchard to protect the fruit. On August 7, the new brigadier and his wife happened along; he was dressed, as usual, in his citizen's clothes with his old straw hat over his eyes. They strayed into the orchard and stopped to pick a dozen peaches. The owner, not knowing Richardson by sight, came out and demanded payment. The general asked the damage and was told fifty cents for the peaches, a very steep price. The money was paid, and as he left, he turned to the guards and told them their services were no longer needed. The soldiers took the hint, and within a week not a peach remained in the orchard.

Each day brought more men and equipment into the area as both the North and South mobilized and trained additional units for the field. Richardson's men were becoming comfortable with his training expectations, and they strived to meet his standards. The enlisted men loved him, and the simple act of personally instructing them in how to build a fireplace in a tent with an underground chimney, as he had learned in Mexico, made them believe that there was nothing he could not do. The junior officers also loved him and worked hard not to disappoint him. But higher up the chain of command, starting with the field grade officers, Richardson remained a strict taskmaster who pounced on any perceived lack of effort or ability.

In this regard, a flaw in his character became more pronounced as he grew increasingly critical of those peers who didn't measure up to the successful past commanders he had served under. Taylor, Scott, Hitchcock, and Alexander had all combined to show him how a leader should behave in his profession, and he would never stray from their example. Israel Richardson, although a steady soldier, was never a brilliant man, and his outspoken opinions of political generals and military policy would became a thorn in the side of the senior leadership in the Army of the Potomac. He remained tactically sound, but he was not a politically correct general. Perhaps his attitude was encouraged by the successful way he solved his problems with Colonel Miles. Whatever the reason, it became clear that any commander who did not lead by example soon earned the scorn of General Israel B. Richardson.

In many ways, he was out of his element when dealing with other generals concerning army politics. Now that he was a senior leader, the art of tact, which he always seemed to be weak in, took on greater significance in daily conversations with politicians and other army leaders. His frustrations drove him closer to Senator Zachariah Chandler, the powerful politician from his home state of Michigan. To Chandler, Richardson represented the aggressive spirit, as well as competence and experience, that the Army of the Potomac lacked with the current leader, General McClellan. Chandler may have been a genuine friend to Richardson, but he also took advantage of Richardson's unpretentious character.

For Richardson, Senator Chandler represented an attractive source of patronage, power, and wealth in his home state. Just nine months earlier, Richardson had been an unknown farmer from Pontiac. That he was now suddenly thrust into the inner circle of state powerbrokers was exciting to him and overwhelming to his wife. All of these dynamic men deferring to his own opinion was a powerful pull for a relatively unsophisticated Richardson, not to mention his young bride, Frances.

The days following Bull Run were challenging for the new brigadier in every area of leadership. A new problem arose within the Army of the Potomac in August. Several regiments complained that because they had not legally been sworn into federal service, their terms of enlistment had expired after three months. Some had grown tired of playing soldier and longed to return home. On August 16, when the 12th New York was ordered to fall out for morning company drill, they refused. That evening, Richardson again ordered the regiment to turn out for drill, which was again refused. In response, the general ordered out the 2nd Michigan and marched them over to the campground of the New York regiment. As Richardson bellowed the commands to load and cap the guns and fix bayonets to the Michigan regiment, the men of the 12th New York rapidly fell out in formation. Marching to the parade field, the 12th New York went through the motions of brigade drill with the threat of two brass twelve pounders loaded with grapeshot stationed in front of them. During the drill, Richardson acted very kind and mildly to officers of the regiment. After the exercise, and in private, he gave them a severe reprimand, attributing the disorganized state of the regiment to their laziness. Even this negative was viewed in a positive manner by the rest of the men in Richardson's brigade. The men bragged that to quell disturbances in other regiments of the army, Colonel William T. Sherman, of the regulars, was sent for, but in his brigade, Richardson says he prefers to do it himself.[2]

On August 23, the 12th New York was replaced by the 37th New York. The brigade training continued without pause on the next day, when General McClellan, President Lincoln, and Secretary Seward inspected Richardson's brigade. As the Union leadership trooped the line, the men heard Richardson talking to Lincoln. "These men can be relied on. We could have held Blackburn's Ford that Sunday if it had been allowed." The results of the inspection inspired the soldiers: "McClellan is taking a personal view of every regiment in the army. I have confidence in him and all of our men think Richardson is almost a God."[3]

Richardson's brigade was stationed on the Virginia bank of the Potomac River, near Munson's Hill, the closest Confederate outpost to the Union position, and McClellan paid a great deal of attention to it. The men remarked that Richardson and McClellan rode out with their escort to inspect the enemy lines every day. In a letter to the family, Richardson described his relationship with his new commander. "Some three weeks ago, I tried to bring to the notice of some of our officers of engineers the importance of occupying a high hill covered with timber and commanding both Forts Albany and Runyon, and 800 yards in advance of the former. They said it would throw our line of defense too much in front. General McClellan came over and I immediately proposed the plan to him and going up on the hill, he made up his mind in less than five minutes and told me to go to work. Gen. McClellan says now it is the most important work in the whole line on this side of the river."[4]

The area attracted a heavy amount of picket fire from both sides. Usually, a gentleman's agreement between company grade officers from each side could stop this kind of behavior, but in this sector, the activity was hard to control. When he learned to his delight the identity of the enemy force facing him, Richardson made a personal effort to quell the problem by contacting his Confederate counterpart, his old friend Brigadier General Longstreet, and cordially inviting him to a dinner party, to be given at his headquarters. Longstreet later would recall: "He (Richardson) was disappointed when I refused to accept this amenity, and I advised him to be more careful lest the politicians should have him arrested for giving aid and comfort to the enemy. He was my singularly devoted friend and admirer before the war, and had not ceased to be conscious of old-time ties."[5]

Since promotion to brigade command, Richardson had been dividing his time between the brigade headquarters and the 2nd Michigan. On September 16, 1861, General McClellan appointed Colonel Orlando M. Poe to be the new commander of the 2nd Michigan.

Born at Navarre, Ohio, March 7, 1832, Orlando Metcalf Poe entered the U.S. Military Academy in 1852 and graduated sixth in his class in 1856. His first duty was as a second lieutenant of the Topographical Engineers. With headquarters in Detroit, he supervised lighthouse construction, as well as river and harbor improvements, on the upper Great Lakes until 1861.

At the outbreak of the war, Poe was detailed to organize Ohio volunteers, but because of his ability and experience as an engineer, he was added to the staff of General George B. McClellan. Impressed with his staff work during the Rich Mountain campaign, McClellan brought Poe with him to Washington and put him to work laying out the defenses of the capital.[6]

Now that Colonel Poe was in command of the 2nd Michigan, the men had to adapt to a new leadership style. Although he was pleased with the regiment's skill in drill and ceremony, Poe believed that Richardson had been lax in upholding regulations regarding stolen property, which the men of the regiment felt they had a soldier's right to. In other words, while both commanders stressed fighting ability, Poe also put more emphasis on camp regulations and spit and polish than Richardson did. After an adjustment period, the men would grow fond of their new colonel. But Richardson would always remain close to the regiment, and even though brigade command duties kept him away for much of the time, he could still be found in the regimental campgrounds on occasion, talking to the soldiers.

"We could wipe them out in a twinkling, and yet I am ordered to make no demonstration"

From the vantage point of Munson's Hill, enemy pickets could actually view the unfinished dome of the Capitol, as well as the camps of many Union regiments, which continued to grow and drill each day. The rebel fortifications looked impressive, manned with many men and an artillery piece to repel any attack.

From his headquarters at Fort Albany, Richardson was in direct communication with General McClellan by means of telegraph. He was aggressive in probing the enemy position and looking for any weakness. When he thought he had found an approach that would allow him to maneuver a force behind the Confederate works, he telegraphed the suggestion to McClellan but failed to receive permission to launch his attack. His opinions mirrored the remarks beginning to circulate around Washington by the Radical Republicans, who wanted to see immediate offensive action instead of the caution exhibited by McClellan. "Here we are, seventy thousand men within one hour's march of that hill, where there are not over four thousand Confederates, whose nearest supports are at Fairfax Court House. We could wipe them out in a twinkling, and yet I am ordered to make no demonstration, and if attacked, to fall back under the guns of the fortifications along Arlington Heights."[7]

On August 28, 1861, Richardson ordered a two-hundred-fifty-man detachment from his 2nd Michigan to occupy and hold Bailey's Crossroads against any encroachments of the enemy's forces in that vicinity. This force was successful in securing the objective, but they remained under a brisk fire from rebel pickets along the whole line for the next five days. This fire stopped only for periods of darkness.

McClellan arrived with Richardson late in the afternoon to inspect the lines and encourage his soldiers. He asked the 2nd Michigan whether they were "ready for a brush"; when they enthusiastically responded, McClellan replied that he would "risk the night" with them. Richardson led McClellan out along his brigade front, making the argument for more aggressive action; McClellan, however, was noncommittal. Lieutenant Charles B. Haydon wrote, "I do not like to see them exposing themselves so much. They go out in sight of the enemy every day. They went out again today just after dinner."[8]

As the frustration of inaction built, Charles Coffin, a newspaper reporter, accompanied Richardson to the front lines in early autumn. "Dismounted our horses, walked through a corn field and came upon the picket lines. We were so near the Confederates that we could hear them talking, and could see the soldiers behind the breastworks. 'As near as I can make out, there are about seven thousand, and they have no supports nearer than Fairfax Court House. In an hour's time we could pounce upon them with seventy thousand men,' said General Richardson, and added: 'I am ordered, if attacked, to fall back to the forts. I don't understand it.'"[9]

The increased activity led General Joseph E. Johnston to believe that it was only a matter of time before this forward position would be captured, and he ordered the withdrawal of the outpost during the night of September 27, 1861.

The next morning while on picket duty, the 2nd Michigan discovered the enemy pickets had been withdrawn. The report was telegraphed to headquarters, and McClellan wired back to Richardson to move his men forward cautiously. In the afternoon, Richardson and Poe came out to the picket line to take charge of the operation. Lieutenant Haydon describes the action in his journal:

"About four o'clock, General Richardson and Colonel Poe came out. After looking around for a little while, Richardson ordered Capt. Sherlock and myself to take twelve men and occupy a house about thirty rods in front of the enemy's battery. We advanced, occupied the house and scattered along a fence parallel to the battery. We could see about twenty men around their works who fired occasional shots at us. . . . General Richardson and Colonel Poe looked on, not believing the works were deserted. The General swore worse than a corporal. [Second Lieutenant W. H.] Benson and I had not had a chance to get swords and were armed with nothing but pistols. I was fortunate enough to escape his observation, but Benson caught it. "Is there another lieutenant here!" shouted General Richardson.

"Yes, Sir," said Benson, "I am." The general turned around and looking at him a moment said, "Well, by God, you look like one. You'll kill somebody yet. Where in hell is your sword Sir, where have you been? What have you been about, on duty without a sword!?"

Here Colonel Poe interfered in the behalf of the paralyzed lieutenant and explained that Benson only received his commission a week ago.

"Ah well," said Gen. Richardson kindly, "Can you get a sword, Sir?" Capt. Whipple handed him his. "Do you see that barricade on the road?" Yes. "Can you lead these men there?" Yes.

Then, without waiting a second, "Come. Why in hell ain't you off Sir, what are you standing here for?"

When he saw the men running to the works he pretended to be very much enraged but could easily be seen laughing in his sleeve. "There, damn it, Colonel, there goes one of them up to the fort. There go two more. There, by God, goes the whole lot of them. Colonel, all you have to do is to hold these men if you can, till it's time to let them go."[10]

The assault by the 2nd Michigan on the Confederate outpost, abandoned the night before, resulted in capture of the two-dozen-man rebel rearguard that remained. Once again, during a period of relative calm between both armies, Richardson's small action was noted by the Union leadership as an example of something positive in an army that was starting to receive criticism for its lack of aggressiveness. In a letter to his wife dated September 29, 1861, McClellan indicated that he felt relieved by the taking of the fort. "They can no longer say that they are flaunting their dirty little flag in my face."[11]

The media reaction over a sensational discovery in the enemy works at Munson's Hill overshadowed the outcome of this action. The menacing artillery piece that could be seen from the Union camps turned out to be a peeled log painted black with a pair of rickety wagon wheels attached. Politicians, crying for action, coined the term "Quaker gun" to describe this log. The newspapers increasingly began to question the administration strategy, and in turn, Lincoln pressured McClellan to propose a definitive plan for the capture of Richmond. Richardson thought the army would move soon but mentioned in a letter, "Gen. McC. keeps his plans to himself, even from his own staff."[12] In Congress, politicians who had welcomed McClellan two short months ago were beginning to have doubts as to his abilities and qualifications as the leader of the Union forces.

Although it appeared that the commanders in the Army of the Potomac were more concerned with training rather than fighting, some small examples of aggressive leadership were appearing here and there. Richardson's brigade continued to be active, with a reconnaissance-in-force mission toward the Occoquan River in Virginia. He sent the following report to his division commander, Brigadier General Samuel P. Heintzelman, on October 19, 1861.

"In obedience to your instructions, I left this camp yesterday at 3:30 p. m. to make a reconnaissance in the direction of Occoquan. The command proceeded as far as Accotink Creek, taking the Telegraph road.

"On reaching this stream I came to a halt, and sent half a company of cavalry to Pohick Church, the other half to the Accotink Village, and posted a company of infantry to our right on the road leading up to the creek. This company on moving up the road fell in with the enemy's pickets, who gave the alarm. The long roll beat some twenty minutes from three different camps on our right, showing that they were there in some force. After resting the command half an hour, I sent to order in both detachments of cavalry, who soon came in, finding no enemy at the village or at the church.

"The enemy occupies the valley on the right of the road leading from the crossing to the church. From what I could learn, the road from Pohick Church to Occoquan is clear, and but few troops are in the later place. Having finished the object of the expedition, I moved the command back to camp, where it arrived at 12 o'clock, after marching some twenty miles. I took this opportunity of moving forward our pickets, who now occupy a direct line from Windsor Hill to the mouth of Dogue Creek."[13]

One month later, Heintzelman sent Richardson's brigade back into the same area to push out the rebel pickets. At 12:30 A.M., the drums and bugles sounded and Richardson's men prepared to march at 3:00 A.M. to attack Pohick Church. The companies formed up quickly, each man carrying four pounds of ammunition, a day's rations, blanket, and canteen. The brigade moved out on time, followed at 4:00 A.M. by Sedgwick's brigade, and by daylight had covered six miles. Three miles from their objective, Richardson split his brigade in two, detaching two of his regiments, the 3rd Michigan and the 37th New York, along with a battery of artillery, and sent them down another road that entered Pohick Church from the rear. Richardson led the two remaining regiments, the 2nd and 5th Michigan, with another battery of artillery, forward down the Telegraph Road. As he was nearing the objective, Richardson's aide, Captain Norvell, returned to the main body to report that the enemy had just abandoned Pohick Church.

Heintzelman arrived on the scene soon after Richardson entered the church and directed him to send forward a reconnaissance on the Telegraph Road as far as the Occoquan River. Here the cavalry patrol was ambushed by enemy pickets hidden in the woods, and they withdrew with three killed and one wounded. At 3:00 P.M. the brigade received orders to return to camp and, after a hard and disciplined march of thirty-five miles, arrived home at 9:30 P.M. This was a performance far different from the first march the unit had attempted back in July at Blackburn's Ford.

The Joint Committee on the Conduct of the War

On December 5, 1861, Senator Chandler found an opportunity to attack McClellan through an investigation of General Charles P. Stone's conduct during the Union disaster at Ball's Bluff. He moved to create a congressional committee to investigate the causes of the defeats at Bull Run and Ball's Bluff. Several other Radicals offered amendments to include other battles such as Wilson's Creek. In the debate that followed, it was suggested that a joint committee be formed from both houses of the legislature and that it have the power to investigate all lost battles.

Thus was born the Committee on the Conduct of the War. It played a dramatic and powerful role in the political history of the United States. The Radicals could never have initiated and carried on their struggle against Lincoln without the information that the committee furnished in its slanted reports. It became the spearhead of the radical drive against the administration. It investigated the principal military campaigns, worked to undermine Democratic and conservative officers, interfered with the plans of field commanders, and bullied Lincoln into accepting the radical program.

The dominating figure of the committee was its chairman, Senator "Bluff Ben" Wade, of Ohio. He had won his election to the Senate in 1851 by his opposition to the Fugitive Slave Act in the Compromise of 1850. Next to Wade's elbow was Senator Chandler, of Michigan, offering advice and guidance. Together Chandler and Wade determined the policies of the committee. Wade was a consummate artist at manipulating votes in Congress and was entrusted with rallying the Republican machine behind the committee's lead.

Chandler had been a prosperous Detroit merchant before he entered politics. In 1851, while mayor of Detroit, he was sued by an army officer serving at the Detroit Barracks. During a winter night, while returning home from headquarters, the officer slipped and sprained his ankle in front of Chandler's home. The city required all residents to keep the sidewalks clear of snow and ice in front of their homes. Chandler was enraged and insisted on a jury trial, representing himself at the proceedings. He denounced the officer, a young captain by the name of Ulysses S. Grant, by branding him an idle loafer living off the community, "If you soldiers would keep sober, perhaps you would not fall on people's pavements and hurt your legs." Chandler lost his case and was fined six cents plus court costs.

With the birth of the Republican Party in Michigan, Chandler became state party chairman and was elected to the Senate, where he joined Wade in opposition to the slavery interests. President Lincoln had placed the federal patronage in the state at his disposal, and this formed the basis of his political empire.

Having as powerful a friend as Senator Chandler so available was tempting to Richardson. One small example of him going outside the chain of command occurred with a supply problem early in November of 1861. Chandler was always sympathetic to his Michigan constituents, and an eyewitness in the 2nd Michigan described, "General Richardson's urgent letter of yesterday brought Senator Chandler over here early this morning. General Richardson took him around and exhibited to him the ragged tents and old muskets which are our only arms and poured out some very urgent and emphatic complaints."[14]

How quickly Richardson realized the fine line he had to tread between his political guardian, Senator Chandler, and his army commander is hard to pinpoint. He was probably not politically sophisticated enough to understand how his actions were affecting his future. Coming from Michigan, where the local majority views were that of the Radicals, he probably felt very comfortable with their philosophy; and as a soldier, his inclination that attacking the enemy was preferable to going into winter quarters played right into the radical agenda.

Once the committee became operational, their first act of business was to invite General McClellan to testify before them as the first witness. Senator

Wade sent the communication to the general on December 21, 1861. McClellan confirmed this summons the next day, making an appointment before the committee for 10 o'clock in the morning on December 23, 1861. However, on the 23rd, the general failed to show as scheduled. On Christmas Eve, the committee met and read a note from McClellan's staff explaining his absence due to sickness. The committee's next order of business was to interview its first in a long line of Union officers, Brigadier General Israel B. Richardson.

His division commander, General Heintzelman, accompanied Richardson and was also examined by the committee. From the line of questioning, it was easy to see that these two had been handpicked by Chandler and Wade to draw out testimony that might be critical of McClellan. Knowing the close relationship between Richardson and Chandler, it was assured that Chandler would already have an indication as to what questions would have the most detrimental effect on McClellan. Heintzelman's diary entry from December 14, 1861, gives some insight as to the political techniques of Senator Chandler and the committee:

"On that day, Heintzelman came to Washington on business and learned from a friend that Zack Chandler was looking for him. He made an appointment to see the senator at five-thirty that afternoon at Willard's Hotel. 'I went and found him alone,' wrote Heintzelman of the meeting. 'He locked the door and we had a talk of two hours on the affairs of the army. . . . He asked me if McClellan had ever called a council of war. I told him I believe not. He had never consulted me on any military subject. I proposed several theories since the war commenced, but McClellan had not noticed those I left for him. I also told him that if my advice had been taken the Potomac would not have been blockaded and I doubt whether we would have sustained a defeat at Manassas. . . . I also told him my views about carrying this war and the mistakes I thought had been made. He don't want me to speak of our interview.'"

Once Chandler was satisfied that Heintzelman was an enemy of McClellan, he arranged for the resentful division commander to appear before the committee. After a little prodding, Heintzelman spoke out freely against his superior during his testimony. Whenever Heintzelman visited Washington, he hunted up Chandler for a briefing, and the shrewd senator always dangled before him the bait of an independent command to be secured through the committee's influence.[15]

Richardson's testimony, while somewhat disapproving of the fact the army wasn't moving forward, was still neutral in his approval of his commanding general. Whether or not he understood that Chandler was using him as a political tool is hard to say; but he was not the damning witness Chandler hoped for. Heintzelman was more vindictive in his testimony, possibly because he felt his high seniority in the army was not being respected enough by the junior commanding general.

"Fall out to drill"

After ten months of service, Richardson's original regiment, the 2nd Michigan, along with most of the Army of the Potomac, had become fairly seasoned in the ways of field craft. By now, most of the weak and sick had been weeded out of the unit and the men had developed an efficient routine to campaigning. The February 24, 1862, edition of the *Pontiac Gazette* gave the following description of camp life in the 2nd Michigan:

"We are doing nothing in these days of mud and wet, with the exception of once a day when the sun shows for an hour or two, we receive the summons from General Richardson to 'fall out and drill.' We love to have him at our head and gladly 'fall out.' We have obtained the greatest proficiency in all the movements of brigade drill under the watchful eye of the General, and you would be both surprised and pleased to see us now and mark the contrast between our drill at this time and the drill as it was four months ago.

"The General is a staunch veteran and no one better fitted to command; when our immediate commander's voice is drown out in the noise of many moving feet, the voice of the General rises above the din, clear and distinct. He is idolized by the entire brigade, and not a man in our four regiments but would die for him."

The officers of the 2nd Michigan presented General Richardson with a sword and sash as a Christmas present at the end of 1861. Charles B. Haydon described the event:

"The General knew nothing about it until we came in on him. He acted funny and embarrassed as a boy with a new hat. He called on Colonel Terry to help him out by a speech, which he did quite handsomely. We took him entirely off guard. Anything like speech making is a terror to him. He has never been known to talk for more than two minutes consecutively since he joined the regiment. He likes to do things without ceremony."[16]

The soldiers of the brigade were growing fonder of their commander every day. As they became more professional in their duties, the eccentricities that emerged from Richardson's personality were noted with affection. One day General Richardson appeared in camp wearing a new uniform hat. It had a large silver eagle on the side, which he tore off immediately. Finding his aide, he inquired, "Captain Norvell, what do you think of my hat? It had an eagle on it but I thought it would do without any eagle, so I took him off." He then jammed on the hat and went off nodding and shaking his head. Everyone knew it was acceptable for a brigadier general to tear the eagle off his hat, but if any lieutenant appeared for dress parade without all the uniform which belongs to him, boots blacked, white gloves on and not a speck of dirt about him, he would be immediately sent back to his tent.[17]

Fighting Dick made his mark on his men by seeming to be everywhere at once. His presence left a confidence and delight among his soldiers. Private Perry Mayo described the general's character: "his countenance is stern, and when he gives an order, he means it; but, he is a man, every inch of him. He never puts on any extra airs or style but delights to be around his men in citizen's dress."[18] Color Sergeant D. G. Crotty, 3rd Michigan, related another story about him:

"We all claim that 'Fighting Dick' is the plainest general in the army, and one of the best. He never cared much about his dress which consisted of a jacket, an old straw hat, and trousers, in the side pockets of which his hands are generally thrust. This was his every-day attire, without any insignia of rank about him; but, with all these rough outlines, we all know he has a head and a heart. Everyone loved the good natured and plain old 'Fighting Dick.'

"One morning, while walking along the road, the General was accosted by a sprig of a Lieutenant, saying: 'Hello, old fellow, can you tell me where General Richardson's headquarters are?' The General told him that he could, pointing out the direction to him. He then strolled leisurely toward his log hut on the hill, and found the dandy saying all kind of things, for he was mad that no one waited on him. When he saw the general approaching, he told him to hurry up and hold his horse while he went in to deliver the dispatches he had for the General.

"The good natured General took the horse, tied him to a stake, went in by another door, and stood before the dumbfounded Lieutenant with his stars on his shoulders. 'Now,' said he, 'what do you want?' The dandy had to face the music, and handed the dispatches to his late groom with trembling hands. He was doubtless relieved when the good natured General told him 'That will do,' and the sprig of a shoulder-strap was doubtless taught to find out whom he talked to before asking them to hold his horse."[19]

Another trait that his men had noticed was the general's horsemanship in relation to his stockiness. Charles Haydon's journal complained of Richardson's style:

"If General Richardson could only ride on horseback decently he would be one of the finest looking officers I ever saw. He will always take hold of the mane with one hand to keep from falling off. He says he used to ride pretty well when he was in Mexico and can ride well enough now to suit him, but the boys in the Second laugh a good deal about it. Colonel Poe cannot be beat in the army in this, but the General goes jolting along like some clumsy old farmer."[20]

Although his duties kept him at brigade headquarters most of the time, Richardson still managed to come back to the 2nd Michigan's campground and stay in touch with old friends from the regiment. Colonel Poe found it hard to wrestle the soul of the unit away from Richardson, who continued to be preferential toward his old regiment. Poe was a strict disciplinarian who resented the fact that Richardson had a habit of playing fast and loose with regulations while he was in command. One example was the rampant theft that had always occurred in the brigade. Richardson had always looked the other way as his men scavenged materials from around the countryside to make their life more comfortable. With almost fifteen years of experience living in the field, he knew the value to morale and health for any improvement in a soldier's living standard.

The rank and file quickly learned. When the 2nd Michigan arrived at their designated campground, an old veteran recalled, "There were several regiments camped near us, and we had been in the neighborhood but a few hours before we discovered that we must sleep with our shoes on and a corner of our blanket between our teeth, and learn to steal on sight, if one hoped to keep even with his neighbor. Of course, we had to steal something before we were admitted into the circle of their acquaintance, and out of sheer desperation one of our boys went out and hooked a step ladder. On being asked what he was going to do with it, he replied, "None of your damn business. It's a pity a fellow can't steal a little something without you all making a fuss about it."[21]

If higher headquarters ever complained, Richardson stepped in to warn his men. Such was the case when some of his men actually tore down and carried away a barn in the presence of its owner. Soon Richardson was in camp, explaining to his men, "It won't do to hook any more boards around here. They are making a devil of a fuss about it at headquarters." He never stopped his boys from "cramping" until he was obliged to. His orders were that such things "must be stopped as much as possible," which was always understood to mean that the men should not steal anything unless they really needed it.[22]

That Richardson paid particular attention to his old regiment sometimes came as a disadvantage, as evidenced at one brigade drill session that winter. Owing to a misunderstanding, the regiment did not come on line exactly where it was supposed to, and General Richardson was in a hot-tempered mood. He ordered the regiment about face and marched it back to where they had started. At that point he wheeled and twisted the unit into such a shape that they hardly knew which way to go or what to do next. "Now see if you can get onto the line as you ought to," he said as he rode away and left them. The 2nd Michigan finally got into position, but not until the rest of the brigade had a great laugh at their expense, disgracing them for the day.

After the brigade drill, the field officers of the regiment made bitter complaints to the general regarding their treatment on the drill field. Richardson wasn't troubled in the least. Finally Lieutenant Colonel Larned, being a lawyer, and full of expedients, told the general how much the 2nd thought of him and how they would willingly follow him to their deaths, and how bad they felt that he should disgrace them in front of the other regiments, et cetera; the general's eyes grew misty over the matter, and looking at Larned, he said, "Well, well; I don't know but I was a little too fast. Colonel, I'm sorry I did that."[23]

However questionable Richardson's command philosophy was, the resulting high morale was evident by the comments of a private from a Michigan regiment: "Our brigade commander was Gen. I. B. Richardson, or 'Old Dick,' as we used to call him. We remembered him as a man who understood volunteers and appreciated the difference between them and Regulars. His slouchy appearance was anything but military; but he would stay in a fight as long as any one, and looked after the comfort of his men with a fatherly solicitude."[24] Richardson had kept a detail from his regiment after his promotion to brigade command, but he soon sent them back to Colonel Poe, saying, "Colonel, I guess you'll have to take this bodyguard back. I'm afraid they'll tear my house down if I keep them any longer." They had such a passion for boards, bricks, and straw, in fact a passion for everything that was moveable. But the men were never known for malicious destruction of property. What they were unable to carry off, they generally left in as good condition as they found it.

Poe slowly won over the regiment with his own leadership style, and the thefts began to diminish. However, old habits died hard, long after commanders had been transferred, as General Philip Kearny, who became the division commander of the 3rd Michigan, found out months later:

While inspecting Company D, of the 3rd Michigan Regiment, General Kearny came to a man with a very dirty and ragged pair of pants. "You are a pretty looking soldier," said the General. "You would not make a good breastwork. You are too dirty. Is that the best pair of pants you have?" The man replied that he had a new pair, but someone had stolen them. "A hell of a soldier that cannot steal a pair of pants!" replied Kearny.

At the next inspection of the 3rd Michigan, Kearny came to this man, who had a bright new pair of officer's pants on. The General looked him over, front and rear, then looking him in the eye he said, "Where in hell did you get them pants?" "I stole them," he replied. "Why you son of a bitch, they are my pants, my best pants!" "You are the man that told me to steal a pair," replied the soldier. "Not mine, not mine," said the General, and the incident was closed.[25]

Richardson noted his relationship with President Lincoln to his family in a letter: "The President is a great friend of mine, says I am honest and faithful, and tells people that if there is to be any fighting to be done; he expects me to be among the first. I go to call upon him occasionally, and he is always ready to see me; not withstanding the number of office seekers."[26]

On March 8, 1862, Lincoln issued two orders to McClellan. The first was approving McClellan's plan to attack Richmond by way of the Peninsula. The second order organized the army from twelve divisions into four corps commands under the most senior generals, Edwin V. Sumner, Samuel P. Heintzelman, Irvin McDowell, and Erasmus D. Keyes.

During his first few months in command, McClellan appreciated Richardson's aggressive style and his expertise in schooling his brigade. On a professional level, Richardson was exactly the type of soldier McClellan desperately needed, but suspicions of Richardson's political connections kept McClellan from using his talents to the fullest.

Richardson was a Republican, and McClellan a Democrat; Richardson's political patron was Zachariah Chandler, whose sole mission, it seemed, was to destroy McClellan's career. The two division and corps commanders, Sumner and Heintzelman, with whom Richardson closely identified had voted against McClellan's attack plan. Richardson would continue to do his duty as a soldier, to the point of laying down his life, but off the field of battle, he would find his own ways of showing his displeasure at his commander's perceived lack of aggressiveness.

General Richardson was not the only senior leader within the Army of the Potomac to privately find fault with McClellan. In a private letter back home, General Phil Kearny stated his frustration and made this prediction:

"Still, although there is no one to exactly replace McClellan—But I now proclaim distinctly that unless a Chief, a live officer, not an Engineer, of military prestige, (success under fire with troops) is put in command of the Army of the Potomac, (leaving McClellan the bureau duties of General in chief), that we will be in for some awful disaster. . . . McClellan's fault is, that calculating for a future Presidency, he succumbed to the politicians."[27]

On March 10, 1862, the Army of the Potomac began its advance. At a very early stage, the troops discovered the enemy works at Manassas abandoned. As units occupied their new positions, McClellan endured a firestorm of criticism from the Northern press. When the rebel works were entered, guarded only by logs painted black to resemble cannon, the "Quaker guns" became an embarrassment and his political support took another hit.

The editor of the *Pontiac Gazette*, M. E. N. Howell, was visiting Richardson's brigade and received a briefing from the general. Howell's editorial, published on March 15, 1862, was critical of the affair, and stories along the same line were running in Republican papers throughout the nation.

"Well, the advance has been made, and Manassas is ours! General Richardson asked permission to take Munson's Hill six weeks before the enemy evacuated it. . . . Since then, the commander and his 49 aides-de-camp have spent five days in making a critical examination of the *late* rebel camp ground, probably for the purpose of ascertaining the best point of attack that he *might* have selected had he chosen to fight the enemy when he could have done so."

Although McClellan still had the confidence of President Lincoln, members of the president's cabinet were actively campaigning for McClellan's removal. Their goal was to replace him with someone who would be more sympathetic to the type of punishing war they wanted waged on the Confederacy. With all of the criticism against McClellan, if he had only just fought and won victories, all would have been forgotten. But constant partisan bickering soon began to draw him into a political fight with the Republican Party machine that he could not win.

As the Army of the Potomac began to move south on its first campaign, Richardson received his promotion to divisional command. Sumner's division command was opened by his promotion to Corps command. Heintzelman was not measuring up to the type of officer Richardson respected, and the two had their share of disagreements.

The assignment was left in the hands of General McClellan. His first choice was Phillip Kearny who, besides being an excellent pick, hailed from McClellan's home state of New Jersey. Offered the job, Kearny turned it down because he didn't want to leave his brigade command, which consisted of all New Jersey regiments.

Although no record remains of Richardson's feelings toward his old division commander, we could assume that they ran along the same lines of General Kearny's opinions. Like Richardson, Kearny was an aggressive leader who did not tolerate weak superiors well; he also served under Heintzelman during the Peninsula campaign. To him, it seemed that the Army of the Potomac was growing faster than good leaders could be found to command units, and although he served the Union loyalty, privately he was critical of many of his senior leaders. His frustrations are clearly noted by his amusing descriptions of his fellow generals: "As to Heintzelman, a very commonplace individual of no brains, or whose limited apportionment was long since ossified in the small details of an Infantry garrison. . . . There are at least one hundred Brigadier Generals, who are not required. . . . Old General Sumner is a fine old officer, it is true. But then, Banks is a nobody and citizen, although as good a politician as he is a bad soldier. Keyes, a gentlemanly man, and a good friend of mine, was a mere Professor at West Point, during the War of Mexico."[28]

With Kearny's refusal, Richardson received the command. The *Pontiac Gazette* announced the promotion and related Richardson's efforts to bring his beloved brigade along with him into Sumner's command.

"On Saturday, March 13, General Richardson was promoted to command a division and assigned to General Sumner, who is in command of an army corps. General Richardson received this appointment from the President himself who has every confidence in the gallant Michiganian's ability and military skill.

In accepting a Major General's position, 'Fighting Dick,' by which sobriquet he is best known, most deeply regretted the necessity of separating from his late command. He immediately obtained an audience with the President and begged that his old brigade might be transferred from Heintzelman to his own division. Mr. Lincoln said he was willing, but before giving the order he must consult with the Secretary of War. So he accompanied General Richardson to Mr. Stanton's office, but the Secretary had objections to the transfer, which the President did not feel at liberty to overrule. The General then went back to his old brigade, made a feeling address to his old comrades-in-arms, then hastened to his new division at Manassas."

The evidence is that Richardson pulled out all the stops to bring his brigade along with him to his new assignment. President Lincoln took a personal interest in Richardson's request. A telegram in the president's handwriting, but signed by Secretary of War Edwin M. Stanton, was sent to McClellan.

> Major General McClellan:
> As General Richardson takes General Sumner's old Division,
> can he have an exchange of Brigades so as to take his old Brigade
> with him?
>
> > Edwin M. Stanton,
> > Secretary of War

It must have been frustrating to McClellan, in the midst of shifting units for his Peninsula campaign; to have the administration requesting brigade swaps within divisions merely for political reasons and personal favors. He replied immediately, advising no changes to his organization be granted.

Within the 2nd Michigan, rumors of the command changes were hard to explain. The men knew Richardson's habit of speaking his mind to his superiors, and it seemed pretty clear to them that Richardson's transfer was the fallout from a recent argument with General McDowell.[29]

After a quick briefing from Sumner, Richardson left for Manassas with the knowledge that Thomas J. Jackson was rumored to be moving up the Shenandoah Valley. In the midst of all these challenges, a telegraph was received from Fannie on March 18, announcing the birth of a baby boy, Israel Philip Augustus Richardson, in Alexandria, Virginia.

The day before Richardson's appointment to command Sumner's old division, orders had been issued to begin the advance of the Army of the Potomac on the Confederate works at Manassas. This was a screen, planned by McClellan to mask his movement by water to the Peninsula. As the skirmishers of Richardson's division, leading the advance of the army, approached the Confederate fortifications, they found the enemy had recently abandoned the positions.

Colonel Edward E. Cross, commanding the 5th New Hampshire, of General Howard's 1st Brigade, described the operation in his personal journal: "In the afternoon, rode to Generals Beauregard and Ewell's late headquarters and to Manassas Junction. Here were evidences of rapid and disorganized retreat of the rebel army. The depot was a mass of smoking ruins, as was the case with many other buildings. It rained all day; rode with General Richardson to examine the surrounding country."[30]

It was fortunate that Richardson took command of his division while it was actively conducting field operations against the enemy. Although the operation was basically unopposed, it sent a message to his soldiers that the new commander would be identified as a man of action. He used the opportunity to meet and quickly size up his brigade and regimental commanders as they led their men in the field. His reputation of being a no-nonsense fighter met with the approval from leaders like Colonel Cross, who himself would earn the same reputation.

Richardson pushed his division to the Rappahannock River. On March 28, 1862, General Howard's 1st Brigade was sent forward to make a reconnaissance. The mounted pickets of the enemy were soon discovered, and instantly a heated running battle lasting four hours ensued, as the rebels sought to delay Howard's brigade.

About four o'clock in the afternoon, skirmishers from the 5th New Hampshire came on a large body of rebels near the Rappahannock Station. They were loading railcars and preparing to leave. Colonel Cross ordered up Hazzard's battery and formed lines of battle. The skirmish line and sharpshooters had a brisk affair with the rear guard of Ewell's division, as they retreated across the large railroad bridge on the Rappahannock River. As both sides opened an artillery duel and the 5th New Hampshire moved closer, Ewell blew up the bridge and withdrew.

Back in Michigan, the *Pontiac Gazette* told the story in its March 29 edition: "There is a rumor in town last night to the effect that General Richardson's division had met the rebels near Warrenton, Virginia and routed them. Though not confirmed in this morning papers, I am incline to think that if there was an enemy within fighting distance of Warrenton, General Richardson has attacked him, for I know that when the General left Alexandria to join his command, he was fast spoiling for a fight. He wasn't able to see the good of eight months inaction of 200,000 men."

The first campaign of Richardson's division was a success. During the three weeks of advance into the deserted enemy works at Warrenton Junction and the marches toward the Rappahannock River, the officers and men behaved well under fire. However, the staff sections were learning how difficult it was to manage a campaign on the march, and the men suffered badly until experience replaced guesswork. The men were without tents, and some regiments had no cooking utensils. Rations were supplied in limited quantity and in poor condition; and units often went more than twenty-four hours without eating. Regiments marched night and day, wading through streams, and slept in open air so cold that their wet clothing froze to their bodies. After their battle at the railroad bridge on the Rappahannock River; the 5th New Hampshire spent the night in camp "cold, wet and some snow; had roll-call every hour; rations short and many men sick; cavalry went out scouting, but did not see any Confederates."[31] The painful lessons learned in this campaign would be of immense value to the division in later days.

During his first weeks in command, Richardson understood his role as division commander and how to act in front of his soldiers. He portrayed a figure that was expert in all tactics and field craft. He was a tough disciplinarian and held subordinates to the highest standards. Yet he was also a commander who could endear his men by not taking any special privileges that came with his position. He was tolerant of regulations when the lowest private's comfort was at stake. Individual examples of his conduct were passed on between his soldiers, who were anxious to understand the temperament of their new leader. A story making the camp rounds set the men at ease as to the character of the new division commander.

"While we were laying at Manassas, Andy Wilson, Bill Hardy and myself decided one day to go out on a foraging expedition. Traveling a considerable distance we came to a farmhouse where we caught some chickens. Just as we got them, we saw some rebels coming, and we started back to camp, as the rebels were gaining upon us. For safety we took refuge in a swamp, where we were obliged to remain all night. In the morning we managed to elude the rebels and got back to camp with our chickens.

"Shortly after we returned to camp, General Richardson sent for the three to come to his tent. When we arrived at the tent, General Richardson asked Hardy where he had obtained the chickens, and Hardy said, 'I got them from Jake.' Then I was called up with Wilson and asked where I had got the chickens I gave to Hardy, and I told the general that I had bought them from a farmer. The general saw the joke and laughingly said, 'If you boys will fight as well as you forage, I am not afraid of our going to Richmond.'"[32]

On April 1, 1862, Richardson's division was ordered back to Manassas Junction to reinforce the Army of the Potomac, which was moving up the Virginia Peninsula. Lieutenant Josiah M. Favill, 57th New York, of General French's 3rd Brigade, described the benefits of this first campaign in his diary: "The campaign just ended, although without results, (which is not the fault of the troops) has been most severe on both officers and men. It lasted just twenty-four days, during which time we were without a change of clothing of any kind, and without camp equipage, sleeping in the open air, except while in Manassas, and exposed to an unusual amount of rainy weather; notwithstanding the exposure, the command, upon the whole, is in better condition physically than when it started out. Our underwear had to be thrown away as unfit for further use, and the rest of our clothing hung up for ventilation. Arrayed in clean clothes and clean skin, we speedily resumed our former smart appearance."[33]

The enlisted soldiers had by now heard of the new division commander, and stories regarding his reputation where swirling around the regimental campgrounds. Private Jacob H. Cole, from the 57th New York, described the following incident.

"While we lay at Manassas, a number of the boys went to a brook to have a wash. When we were washing we were approached by a man who had every appearance of being an old teamster, or a wagon driver. We did not recognize him and he did not tell us who he was. He asked one of the boys to lend him his soap so that he could have a wash, when the one he had approached turned to him and said, "You go to hell and get your own soap, you old baggage master." Then he came to me and asked me to lend him a piece of soap that he might wash his hands. I gave it to him. When he had finished he handed it back to me, at the same time thanking me for its use. After we were through washing we made a fire, and while standing around it the old farmer, as we supposed, sat down, and began to tell us stories of his experience in the Mexican War. Some of the boys asked him what he was doing down in the army. He said he was working for the government, and that we would all know him better after awhile. We will have learned more about war and what it is to share what we have with our comrades, and before we get home again we will all be more willing to assist one another, and if our comrade desires to borrow anything from us we will be only too glad to let him have it.

"Shortly after this some contrabands, came into our lines. My brother, William Cole, Dad Haggerty and myself were detailed to take them to General Richardson's headquarters. When we arrived at General Richardson's head-quarters we saw many well-dressed officers. As none of us had ever seen General Richardson, we were at a loss to know which one was the general, so we inquired for General Richardson. The officers told us to go to another tent, as we approached we saw the old teamster, as we thought, sitting alone. So I said to him, 'Could you tell me where I can find General Richardson?' and he said, 'Well, I guess I can tell you where he is. Sometimes they call me General Richardson, and at other times they call me "Greasy Dick."' I said, 'I hope you will not try to fool me; you're the man I lent the soap to the other day.' He replied, 'I am not trying to fool you, my boy, but let it rest. You can bring the contrabands here and I will attend to them.' So we brought the contrabands up to the tent, after he looked them over he gave me an order to take them to General Sumner's headquarters.

"We went to General Sumner's headquarters, and after saluting the general, I said: 'General, I received orders to take these people to your headquarters. Here is the order, but whether it was given to me by General Richardson, I do not know. All I know is that whoever the man was he signed his name as General Richardson.' So General Sumner took the order, and as soon as he had read, he said to me, 'Yes, that is General Richardson; you will know more of him and will learn to like him the more you see him.'"[34]

6

———

Distinction

———

*"He has sent us three barrels of whis-
key, we ought to give him a cheer"*

As Richardson probed south from the deserted Confederate works at Manassas, the first of General McClellan's divisions embarked on ships at Alexandria for the journey to Fort Monroe and the Peninsula. During the next three weeks, nearly four hundred vessels shuttled back and forth along the two-hundred-mile route, transporting 121,500 men, 14,592 animals, 1,150 wagons, 44 batteries of artillery, and 74 ambulances. McClellan planned to move rapidly up the Peninsula and force the Confederates to face him in a decisive battle that would decide the fate of Richmond.

Confederate Major General John Magruder, with a force of ten thousand men at Yorktown, was able to bluff McClellan into thinking he was facing the main Confederate force under General Johnston. McClellan changed his battle plan and began siege operations against Yorktown. The delay caused in bringing heavy artillery and equipment to bear on the enemy works bought time for Confederate units to concentrate around Richmond.

With new recruited regiments arriving daily, the Army of the Potomac was reorganized for McClellan's new campaign. The II Corps, under Edwin Sumner, would be composed of two divisions, the 1st, led by Richardson, and the 2nd, led by John Sedgwick. Sedgwick was a West Pointer whose grandfather had been a general in Washington's army during the Revolution. A veteran of the Mexican and Indian wars, "Uncle John" was a proven leader who had the reputation of caring for his men.

One of the first duties of the new 1st Division commander was to meet and review the officers and men of the three brigades assigned to him. Richardson had inherited three strong brigadiers from Sumner. The 1st Brigade was led by Oliver Otis Howard, a former first lieutenant and mathematics professor at West Point. A deeply religious man, he was also an intelligent officer who could lead by example. General Howard was equally pleased with his new division commander. He described meeting Richardson as his brigade was boarding the transports for the Peninsula. "Here our division commander, General Richardson, joined his division. He was a large, fleshy man, generally careless in his attire and toilet; an officer who knew him said: 'He is inclined to lie abed in the morning.' I soon learned to prize him for his pluck and energy that came out in battle and on an active campaign. In the fight he was a capital leader, very cool and self-possessed."[1]

A true political soldier, Thomas Francis Meagher, commanded the 2nd Brigade, known as the Irish Brigade. Meagher was an Irish American lawyer and newspaper editor from New York City. In Ireland he had been convicted of treason and sentenced to banishment in Tasmania. From there he made his escape to New York, where he became a popular spokesman for the large Irish community living in the city. Meagher served as a captain in the 69th New York at Bull Run and became its colonel with the reorganization of the unit in the following months. As a reward for recruiting other Irish regiments, he was given a brigadier general's commission. As a professional politician and amateur soldier, he was the weakest brigade commander, but he was proving to be an effective officer who could follow orders and was loved by his men.

William Henry French was the oldest of the three and one of the few veterans that Richardson could rely on. He commanded the 3rd Brigade. French graduated from West Point in 1837 and had seen service in the Seminole and Mexican wars. French was a feisty old regular who had much in common with his new boss. His personal appearance was that of a heavy man whose face was so red, "one would suppose that someone had tied a cord tightly around his neck." He also had a nervous twitch that caused him to blink his eyes excessively. His men nicknamed him "Old Blinkey."

Captain Jack Gosson, from the Irish Brigade, was one of the first officers Richardson met upon taking command of his new division. The captain thought it was important for the 2nd Brigade to make a good impression on their new commander. Before Richardson's review, Captain Jack rode along the line and informed the boys that General Richardson was on his way to take command "and what do you think of the brave old fellow, but he has sent over three barrels of whiskey, to treat the boys of the brigade; we ought to give him a thundering cheer when he comes along."

As the general and his staff rode along the lines, Gosson took off his cap, which was the signal, and a wild cheer ran through the brigade that nearly startled the whole army. Richardson took the compliment paid to the three barrels of whiskey all to himself and became deeply attached to the Irish Brigade, making a special favorite of Captain Jack. The men were sorely disappointed when they got into camp and found no whiskey but, with true Irish humor, enjoyed the joke.

Upon their arrival on the Peninsula, Richardson's regiments spent the first several days detailed to fatigue duties. Until the entire division had landed and reorganized, the men suffered chronic shortages of tents and rations. For their second evening, Richardson scraped up a dinner of potatoes and pork and invited General Meagher to share it with him. To prepare this simple dinner, the general had to borrow the only pot in camp from General Howard. After dinner, when Meagher had taken his leave, Richardson sat near the campfire by himself, with a soldier's overcoat wrapped around him. A servant of General Howard's came up and slapped him on the back, exclaiming, "I say, old boy, General Howard wants the pot he lent old Dick Richardson to boil his taters in." Richardson jumped up, seized a burning brand from the fire and aimed it at the intruder's head, who hastily dodged the stick and fled.[2]

As the division was collecting itself at Ship Point, orders that further reduced officers' baggage were received. Regimental, field, and staff headquarters were not to have any wagons but must put up with packhorses. The men in the 57th New York noted that the new regulation made General French blink worse than ever.

By April 15 Richardson moved his division into the Union lines at Yorktown, joining the II Corps under Sumner. His division was again detailed to supply work parties building corduroy roads and bridges and digging trenches to support the siege operation. The frustration was exemplified by a letter sent home from Colonel Francis C. Barlow on April 23. "Richardson turns out to be a damned miserable Division Genl., never knowing or caring for his command. Other Divisions have had all manner of military instruction this winter & the Division Genls. visit their Brigades daily—Nothing of the kind has been done with us & I believe we are the most miserable Division, Brigade & Regiment in the Army."[3]

Richardson was preparing his division for the assault on Yorktown scheduled for May 4. The night before, a Confederate bombardment signaled the evacuation of Yorktown and the withdrawal to positions farther up the peninsula. The next morning, some of Richardson's regiments entered the Confederate works and helped to mark the locations of enemy "torpedoes," artillery shells that were left buried in the ground and attached with wires to the fuses. This first use of the land mine caused a great resentment by the Northern soldiers, who looked on them as a criminal and cowardly invention.

On May 5, 1862, General Longstreet met the Union advance guard at the old colonial capital of Williamsburg. As units from both sides entered the fight, McClellan sent dispatches to Richardson and Sedgwick to speed their divisions forward at all costs. The booming of cannon indicated that a heated battle was being waged in the direction of Williamsburg, and the intensity of the firing rose throughout the day. Richardson was able to get his division moving along the Williamsburg Road late in the afternoon.

A message from McClellan's headquarters that came during the march told Richardson of a Union victory and a change of orders. His division was to return to Yorktown and prepare for a movement by water that was meant to flank the rebel lines, cutting off the Confederate retreat. The next morning dawned bright and clear, and the sun rapidly dried the men and the roads.

By late afternoon Richardson had his division bivouacked closely together in a beautiful location on the wide bank of the York River. A beach of beautiful white sand formed the shoreline, and the water was shallow. As soon as every tent was pitched and the guard established, Richardson granted leave to everyone not on duty and permission to go swimming. Everyone went and enjoyed themselves immensely; this had been the first time the men were allowed to swim since their enlistment. It was a lively scene, nearly ten thousand men splashing and swimming in the river together.

Richardson was a plain, rather slovenly dresser. He often meandered through the campgrounds wearing the plain blue pants and overcoat of an enlisted soldier, without any insignia of rank. Those who did not know him personally often mistook him for a private soldier. "Some of our men were bathing, and one stepped up to a stranger in the water, and requested him to rub his back, which he agreed to do for a similar favor, after they went out, our volunteer was astonished to see the stranger put on a general's coat and walk away, saying nothing. It was General Richardson, our division commander."[4]

"While walking through his camp, he met a soldier from the Irish Brigade staggering to his tent. 'What unit do you belong to?,' Richardson asked the soldier. 'What do I belong to, is it? Aah now, that's a good one, I belong to the Irish Brigade; and what, if a body may ask, do you belong to?' inquired the soldier.

"'Oh, I belong to General Richardson's command.'

"'You do; I don't know the ould fellow, they say he is a rum one; Dirty Dick we call him.'

"'Indeed; how do ye like him?'

"'Oh, very well; I hear the boys say he is a brave ould fellow; all the boys like Dirty Dick well enough; but wouldn't you have a drink?'

"'I thought there was no whiskey to be got in camp now.'

"'Isn't there, indeed; come along, ould chap,' and Pat took the general familiarly by the arm.

"The two walked over to the quartermaster's hut, where a woman who accompanied the brigade and worked as an assistant in the supply section was doing a decent business selling whiskey for three dollars a bottle. 'I say, Mrs., let me have another bottle of that firewater of yours.' From the back of the store, she responded, 'You have enough, Paddy.'

"'No, I want a bottle; I have a frind wid me.'

"The lady was in the act of handing the bottle to Paddy, when she seemed taken with the appearance of his friend.

"'Paddy Doran, you villain, may my curse light on you,' and she aimed the bottle at Paddy's head; but he dodged it, and in the process, knocked against his friend, sending him tumbling.

"'Oh, General Richardson dear,' she exclaimed running to help him up, 'don't mind that—'

"Whatever she was going to add remained unsaid, for Paddy Doran, hearing who his friend was, made a dart for the door. It so happened that the lady was between him and the door, so Paddy, in his fright, knocked her over on his way out, completely rolling her over on top of the general. Much to the relief of Private Doran, other than shutting down the whiskey distribution point, no disciplinary action was taken."[5]

"We should get into a big fight within the next few days"

Due to the lack of shipping, Richardson's division was able to spend several days in their camps at Yorktown while the divisions of Sedgwick and Porter were transported ahead of him. From May 9 through May 13, various regiments were moved, as the steamships became available. By nightfall on May 13, Richardson had all of his brigades together again; the whole division encamped in a giant cornfield surrounded on three sides by a dense pine forest. That evening General Richardson held a reception for his officers at headquarters, he was optimistic, congratulating his men on being within such a short distance of the rebel capital and having them all united again.

Everyone that is, with the exception of Colonel Barlow; in another letter to his brother on May 15, he writes from "a damn little hut of an Indian rubber blanket, in a wood in a pouring rain." Describing his problems with a bad tooth, "which for two nights kept me awake nearly all night. The Doctor has made 4 more attempts to extract it (besides the 3 attempts made some days ago). He has, however, broken off everything which can be seen or appears above the gum besides cutting into the gum largely & he's now give it up in despair & I am to grin & bear it until I return to civilized parts."

The Army of the Potomac was steadily moving toward the rebel capital and a showdown with Johnston's army. One positive aspect of this deliberate advance was to work out kinks in the supply system and have the somewhat green soldiers build more confidence in their leaders and duties in enemy territory. Lessons in discipline were still being carried out on the march as illustrated by

Private N. D. Corser of Co. C, 5th New Hampshire. "General Sumner invited our squad to march with the Corps headquarters one day, with the hams and bacon he found speared on our bayonets, where we were forced to carry them all day. Whew! My shoulders ache when I think of it now."[6]

A soldier in Howard's brigade gave his approval of Richardson's command style during this time: "Sunday, the 18th, we again started and marched five miles and went into camp. By this time the men had become somewhat familiar with General I. B. Richardson, our division commander. He was a large, heavy, powerful man, a West Pointer, and commanded, I think, the 2d Michigan at Bull Run. He put on no military style; generally he was clothed in a private's blouse, which, if I remember correctly, did not have on shoulder straps. His speech, when not aroused, was slow and drawling; he did not care for salutes and the men began to regard him as one of them; he had their confidence and affection, and they willingly followed him. As our regiment was marching, he was along side of it, and a newspaper man with him, remarked: 'If you have got as good a division as you had a regiment at Bull Run, it will make some dead rebels before long.' The general smiled and drawled out, 'I guess they'll do.'"[7]

One day, Richardson was riding when he came across a soldier that was tied to a tree by his thumbs. He said to the man, "Well, well, who tied you there?" The man replied, "There was some general passing along here and he asked me what command I belonged to, and he winked and blinked with both eyes and drew his mouth in such a shape that I could not help but laugh at him, so he ordered me tied up by the thumbs." Richardson got down off his horse and cut the man loose, saying, "You can return to your command as I think I know who the general was, but the next time you see a man commence to wink and blink, be sure to get out of his way for he is getting ready to shoot."[8]

A growing resentment of McClellan's tactics was becoming evident. General Phil Kearny privately referred to McClellan as the "Virginia creeper." In Sumner's corps, opinion was divided. Although it was well known that General Sumner had the support of the Radicals, he steadfastly remained above politics throughout the war. In fact, when testifying to the Committee on the Conduct of the War on February 18, 1863, just before his death, he remarked, "There is too much croaking in the army," a reference made to the political backbiting among his officers. An example was Oliver O. Howard, probably the least political general within Richardson's division. He wrote home, "I don't know what Genl. McClellan is doing. I wish he would wake up to the impatience of the country a little and make us move with a little more rapidity. I do not believe he lacks genius for his profession, but I think he inclines too much to engineering."[9]

Of his two division commanders, Richardson was firmly in the radical camp, while Sedgwick was a Democrat and a supporter of McClellan. But Sedgwick was also concerned enough to write on May 17, 1862, that "McClellan is acting with much prudence and caution. . . . Six weeks will tell the story, in that time we will beat them badly or will be beaten ourselves." Within Richardson's 3rd Brigade, the diary of a company grade officer noted the following:

"Why we remain inactive all day long so near the enemy I can't find out, unless it is to give him a chance to entrench; it is clear we are not going to surprise anybody. . . . Jackson has been detached from Lee's army, and is making things lively near Washington. What a shame it is that McClellan does not pitch into them here promptly, and take advantage of Jackson's absence."[10]

By May 24 the result of his deliberate maneuvering had put the army's right flank just five miles from Richmond. Soldiers could clearly see the church spires and hear the church bells and clocks chime. This positioning caused the Army of the Potomac to be split into two parts divided by the Chickahominy River. The little river would not normally be a problem regarding the movements of the army, but in this rainy season, its low banks would overflow and the bottomlands would quickly flood, turning the immediate area into a swamp.

On May 26 Richardson assigned Howard's brigade the job of repairing the bridges in his sector and ordered Colonel Cross and his 5th New Hampshire to report for fatigue duty. His task was to build a bridge passable for artillery. This bridge, along with Bottom's Bridge farther south, repaired by Colonel Miller and his 81st Pennsylvania, provided the only links over the river. Cross surveyed the area and laid out the construction. The whole regiment soon began the work in cutting and dragging logs to corduroy the approaches and the bridge. When it was completed, it was one continuous corduroy road for twelve hundred feet.

As the men lay in camp waiting for orders, news of General Porter's attack on the Confederate position at Hanover Court House to the north was announced. Colonel Samuel K. Zook and Captain Josiah Favill, of the 57th New York, rode over to Richardson's headquarters to hear more of the battle. General Richardson talked freely with Zook and said he was sure that "we should get into a big fight within the next few days, beyond a doubt."[11] After this meeting, Favill recorded his first impressions of his division commander: "Richardson is a dark, slim man, with stooping shoulders, and a pronounced nasal voice. He looks like a farmer more than a soldier, and is utterly devoid of style; but has good common sense, a rare commodity apparently, and is very popular with his command. He is a West Pointer, notwithstanding his lack of style, and served in the old regular army. He made me think he smelt something disagreeable all the time, by the way he moved the muscles of his face. He is a typical Yankee."[12]

Richardson watched the bridge-building progress slowly and added details of 250 men from the 64th New York and 150 men from the 69th New York to help Cross with his work. On May 29 General Sumner inspected the completed structure and christened it Grapevine Bridge. Late in the afternoon of May 30, a terrific thunderstorm in what had been several weeks of rainy weather hit the area. Soldiers tried to rest in the face of this torrential rain, which flooded out their camps and turned every brook and river into a raging torrent far above its natural level. Richardson was relieved to hear from Cross and Howard the next morning that the Grapevine Bridge had survived the flood.

May 31 dawned with a beautiful morning, and while Howard's brigade had been busy on fatigue duty, the Irish Brigade and French's brigade had passed the last few days performing regimental drills. To celebrate the end of the week, General Meagher scheduled a day of entertainment consisting of horse races and athletic contests. The first prize for the horse race was a tiger skin donated by General Meagher. General Richardson and General French were on hand, acting as judges for the events.

As the activities were getting under way, faint sounds of artillery and musketry were heard coming from the far side of the Chickahominy. On his own initiative, Richardson took the precaution of issuing ammunition and having his brigades prepare to march immediately if Sumner received instructions to move to the relief of the heavily pressed IV Corps under Major General Erasmus Keyes.

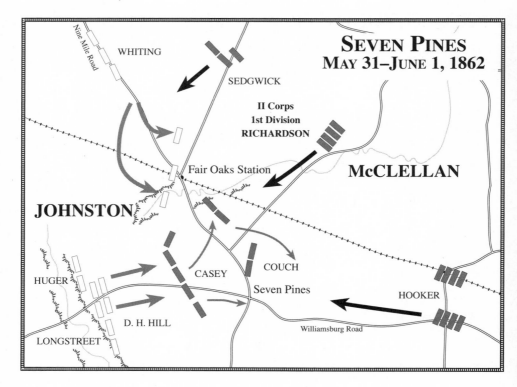

"I have refused handsomely two attacks upon my lines"

By afternoon, reports were filtering back that the Federals were losing ground and the camp of General Casey had been overrun. Both Richardson and Sedgwick waited impatiently with Sumner at the II Corps headquarters for an order from McClellan to move.

At 3 o'clock in the afternoon, an aide from McClellan's headquarters arrived, bringing the word that Sumner was waiting for. Instantly each division commander galloped toward his own command. As soon as Richardson came close enough to be heard, he shouted to Colonel Cross, "Right face, Forward!" and the division was started toward the lower bridge, a mile and a half downstream, while at the same time Sedgwick turned his division toward the Grapevine Bridge.

The Chickahominy had continued to swell through the day from the run-off of the torrential rain the night before. Now, both bridges were in danger of being swept away as the water level continued to rise. An engineer officer rushed up to General Sumner as his units were approaching the Grapevine Bridge:"General Sumner, you cannot cross this bridge!" Bull Sumner had been in the army forty-three years and had seen it all, and no upstart engineer officer was coming between him and his duty. "Can't cross this bridge!" he roared. "I can, sir; I will, sir!" But the bridge was breaking up before their eyes, the engineer said; it would be impossible to make it to the other side. "Impossible!" Sumner roared, "Sir, I tell you I can cross. I am ordered!" That closed the debate, and Sedgwick's men started across.[13]

As Sedgwick's division was camped next to Grapevine Bridge, Sumner sent Richardson to the lower bridge in hopes of speeding the crossing of the Chickahominy. The separate columns would unite on the road leading to Casey's camp, which Sumner and Richardson had personally reconnoitered previously. With French's brigade in the lead, and frequently breaking into a double-quick march, the brigade arrived at Bottom's Bridge only to find its foundations completely undermined. Richardson sent French across by wading, but soon found the going so slow that he turned his other brigades and artillery batteries back to cross at the Grapevine Bridge. These units reached Grapevine Bridge just as the last of Sedgwick's division was crossing. The water was now so high that the bridge seemed to be floating on the surface. As the men crossed, some of the logs that made up the floor would roll and dip, but somehow, the construction held together.

French had a rough time getting across in the strong current. The soldiers were forced to balance their weapons and ammunition over their heads as they slowly made their way across. Once the head of the column reached the far side, a continuous line was formed, making the passage easier for the remainder.

The men took pride that when Richardson crossed the river, he jumped off his horse and took it on foot through the water, saying to all who could hear that he was no better than the privates. Spurred on by news that Casey's division had been routed, it took the brigade two hours to get across and reform. The bad roads leading to the battlefield and the soldier's wet uniforms combined to make it a miserable march and kept the brigade from reaching the battlefield until just after dark.

Between eight and ten o'clock, as the brigades of Richardson's division reached the scene of the day's fighting, they were surrounded by mass confusion. It was an eerie sight as they groped their way to the front lines. Nothing could be heard but the groans of the wounded or the smothered words of commands as the division moved into its assigned position. Many lanterns glowed in front of them as surgeons and chaplains searched the ground for the dead and wounded. Richardson gave permission for his regimental surgeons to help in this task as his division was being placed into position.

The Confederate attack that began that morning was General Joseph E. Johnston's attempt to destroy the IV Corps before the rest of the Union Army could cross the Chickahominy River and reinforce them. By the end of the day he had pushed back the divisions of Couch and Casey but could not destroy them. Late in the afternoon, Johnston was struck in the shoulder by a bullet. In the next moment, he was blown off his horse by a shell burst that slammed a large fragment into his chest. Major General Gustavus W. Smith, the next senior officer, suddenly found himself in command of the Confederate army.

General Smith decided to continue the battle at the earliest possible moment in the morning, turning his army toward the railroad line on which Richardson was laying out his defensive positions. Longstreet was directed to push his successes of the previous day as far as practicable, attacking with his division at first light, joined by the divisions of Henry Whiting and Benjamin Huger once the battle was fully developed.

Richardson was hard at work placing his division along his assigned sector. Fortunately, Sumner placed his division along a prominent man-made feature, the Richmond and York River railroad line. This eased any coordination confusion as Richardson covered his sector with three defensive lines, each by brigade, with French's Brigade holding the front line, followed by Howard and finally Meagher. The 5th New Hampshire was detailed to picket in front of the defensive position, and the 63rd New York was sent back to help get as much artillery forward as possible before morning. The heavy rains of the day before and the fact that Richardson had trailed Sedgwick on the march had turned the roads into quagmires, which left the artillery pieces far behind, occasionally sinking up to their axles in the mud. Captain George W. Hazzard, Richardson's chief of artillery, worked all night to get his guns forward and, through the greatest of struggles, arrived at 4 o'clock in the morning.

The leaders and pickets stayed busy for the remainder of the evening, trying to get a better understanding of their position and what was out in front of them. When Cross marched his regiment to the front of French's brigade, he met General Richardson, who had already personally scouted the enemy positions in front. Richardson clearly delivered his intent; "Colonel Cross, I am giving you the advanced guard. Hold your position until you are whipped or relieved." Understanding the tension the men were feeling on the eve of their first battle, as the regiment filed past, Richardson said, "Fifth New Hampshire, remember your granite hills; you will stand firm like your own stone walls." He gave directions about the lines of battle to Cross, left a staff officer to show him the ground, and departed to look to his other lines before morning.[14]

Sergeant C. W. Gilman of the 5th New Hampshire recalled the confusion as his regiment moved into the unknown darkness: "We relieved the 7th Michigan in the dark, and came within a jiffy of having a terrific encounter with them by mistake. Just over the railroad were two Texas regiments and a Mississippi regiment, and all through the night the rebels were busy with lanterns around the station taking care of their wounded. Feeling thirsty in the night, I wandered a few yards to the front in search of water, and having found a puddle, shared it with others. At daybreak I went to refill my canteen, I discovered that the puddle was about ten feet wide, and in it lay two dead Confederates."[15] The lines between the two armies were very close. Reinforcing units sent to the front in the darkness didn't realize how near the enemy positions were to their own. Around two o'clock in the morning, in front of the 57th New York, the men were amazed to see a string of campfires suddenly become lighted within 100 yards of their positions. Colonel Zook sent a party of six volunteers to reconnoiter the area and bring in some prisoners. Within half an hour, the scouts returned with three enemy soldiers, wearing immense bowie knives, slouched hats, and butternut clothes. They belonged to a brigade of Texans that had recently arrived from Richmond and had no idea how close they were to Union lines.

Farther out in front on picket with the 5th New Hampshire, Colonel Cross also went forward to investigate the fires. As he crossed a road, he was halted by a click of a rifle lock and a sharp voice calling, "Who goes there?" Cross answered, "Wounded man of the 5th Texas. Who are you?" "Picket of the 2d Alabama," was the reply. "I wish to go to your fire," said Cross. "Pass around by the depot, and you will find the doctors," was the answer. Cross then drew off into the darkness and rejoined his regiment.[16]

Richardson expected to receive a Confederate attack at first light and ordered his units to stand to at three o'clock in preparation for the assault. As his men were getting into position, Colonel Cross finished a busy night with the picket force by personally capturing a rebel courier who rode up, inquiring where he could find General Pryor. "Yes," said Cross, "this way, sir," and with a drawn revolver made him his prisoner. The courier had a bag of dispatches indicating that a Confederate division commanded by General Benjamin Huger was approaching from Richmond. Richardson quickly forwarded the dispatches to General Sumner.

As dawn was breaking, General French made the startling discovery that a gap of half a mile existed on their left, covered only by pickets, between his brigade and the area assigned to the brigade commanded by General David E. Birney, of General Kearny's division.[17] Richardson had stressed this very point of making sure his flanks were locked in with adjoining units when he briefed French during the night. Sumner was notified, and he approved Richardson's solution of extending French's brigade to fill the gap, with the addition of the 81st Pennsylvania from Howard's brigade and moving the 5th New Hampshire back from picket duty to the rear of this new line.

Hardly had these improvised arrangements been completed when enemy activity was detected to the front. Longstreet, after receiving his orders from General Smith to renew the attack at dawn, went to General D. H. Hill, who had set up his headquarters in the bullet-riddled tent occupied the previous night by Silas Casey. Longstreet's orders to Hill were to "develop the situation." Hill sent forward three brigades: George E. Pickett's brigade from Longstreet's division and two from the division of General Huger, William Mahone's and Lewis A. Armistead's. The instructions given to these commanders were vague at best, with Mahone being told by Hill, "Take your brigade in there," pointing off to the north. Pickett later recalled, "I asked General Hill of the whereabouts of the enemy. He said they were some distance in advance—in fact, I had no definite idea where."[18] Further complicating the advance was the fact that each brigade was ordered forward separately so their attacks were not coordinated together, or their flanks connected.

The first sighting of enemy troops in Richardson's sector came not from these three brigades but from John B. Hood's brigade of Whiting's division. At first light, on the extreme right of Richardson's position, enemy pickets were spotted deploying and moving forward across a large open field. The head of a column of cavalry was also seen just inside the edge of the woods along with a group of mounted officers. Richardson turned to Captain Rufus D. Pettit, who had just finished bringing up his battery minutes earlier, and ordered him to fire. The shells and spherical case shot were accurate, and immediately Hood's men retreated to the safety of the forest. Whiting's orders were to make no advance until the attack by the right wing was well developed. For the rest of the day, Whiting would remain in position, because he felt these conditions had not been met. Richardson believed that "this no doubt was intended as the head of the real attack, to come down this open field, but no movement of the enemy in that direction after our firing had ceased could be seen during the remainder of the day."[19] In this short affair with Richardson's artillery, witnessed by the entire front, Hood lost thirteen men wounded.

At 6:30 A.M., soon after French had finished thinning his line to stretch across the area covered only by pickets, Mahone's brigade appeared in front of Richardson's sector, followed almost immediately by Armistead's brigade, farther on the left. They moved forward at a brisk walk and, because of the woodland, drew very close before being discovered. French's men strained to catch a glimpse of the rebels approaching their front. Voices could be heard forming men for an attack, along with the crackling of boughs. Suddenly, a rolling fire of musketry erupted along the line. Opposing regiments started to engage each other at a range of fifty yards.

An eyewitness account by a member of the 57th New York described how the men behaved under massed fire for the first time: "The noise was tremendous; and the bullets whistled about our ears like hailstones, tearing branches, twigs, and leaves from the trees. General Richardson came up just at this time, and immediately ordered the whole brigade out of the woods, so the batteries could sweep it clear with canister and shell; we filed out in quick time, forming behind the guns, which opened up at once, filling the woods with bursting shells and showers of iron hail. It was a dreadful thing for the wounded men, who were unable to move, but it seemed a necessary evil.

"Very soon the woods took fire, and many men who were not killed outright were burnt to death. The general did not seem to think of this, however, and was concerned only in clearing the woods of rebs; the artillery fire lasted about half an hour."[20]

The 81st Pennsylvania, commanded by Colonel James Miller, anchored the extreme left of Richardson's line. Through the trees on his left, Miller spotted a formation of troops moving toward him. He immediately put his men into a firing position and gave the command, "Ready!" An officer near him said: "No, no, colonel, they are our men!" Probably thinking that they belonged to Birney's brigade, Miller ordered his men to "Recover arms!," and shouting out to the strangers, "Who are you?" They responded, "Virginians," and instantly fired a volley from a distance of a hundred feet.

The volley by the 14th Virginia, of Armistead's brigade, killed Colonel Miller and staggered the whole 81st Pennsylvania. The regiment separated into two wings but managed to return a decent rate of fire. Meanwhile, the 3rd Alabama advanced out of the woods right where the 81st Pennsylvania and the 52nd New York had tied into each other's flanks. This was the weakest point in Richardson's line, and the best regiment in Mahone's brigade moved forward to take advantage of it. The 3rd Alabama, commanded by Colonel Tennent Lomax, concentrated its fire into the left flank of the separated wing, and slowly both portions of the 81st Pennsylvania fell back toward the railroad.

As the 3rd Alabama moved forward, it was able to put some fire into the rear of the 52nd New York, and a portion of this regiment had to fall back and turn its flank to deal with this threat. Looking back on this action, General Mahone remarked that "the impetus of the charge of the 3rd Alabama, a splendid regiment, I am satisfied must have severely shocked and disordered Richardson's line, and if there had been any intelligent understanding of the position of the enemy, and instructions as to what we were to do, it can be seen now how easy a destructive blow might have been given."[21]

The engagement lasted for just about an hour, with Richardson describing it as "the heaviest musketry firing I had ever experienced."[22] As soon as he received reports on the situation with his left flank, Richardson ordered General Howard to reinforce that sector with two of his regiments in the second line, the 61st and 64th New York. Howard personally led these regiments forward and soon met General French, who welcomed the help.

Conducting a passage of lines, Howard's men advanced, pressing the rebels back across the road into the camp that Casey's division had occupied the day before. Here the rebels made a stand, and soon the two opposing lines were firing at each other from a distance of thirty yards in some instances. On learning of the 81st Pennsylvania being split into two wings, Howard dispatched his aide, Lieutenant Nelson A. Miles, to collect the companies and make the best disposition he could. Although wounded in the foot, Miles rallied the unit and stopped the advance of the enemy to his front.

Howard had been slightly wounded in the arm just after he started forward with the 61st New York. At the outskirts of Casey's old camp, his horse was wounded, and as Howard was dismounting, he received his second wound to his right arm, which shattered the bone. Howard put Colonel Cross in charge of the brigade, as he made his way to the rear. "The regiments in his brigade are not sorry. Glad to get rid of him," Sergeant Charles Phelps of the 5th New Hampshire wrote afterward.[23] Richardson ordered two regiments of Meagher's Irish Brigade forward to the railroad tracks with Cross to relieve French's units, which were running low on ammunition.

Cross continued the advance until the Confederates started to make a stand. Sergeant C. W. Gilman recalled, "We had traversed about one-half across the swamp, when, in the midst of a swampy brook that ran through the center, we received the first intimation that we were close up to the rebels. It came in the shape of a blinding flash and a most terrific crash of musketry directly in our front, and less than thirty paces away. With one bound we cleared the slough and saw before us three rebel lines of battle—one lying, one kneeling and one standing—intent on hurrying us into eternity by the shortest cut. We dropped on one knee and gave them volley for volley."[24] At this close range the effects of each volley was awful. Judging that the rebel firing was slackening, Cross decided to order another advance, but while shouting the command, he was hit by a minié-ball in his left thigh. Falling down, he lifted himself up again, leaning against a tree. While in this position he was hit by a load of buckshot, which struck him in the left temple.[25] With this wound, he took himself out of the fight and turned command over to his executive officer, Lieutenant Colonel Samuel G. Langley. Langley surveyed the scene and chose to fall back and reform his unit.

A soldier from the 53rd Pennsylvania noted, "The 3rd Allabamer Regt suffered severely. I have seen a good many of them; they are mostly fine looking men and are said to have been the flower of the Southern army. Some of the rebel prisoners are very bitter. They say they would rather see the Southern States in hell than in the Union; others appear to be very thankful for the kind treatment which they receive."[26] Colonel Lomax, commander of the 3rd Alabama, was dead, and his crack regiment had lost 175 men, as confusion in the thick woods began to take a heavy toll on the brigades of Mahone and Armistead.

The fight broke down to individual regiments firing at point-blank range into each other. The 53rd Virginia, under Colonel H. B. Tomlin, arrived late to the fight. As it was rushed into the dense woods to reinforce the brigade, it stumbled into the left of Mahone's brigade and the two friendly units opened fire on one another. Simultaneously, Cross was moving aggressively to their front. Under these circumstances, Armistead's men fell back, leaving Pickett's brigade without any protection on their left flank. Pickett stopped, unwilling to advance any farther without support from Armistead, and went over to the defensive. Repeated requests for reinforcements to D. H. Hill went unanswered, resulting in the Confederate advance stopping completely.

Parts of the 69th and 88th New York advanced, continuing to put pressure on Mahone's brigade. Lieutenant Colonel Patrick Kelly, 88th New York, led his regiment into a "tangled underwood, encumbered with fallen and decayed trees, interspersed with heavy patches of mire and swamp."[27] The regiment became separated, coming through the woods, and was attacked by swarms of bees in the process. Kelly emerged from the woods with only two companies, but he occupied a good firing position, stopping any Confederate advance to his front.

After the 57th and 66th New York were resupplied with ammunition, they moved forward into the woods, accompanied by their brigade commander, General French, on the extreme right. After advancing about three quarters of a mile into the woods, unnoticed by the Confederates, they came on the unprotected flank of the 41st Virginia. A heavy flanking fire was opened, quickly followed with an advance, forcing Mahone's brigade to break off the advance and retreat.[28] During the engagement the 41st Virginia suffered 112 causalities. The Confederates retreated to the Williamsburg Road, from where they had started. It was now 11:30, and the Confederates had lost 1,132 men and failed to accomplish anything.

As the 5th New Hampshire moved out of the woods and reformed, the sound of musketry had diminished to only scattered firing. The regiment lost 186 men, about a fifth of its total. As the men stood in formation, old Fighting Dick Richardson was seen coming out of the woods with his coat off, looking very much exhausted. This marked the end of any organized fighting for the day, with both sides content to take up defensive positions where they were. McClellan arrived on the scene and witnessed Richardson's artillery pounding the wood line. Sumner asked him if he had any orders to give. McClellan, acting as if satisfied with the actions that had been taken, remained at the front only a few minutes, before riding back to his headquarters without directing or influencing the fight in any way.

In the afternoon, after the fight was over, General Sumner rode up to Richardson's headquarters to congratulate him on his success. Richardson refused to accept the compliment from Sumner, saying he had done nothing; his men had done everything. During the fight, it was true that Richardson, French, and Meagher were unable to coordinate the action and, at best, could only react by sending reinforcements in a general direction. But Richardson could be praised by his well-known trait of actively managing the battlefield, along with his determination in sending back regimental work details to drag his artillery through the impassable roads, allowing them to reach their position with only minutes to spare in the morning. He also personally set the example for his leaders and his men by moving up with the advanced pickets at night to get a firsthand look at the position he was expected to defend and spent the remainder of the night preparing for the Confederate advance expected at first light. Once the battle was in progress, he worked hard to ensure all his firepower was maximized by personally ordering Colonel Zook's 57th New York out of the woods in order for Hazzard's battery to shell the advancing rebels.

Following the battle, a letter from Richardson was published in the *New York Daily Tribune*, dated June 16, 1862. Although not as detailed as his official report, it gave a general account of the battle of June 1, albeit flavored with some personal criticisms: "the enemy brushed away the division of Casey like chaff. I don't care to know anything of this most disgraceful rout. Suffice it to say they not only ran then, but have not since been heard from, and have abandoned their whole camp, wagon teams and seven pieces of artillery." He then went on to stress the timely arrival of Sumner's corps to the fight, which in his opinion, saved the day; "half an hour more would have cut our column into two, which would have insured the total defeat of our army"; he praised the bravery and coolness of his men as they went into action and lamented their loss, concluding with, "For myself, I claim no other consideration than that of throwing in the reserve regiments at the right time and in the proper place."[29]

The following morning, on June 2, by McClellan's order, army engineers staked out a line of fortifications that stretched down the length of the frontline. Everyone that could be spared was employed digging ditches, felling logs, and building parapets. The picket line was sent out two hundred yards, and both sides engaged in active sniping at the other.

The governments of both armies proclaimed the Battle of Fair Oaks (Seven Pines) as a victory for themselves. Total casualties for both sides in the two days of fighting were 6,134 Confederates and 5,031 Federals. A soldier in Longstreet's division, who looked over the skimpy ranks of his unit after the battle, remarked that if this was being called a victory, "I never want to be in a battle that is not a victory."[30] On the Federal side, most of the soldiers wondered why the successes of the second day were not immediately followed up. A diary entry by a member of Richardson's division shows the frustration that most men were beginning to feel: "We cannot understand why we should entrench ourselves so powerfully, when we came here for the purpose of attacking. Our commander-in-chief is very timid, certainly, and the prospects for a further advance upon Richmond seem extremely slender."[31] Sergeant Seth G. Evans, 57th New York, wrote home, "I have seen my first real battle and hope it is the last. I never want to see men die in heaps as I did Sunday."[32]

The feeling that McClellan was not pursuing an aggressive campaign was becoming more pronounced at the senior leadership levels within the Army of the Potomac, as well. Privately, in both conversations and letters home, regimental, brigade, and division commanders were showing their displeasure with McClellan's strategy. Colonel Barlow wrote, "I don't know if we are to be the attacking, or the attacked party. We are frequently turned out by alarms but no enemy appears. . . . We are now encamped behind the works, which have been thrown up along the whole line. One would think we are acting on the defensive instead of the offensive."[33] General French stated, "Why we should have remained at Fair Oaks passes understanding. If we could not advance and attack advantageously, on the first of June, how could we do so subsequently, when the enemy had fortified himself?"[34]

None of Richardson's private correspondence openly criticized McClellan's actions after the fight at Fair Oaks directly; however, many instances within his own 1st Division can be documented. Since tact was never one of his strong points, it is likely his displeasure would be shared with his subordinate commanders, hinting at his own opinions.

On June 15, Senator Wade made a hastily arranged trip to visit the army on the Peninsula. He visited with the radical generals, including Richardson, and all agreed that McClellan was not advancing fast enough. In his diary, General

Heintzelman described the senator's comments: "McClellan was trying the patience of the country too far."[35]

"We did not come here to salute; we came to fight"

Replacements were always on the mind of General McClellan. On June 14 he inspected the line, escorted by General Richardson, and was told, "This is the 5th New Hampshire, in command of a Captain."[36] Since arriving on the Peninsula, McClellan had been demanding additional troops to match the Confederate force he believed he was facing. In the days following Fair Oaks, replacement units began to filter into the II Corps and Richardson's division. Three newly recruited regiments; the 29th Massachusetts, the 2d Delaware, and the 7th New York, were assigned to Richardson to ease his losses. He split them between each of his brigades, the 29th Massachusetts to the Irish brigade, the 2d Delaware to French's brigade, and the 7th New York to Howard's brigade.

An old veteran from Richardson's division noted the arrival of the new replacements: "The 7th New York was standing at rest, when the men saw a slouchy fellow, wearing an old blouse, pantaloons torn on one leg from the knee down, and an old black hat, walking in front of their line; they commenced laughing at him, but were checked when their colonel saluted him, and it appeared that he was General Richardson. I heard them cheer, and he answered, saying, 'You must not cheer me; it's the men who do the fighting you must cheer.' The 8th Illinois was in our vicinity, and one of their men met old 'Dick' on the railroad and accosted him with 'Halloa, old fellow, can you tell me where there's a sutler?' The dear old general answered that he could, and conducted him to where he could see one, pointed it out to him with pains, and left him without disclosing his rank."[37]

Private Cyrus H. Forwood, of the newly arrived 2nd Delaware, wrote down his first impressions of his new commander. "Gen. Richardson is a fine portly looking man, and a good soldier; plain, unassuming and always at his post when duty calls. The day we arrived, he reviewed us. He looked more like a teamster than a general. His pants were torn down the leg as if old Rough and Ready was reproduced in his person. He is greatly loved by all the men in his division, and showed great bravery in the recent battle. As he was passing our camp, one of our sentries saluted him by presenting arms. He returned the salute and said in a good humor, 'My man, that's played out; we did not come here to salute, we came to fight.'"[38]

Brigadier General John C. Caldwell was assigned to replace the wounded Oliver O. Howard as 1st Brigade commander. Caldwell had been a school principal in Maine before the war. In 1861 he was commissioned colonel of the 11th Maine. His promotion to brigadier general came on April 28, 1862. This would be his first test at commanding a brigade.

Because the opposing lines were so close together, picket duty was lively and their fire kept the main positions nervously alert. To guard against surprise, Richardson had his division "stand to," or aroused and called out, by 3:30 A.M. every night. The men took their places behind their works, guns in hand, and stood there until sunrise.

The drawback to the Federal position was that the troops were quartered on the edge of the great White Oak swamp, in the rear of their defensive positions. The drinking water was generally bad, and the unhealthy conditions began to take its toll on the men. The number of dysentery cases jumped dramatically. Richardson, from his experiences in the Mexican campaign, made sure hot coffee was served to the men as they stood on guard.

The new Confederate field commander, General Robert E. Lee, gathered his division commanders to receive opinions on how to counter the Union threat to the Confederate capital. Valid arguments were given to evacuate the city and choose a better location to make a stand. Lee stopped this talk with a statement that would stand as a summary of his command philosophy: "If we go to ciphering, we shall be whipped beforehand."[39] He sensed that the only possible way to save Richmond was to gain the initiative, no matter what the odds.

Lee sent instructions to General Thomas J. Jackson, operating in the Shenandoah Valley, to move quickly and strike McClellan on his right flank. To put an overwhelming force at the point of attack, Lee had to silently shift his forces in the entrenchments facing four Union corps, under Keyes, Heintzelman, Franklin, and Sumner, and move them to the right. The danger in this was that a Federal discovery of his weakened positions would leave the defense of Richmond wide open for attack.

The Confederate line facing Richardson was under the command of Major General John B. Magruder, the commander who had bought the rebels time by bluffing McClellan at Yorktown. He continued the same strategy by creating as much action as possible on the picket lines to keep the Federals in the dark.

The editor of Richardson's hometown newspaper, M. E. N. Howell, of the *Pontiac Gazette*, was visiting Michigan regiments along the front lines and became the guest of General Richardson during the night of June 20, 1862. His dispatch back to the newspaper was published the following week, and it gave a flavor of the nervousness that was occurring along the frontlines:

"General Richardson's division is in front and holds the earthworks for perhaps a half a mile extending from the railroad to the right, in front of which the heaviest rebel columns are posted. As we walked down to General Richardson's headquarters, we could hear extensive musket firing along the picket lines, and when near the General's tent in Fair Oaks Groves, the bodies of seven killed or wounded men were carried past us to the rear. The rebels had appeared in force, drove in his pickets, and threatened an attack. Matters looked decidedly interesting to us. However our pickets were reinforced, the rebels were driven back and comparative quiet was restored.

"General Richardson and his aide, Lieutenant Charles S. Draper, extended a cordial welcome. The General's headquarters are near the railroad station and only a few rods from our outer fortifications, and almost within rifle shot of the picket lines. Rebel shells are thrown all around him, in and beyond his camp. Soon after we had become comfortably seated in the General's tent, a prisoner was brought before him—a private from the 44th Georgia, just taken on picket. He had a villainous, hang-dog look and in reply to the General's questions, said he came down into the woods with his regiment, feeling stiff and rheumatic during the storm, his captain gave him permission to go back to camp. He started down the same track he came, he supposed, and before he found out his mistake, came upon our pickets who forthwith sent him in. He 'reckoned' there were about 100,000 Confederate troops in front of our lines. General Richardson sent him over to General Sumner's headquarters.

"About six o'clock the General invited us to take a stroll along his fortifications, and having an eye on a point in the woods in front, which he remarked were full of rebels, he ordered Harris' battery of Napoleon guns to throw a few shells in that direction, which was done most beautifully. As the first shell darted swiftly to its destination and exploded just above the treetops, three brigades of the division a rose in three long lines, in battle order, as if by magic, showing the perfect discipline in General Richardson's division. When the rebels undertake to surprise 'Fighting Dick' as they did Prentiss and Casey, they will find the surprise to be on the side of the least expected."

Richardson summarized his views of the situation with a hint of disappointment to his family in a letter dated June 23. "My division holds the right angle and I have thrown up entrenchments flanked by two strong redoubts, and the whole protected by an abatis a quarter of a mile wide. I have built an infantry parapet, with a ditch in front; one of my brigades is continually at the parapet; and the artillery men in the redoubts at their guns, and I have 13 companies on picket in front of the abatis. My second line, of one brigade is 200 yards in rear of the first, and my other brigade, (the best; Gen. French's) is 600 yards in rear of the second. I have refused handsomely two attacks upon my lines since throwing up the entrenchments.

"Now, we must wait for reinforcements, it will be now more than six weeks before we get into Richmond, when if we had had 30,000 more troops we might have ended the war."[40]

Convinced that a tactical pause had been forced upon them, Richardson felt comfortable in allowing a visit by his wife to his headquarters camp at Fair Oaks. It appeared to be Fannie's idea, and her doting husband could not refuse. "Dear Marcella, You will be surprised to hear from me here, but I think the move was the best one I could make. I was quite sick and everyone seemed to think the journey would do me more good than anything else, so I obtained from your brother permission to come, and have been better ever since I commenced the journey."[41] The visit was destined to be a short one however, and she was sent back to Washington as signs that the campaign was about to intensify quickly grew.

The picket line in front of Richardson's division was detailed to the 57th New York, under Colonel Zook, on June 27. Fighting could be heard coming from Gaines' Mill, in front of Porter's corps. By early afternoon, the attentive Zook detected a change in activity on the picket line and decided to investigate personally. He crept out past the friendly pickets and found most of the enemy's force had disappeared. He witnessed a large number of slaves parading, beating drums, making constant noise. Richardson sent Zook to General Sumner to report that all available Confederate troops must be involved with the attack on Porter and the road to Richmond was open.

General Sumner saw the importance of the situation but refused to act on his own authority. At three o'clock Richardson received orders not to advance but to send two-thirds of his division to support Porter's corps, under pressure from Lee's attack. The two brigades under the command of General French moved to the sound of the fighting, while Caldwell's brigade, under the direct command of Richardson, stretched out along the division front to cover any advance from Magruder.

With the coming of dusk, the Confederates stopped their attack and the battle was over. McClellan appeared at Porter's headquarters and announced his decision to give up the ground on the north side of the Chickahominy River and transfer his base of operations from White House Landing on the Pamunkey River to Harrison's Landing on the James River. At midnight, Porter directed French to hold the defensive position as rearguard while the V Corps crossed the Chickahominy River on their march to the new base on the James River.

French managed to pull his brigades out of their position and on the road back to Fair Oaks by four A.M., following the V Corps to the south. By the break of dawn, everyone was safe on the south side of the Chickahominy and the 88th New York of the Irish Brigade destroyed the bridge behind. When the two brigades returned to Richardson's command, they marched directly to their camps and struck their tents. Only after the camp was broken down were the men allowed to rest while awaiting the Confederate pursuit, which all knew was sure to come.

McClellan's decision to change the base of operations for his army from the York River to the James River took Lee by surprise. He expected McClellan to move back to protect his base at White House or retreat down the Peninsula the way he had come. As a result, Lee's forces were not in position to attack the retreating Federals in their vulnerable condition. It took twenty-four hours before Lee understood the situation and made adjustments.

As Porter's men and the army trains moved south across the rear of Richardson's defensive position, the Confederate forces under Magruder and Huger were unaware of what was going on. Richardson understood the importance of aggressiveness on the picket line to mask the movement in his rear. In his report General Lee stated, "Late in the afternoon of the 28th, the enemy's works were reported to be fully manned. The strength of these fortifications prevented Generals Huger and Magruder from discovering what was passing in their front."[42] It was not until late that night, when Richardson finally pulled his men out of the works, that Lee discovered McClellan's movement.

Richardson was trusted with the rearguard command, and he prepared for this movement well. All sick personnel were sent to the hospital at Savage's Station, and the men were put to work throwing up rifle pits at right angles to the main defensive line. Under cover of a slight morning fog, the II Corps pulled out, leaving the 69th New York on the picket line as long as possible to help screen the movement from Magruder's men.

The commissary depot in the rear of the division was put to the torch, destroying millions of dollars of supplies. Tons of ammunition, burning and exploding; barrels of beef, pork, molasses; boxes of hard tack, soap, and candles in great piles were all being destroyed as some of Richardson's men slipped out of the ranks and loaded themselves with whatever they wanted.

The secrecy of Richardson's withdrawal from the Federal fortifications is evident from the messages sent from Magruder to Lee on June 29. Magruder still believed that Richardson was at full strength opposite him, though, actually, only the thinnest rearguard of the 69th New York remained. At dawn word came from the pickets that the Federals lines were abandoned. Magruder dispatched the news to General Lee, adding that he was preparing to attack. The note was returned by Lee, offering his thanks and a sarcastic request that when the Federal works were attacked, he hoped Magruder would not injure the two engineers from Longstreet's division who had already crossed the river and entered the empty fortifications.[43]

The first stopping point on the march was a large clearing two miles down the Williamsburg stage road, next to the railroad line called Allen's Farm. There was a peach orchard planted on the farm, and the following engagement became known as either Allen's Farm or the Peach Orchard. As the division was regrouping, men from the 2d Delaware rested near the edge of the woods. A soldier recalled the following incident years later:

"The rebels soon learned that we were falling back, and were soon heard from. As we lay near the edge of the woods, exposed to a very hot sun, some of us made a shelter of our blankets held up by our muskets. A rebel battery opened upon us from the opposite woods. A round shot came ricocheting across the field, seeming to make bounces several hundred yards at a time, struck our blanket shelter under which several of us lay, and swept it away from our heads.

"Just then General Richardson came riding up and asked a group of officers lying on the ground, who belonged to the regiment next to us in line, 'Where is the commanding officer of this regiment?' One man, who I suppose was the colonel (although he had his coat off at the time), came forward saying in an off-hand way (and without saluting), 'What do you want?' 'Consider yourself under arrest,' came the answer, short, sharp, and decisive. That was a lesson that officer probably never forgot. My recollection of General Richardson was that when on the front he had more the appearance of a farmer than a major general; but he was one of the fighting generals and more is the pity he lost his life at Antietam a few months later."[44]

General Sumner ordered Richardson to form a line of battle facing Richmond, with his left flank connecting to the right flank of Sedgwick's division, both units on the right side of the railroad. French's brigade formed the first line, and Caldwell's brigade formed the second. With the establishment of this new line, Richardson went to the 5th New Hampshire and sent the regiment back to the original defensive line to act as pickets. Slowly but steadily Magruder's men moved forward, finally making contact with Sumner's corps about nine o'clock that morning.

The pickets of the 5th New Hampshire fell back slowly and moved through Richardson's first defensive line, taking their place in the second line with the rest of Caldwell's brigade. The rebel brigades of D. R. Jones and Joseph B. Kershaw could plainly be seen forming their columns of attack and moving toward Sedgwick's front. Very shortly two enemy batteries opened up on Richardson's Third Brigade. Richardson's two artillery batteries under Captain Hazzard and Lieutenant Petitt answered the enemy batteries. In two hours they combined to fire three hundred shells at the enemy batteries and infantry formations, forcing the batteries to retire. Magruder's assault was tentative and easily stopped.

Sumner ordered his corps to stop the retreat on his own initiative. Each Union corps seemed to act independently. As the rest of the army began its withdrawal, generals Franklin and Baldy Smith arrived at Savage's Station, the large Federal supply base and hospital complex used to evacuate Federal wounded down the railroad to awaiting ships. They found it guarded by only the 15th Massachusetts and Meagher's Irish Brigade, which had been detailed by McClellan to destroy supplies.

An alarmed Franklin rode to Sumner with a plea for him to concentrate his corps at Savage's Station. This defensive position would stop the danger of individual units being cut off from the Confederate pursuit. At noon, after

Richardson had beaten off the half-hearted assaults from Magruder, Sumner personally gave the command to fall back, and the retreat continued. Richardson's division arrived at the large logistic base at four o'clock that afternoon.

With Sedgwick's division arriving first, Sumner posted him in the middle of the clearing, protecting the likeliest enemy avenue of approach. As Richardson arrived, he was stationed to the rear of Sedgwick, next to the hospital, in reserve. His artillery batteries, under Pettit and Hazzard, were placed in support of Sedgwick. When Franklin's corps arrived, Smith's division was positioned to the left of Sedgwick, extending into the tree line. Further to the front and left, in the woods, was a position reserved for Heintzelman's III Corps.

The Federal commanders knew the importance of holding their positions here to allow the artillery units and field trains, which included a five-thousand-head cattle herd, to work their way through the White Oak swamp. As the men settled in and continued to improve their defensive line, generals Franklin and Sedgwick went first to visit the hospital, then rode over to coordinate plans with Heintzelman. As the two generals rode over the open field, they saw a group of men come out of the woods on the north of the railroad. Franklin thought they were Federal soldiers, but Sedgwick looked at them more closely, stopped, and exclaimed, "Why, those men are rebels!"

Heintzelman had made his own decision that there were enough troops already at Savage's Station to defend the area and ordered his corps to continue the retreat. He did not coordinate with his fellow corps commanders and left their flank uncovered as he continued through White Oak swamp. It was five o'clock in the afternoon when the Confederates opened with artillery fire from a two-gun battery and were soon accompanied by a huge thirty-two-pound rifled gun mounted on a railcar that had come down the Richmond & York rail line from Richmond. This piece of naval ordnance was nicknamed the "Land Merrimac" and was protected from cannon shot by a sloping iron-covered roof in front, through which portholes had been pierced. It easily outranged any artillery piece on the field that day.

Sedgwick's division, in the center of the Federal line, became the target of a furious assault from regiments in Kershaw's and Barksdale's brigades. His center began to give way to the Confederates, and a frantic appeal was sent to Sumner for reinforcements.

Sumner grabbed the first two regiments that he came upon, the 88th New York of the Irish Brigade and the 5th New Hampshire, both from Richardson's division, and threw them into the gap. The defensive line stiffened with these reinforcements, and the danger subsided. The 88th New York played a considerable part in the battle by charging a Confederate battery deployed along the Williamsburg road that was supporting the enemy assault. The charge of

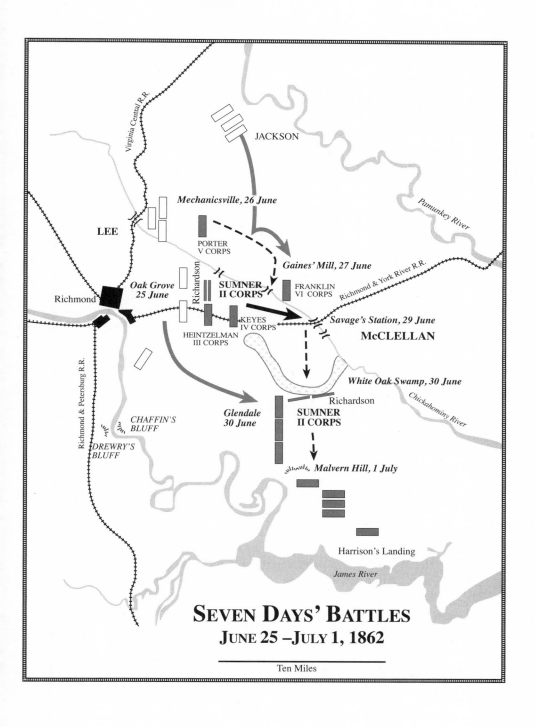

JACKSON

Mechanicsville, 26 June

LEE

PORTER
V CORPS

Gaines' Mill, 27 June

Richardson

*Oak Grove
25 June*

Richmond

SUMNER
II CORPS

FRANKLIN
VI CORPS

Richmond & York River R.R.

KEYES
IV CORPS

Savage's Station, 29 June

HEINTZELMAN
III CORPS

McCLELLAN

White Oak Swamp, 30 June

Richardson

Chickahominy River

*Glendale
30 June*

SUMNER
II CORPS

CHAFFIN'S
BLUFF

DREWRY'S
BLUFF

Richmond & Petersburg R.R.

Virginia Central R.R.

Pamunkey River

Malvern Hill, 1 July

Harrison's Landing

James River

SEVEN DAYS' BATTLES
JUNE 25 –JULY 1, 1862

Ten Miles

the Irishmen forced the battery to limber up and leave the field. With that, the infantry attack stalled and the Confederates finally retired.

Richardson's division was the army reserve at Savage's Station, and Sumner was grabbing his regiments piecemeal to plug danger spots all along the line. Richardson posted himself with his two artillery batteries, engaging the infantry attack and directing counter-battery fire. After expending nearly four hundred rounds, the batteries stopped their firing for the day and rested. The journal of a sergeant in the 57th New York described Richardson's actions working with these batteries:

"The rebels brought out a gun mounted on a railroad car that was known as the Land Merrimac. One of our batteries was firing at it without doing any damage. General Richardson, noticing this, got off his horse. After the gun was loaded, he sighted the piece and fired it himself, with the result that the car was knocked off the track and the Merrimac was put out of business for the time being.[45]

The lateness of the day and a thunderstorm brought an end to the Confederate attack. Magruder committed only two and a half brigades out of the six he had present, in part because he was still afraid of a Federal attack on his own force. Magruder would spend the rest of the evening searching for good defensive positions for his regiments instead of probing the Federal lines until his expected support from Jackson arrived.

"Whatever he did was done with all his might"

Colonel Daniel Hand, II Corps surgeon, was working in the hospital next to General Sumner's headquarters when he noticed generals Sedgwick, Richardson, Meagher, and Burns collected together, discussing the current situation. From what he could make out, the generals were all in agreement that they should hold their present positions.[46] Half an hour after the fight was ended, General Franklin suggested to Sumner that if he had no objection, he would carry out McClellan's orders and cross the White Oak swamp. Sumner's answer was, "No, General, you shall not go, nor will I go; I never leave a victorious field. Why! If I had twenty thousand more men, I would crush this rebellion." Franklin told Sumner that McClellan's orders left them no choice, producing a dispatch directing the army to move across the swamp during the night. Reading the message, Sumner exclaimed, "General McClellan did not know the circumstances when he wrote that note. He did not know that we would fight a battle and gain a victory."[47]

McClellan's inspector general, Colonel Delos B. Sacket, arrived with written orders for Sumner to take up the retreat. Sacket had his own orders as well: "If he fails to comply with the order you will place him in close arrest and give the necessary orders to Generals Richardson and Sedgwick and tell them that the orders must be complied with at once."[48] Faced with this ultimatum, Sumner backed down. To his division commanders, he sent new instructions; Sedgwick would pull out first, leaving Richardson to once again act as rearguard for the Army of the Potomac and responsible for burning the White Oak bridge.

On his own initiative, Sumner had twice tried to stop the Federal retreat; at Allen's Farm and Savage's Station. Whether the outspoken Richardson influenced his mind is not clear. But from his perspective, the II Corps had saved the day for the Federals at Fair Oaks, a month ago. Now following a doubtful policy, it had stopped the pursuing rebels with ease on two occasions at the Peach Orchard and Savage's Station. Ordered again to continue the retreat, thus abandoning tons of supplies, not to mention allowing twenty-five hundred wounded soldiers along with their medical staff to fall into the hands of the enemy, simply was intolerable to the old soldier.

McClellan thought that "Old Bull" Sumner was a dangerous man to have as second in command of the army. He remarked in a letter to his wife that if ever he should become disabled, "Sumner would ruin things in about two days."[49] Writing privately, he noted in many respects Edwin Sumner was a model soldier, "but unfortunately nature had limited his capacity to a very narrow extent."[50]

In hindsight, making a stand at Allen's Farm caused the timid pursuit by Magruder at Savage's Station. With the Confederate columns under Jackson, Longstreet, and Huger moving to intercept McClellan's march, they could not support each other effectively. Magruder, with eleven thousand men, mistook Sumner's stand at Allen's Farm as a fortified position. His messages to Lee for reinforcements forced the diversion of two brigades from Huger's column and added more time to the pursuit. Magruder, who had been so masterful at conducting feints and holding McClellan at bay at Yorktown with a skeleton force, now became a victim of his own strategy.

Richardson must have become filled with disgust at the reluctant order he received from his corps commander. The two men thought alike, and Richardson's opinions might have encouraged Sumner to question the reasoning behind McClellan's plans. The thought of giving up twenty-five hundred wounded men from the hospital at Savage's Station had to be hard to swallow. However, Edwin Sumner was the ultimate loyal soldier. Commissioned in 1819, he had spent fourteen years as a lieutenant and thirteen years as a captain, toiling for what equated to a full career of twenty-seven years as a company grade officer until the war with Mexico rescued him from obscurity. He was admired as a brave leader who led from the front, but his weakness was his regimented thinking.

This systematic thought process may have worked for him during his first twenty-seven years of commissioned service; in fact, this bullheadedness saved General Keyes at Fair Oaks, when Sumner refused to take no for an answer in crossing the flooded Chickahominy River, going to his support.

Sumner's greatest strength was his power to inspire his subordinates by leading from the front. Serving on the frontier with the 1st Cavalry, he watched as Lieutenant Lunsford Lomax was in charge of a work detail engaged in stretching a rope across the Platte River to connect a ferry cable. Lomax gave the order, "Go in, men." Sumner overheard him and called out, "Never say *go* in, Mr. Lomax, but *come* in." Lomax understood the point and went into the water first.[51]

"Make haste, men! Make haste! Every minute is an hour!"

The II Corps was the last to leave, and Richardson's division again became the rearguard of the army. The beginnings of fatigue and straggling men were becoming a noticeable problem. Richardson's men, along with the rest of the army, had been up close to forty-eight hours now, withdrawing, fighting two engagements, and withdrawing again. Staff coordination began to break down with the constant confusion of fighting, pursuing Confederates, managing the army's withdrawal, and destroying supplies.

The wounded men at Savage's Station soon realized they were being abandoned. Before long an army chaplain saw a "long, scattered line of the patients staggering away, some carrying their guns, and supporting a companion on an arm. . . . They retired one by one across the fields, and were lost in the forest. . . ." Major Thomas Hyde, wrote home: "Their cries are yet ringing in my ears."[52]

As the division trailed the rest of the army, the march became a confusing series of starts and stops. The night grew pitch dark, and on the bad road even the breakdown of a single wagon would stop the entire column until it was cleared off the road. An exhausted Lieutenant Thomas Livermore of the 5th New Hampshire had a dim recollection of hearing General Meagher's voice to his front at one of these road jams. At two o'clock in the morning, the 5th New Hampshire caught up with a large body of troops at a complete stop. In the darkness, Livermore heard the voice of General Richardson swearing like a trooper. Arriving at White Oak bridge, thousands of soldiers were jammed on and around the structure, with no one moving. Old Dick, with his fusillade of oaths and curses, was clearing them out so effectively that by daylight all organized bodies of men in the column were across.

Officially, in his report, Richardson described the incident in softer terms. "My march commenced about one o'clock on the 30th of June, and marched until nearly daybreak. Coming up to the bridge I found a mass of stragglers from other parts of the army wedged in so as to be unable to move. I impressed them with the necessity of crossing as rapidly as possible or the enemy would be upon us and the rear of the army cut off. By the greatest exertions of myself and my staff I succeeded in getting this mass over by sunrise, and the bridge was broken up and burned by about 10 o'clock A.M."

The 5th New Hampshire was detailed to destroy the bridge to prevent any pursuit by the Confederates. Lieutenant Livermore remembered:

"We hurried down the hill to tear up the bridge, but when we got there a stream of fugitives hurrying across forbade our touching it, and we waited. Here came a regiment of stragglers in disorderly haste, some hobbling with sore feet, some too lazy to move very fast in other circumstances, and some loaded with too many traps. Among the last was a gray-haired old sergeant of the Irish Brigade, with many years of service indicated by the chevrons on his arm, and the cause of his straggling made evident by a woman and child—his wife and child, probably—whom he guarded. It seemed a cruel time for them. Sutlers and bummers, drummers and cooks, came filing along in a stream which grew thinner and thinner, and then the astonishing spectacle of a noble battery greeted our eyes, unattended by infantry, and drivers urging their horses toward the bridge; they had been left by mistake."[53]

The battery was commanded by Captain George W. Hazzard, of Richardson's division. After the fight at Savage's Station was over, Hazzard ordered his guns unhitched, believing there would be no further movement during the night, and the men and animals went to sleep, as usual whenever they had the opportunity. In the confusion of the night, Richardson pulled his division out of position and no notice was sent to Captain Hazzard.

As dawn broke, Hazzard awoke to the sound of reveille played by drums and trumpets; his first thought was that the sounds were coming from areas that he knew were not occupied by Federal units the night before. As he scanned his immediate area, he found everything was quiet. He quickly understood that his battery had been left behind in a retreat, and the enemy might be upon him at any second. He ordered the battery to be quietly hitched up, sending the caissons off in advance. Hazzard brought up the rear with a pair of guns loaded with canister in the event the Confederates discovered him.

The battery moved off in good order, the horses going at a walk for the first mile; then the command was given for the head of the column to move at a trot. The battery moved along in fine style, hurrying along stragglers with the information that no other friendly units were behind them. They came on the bridge just as the 5th New Hampshire was beginning to destroy it. The battery crossed and finally halted on the top of a hill as the 5th New Hampshire plunged into the water and dismantled the bridge.

As the Army of the Potomac continued on its journey to the James River, Richardson's and Baldy Smith's divisions remained the army rearguard. General Franklin was left in overall command. The area they occupied was a good defensive position that dominated the ground where the swamp road exited into open country. As the morning grew hotter, most of the men in both divisions were trying to grab the first few hours of sleep they had in the past two days. The 61st New York, under Colonel Barlow, acted as pickets. Most of the army's field trains had departed, but there were still over one hundred wagons waiting orders to move. The only signs of enemy activity were several squads of rebel cavalry, searching for stragglers and reconnoitering the Federal positions.

General Jackson's corps had passed through Magruder's forces and taken over the pursuit. Taking possession of the vast hospital and supplies at Savage's Station had delayed the Confederates, and several regiments had to be detailed to guard and escort all of the prisoners taken there.

By noon Jackson's men had advanced up to the destroyed bridge on White Oak Creek. Sergeant Russell Frost of the 3rd New York battery remembered, "Some of our men had small spyglasses, and we could see rebel cavalry in the dense woods on the opposite side of the swamp, it turned out to be rebel artillery getting into position to give us a right royal surprise."[54] Jackson was able to mass over thirty guns to shell the Federal camp without being seen. As the artillery started firing on the Federals, Jackson, D. H. Hill, and Colonel Munford crossed the creek to reconnoiter.

Lieutenant Livermore awoke from a deep sleep to the "thunders of artillery, the shriek of shells, and the horrid humming of their fragments."[55] Captain Favill was also sleeping. "Suddenly I jumped to my feet, awakened by what seemed to be a most terrific earthquake shock."[56]

Confusion was everywhere as regiments struggled to fall in, batteries were unlimbered to provide counter-battery fire, and teamsters from the supply trains still parked in the rear scrambled to hitch up their teams and pull out. At the sound of the shelling, mules stampeded and many teamsters panicked, leaping on the runaway animals and galloping to the rear at full speed, knocking over anything in their way. Richardson appeared in the middle of this disarray, quickly took charge, and soon had the wagons moving out in good order.

Lieutenant Rufus King, 4th U.S. Artillery, gives the credit to Richardson for selecting an excellent position to return the Confederate fire: "General Richardson rode forward and ordered the battery immediately into position on the left of Nelson's house. General Richardson directed four guns to be placed in a small gorge to the left and front of the first position, covering the bridge across the White Oak Swamp. . . . The enemy was completely covered by a thick wood, and the only indication we had of their position was from the smoke of their guns.

"Their fire was very rapid and precise, most of their shells striking within twenty feet of us and a perfect shower of grape passing through the battery. Were it not for the splendid position we had, few of us would have left the battlefield that day without a serious wound. The brow of the hill forming a natural breastwork, our guns, just pointing over the top of the hill, were in a manner sheltered, and most of the solid shot fired by the enemy struck the brow of the hill and ricocheted harmlessly over our heads."

A shell burst in the middle of the battery, and a fragment struck Captain Hazzard in the leg, mortally wounding him. General Meagher stood by one of the pieces, running it forward, exposed to the hottest of the fire. If Jackson, who had a two-to-one superiority in men and artillery, could force a crossing at this point, McClellan's change of base maneuver might become a disaster. The army, stretched out for miles, would have to defend itself from Jackson in his rear, and from Lee, who was even now attacking his flank at Glendale.

Generals Jackson and D. H. Hill witnessed the initial confusion at the onset of the artillery attack. Their first impression was that the Federals could be easily brushed aside by quickly pushing the Confederate infantry regiments across as they arrived on the scene. Suddenly the rebel generals were taken under accurate fire from Hazzard's battery, which Richardson had just placed on the crest of the hill. D. H. Hill described the encounter: "Munford crossed his regiment over the ford, and Jackson and myself went with him to see what had become of the enemy. We soon found out. The battery had taken up a position behind a point of woods, where it was perfectly sheltered from our guns, but could play upon the broken bridge and ford, and upon every part of the uncultivated field. It opened with grape and canister upon us, and we retired rapidly. Fast riding in the wrong direction is not military, but it is sometimes healthy."[57]

Jackson's quick glance at the Federal positions and their rapid reaction to his probe convinced him that forcing a crossing in front of Richardson's position would be too costly. He returned to his headquarters and fell asleep under a tree. Convinced that Richardson's strong position with infantry and artillery limited his options, Jackson failed to take any action to move through or around the Federal position at White Oak swamp.

After the initial bombardment had concluded and no infantry attack materialized, General Sumner ordered reinforcements from Richardson's division to move to his aid. Richardson detached Caldwell's 1st Brigade and Meagher's Irish Brigade, along with his artillery, and remained at White Oak swamp with only French's 3rd Brigade. Both of these brigades saw severe action late in the afternoon and evening and were instrumental in plugging weak spots in the defensive line just before the Confederate attacks at Glendale. After a costly fight, the Federals remained in control of the road system and the retreat continued on to Malvern Hill.

Franklin was ordered to hold the White Oak swamp crossing until nightfall. French's brigade and two pieces from Pettit's battery, with Richardson in overall command, covered the crossing. Franklin's withdrawal was hidden from Jackson's men by the covering fire of the two guns that targeted the broken-down bridge with fused shells that burst directly over it, effectively stopping any repair efforts. At 11:30 P.M., with the rest of Franklin's corps safety away, Richardson ordered French's brigade, minus one infantry company and the two field pieces to form a column and move away quietly.

A half hour later, at midnight, the two field pieces defending the crossing fired their last shots simultaneously, quickly limbered up, and moved away toward the main column at a trot. The Confederates were now free to repair the White Oak bridge and pursue as fast as they chose. The only safety for Richardson's men was the prepared positions on Malvern Hill and the protection of the naval gunships on the James River, which they reached just after dawn.

For the first time in a week, the Army of the Potomac was able to concentrate again at Malvern Hill. Richardson's division was united on July 1, after another all-night march. The division quartermaster train lost twenty-two teams after starting the withdrawal with fifty-one, giving an idea of the damage caused to the army by five days of fighting retreats. Sumner's corps, the last to arrive and concentrate, acted as the army's reserve. Malvern Hill was the dominating terrain feature in the area that could also be supported by Federal naval gunfire from the James River. The infantry positions, with their organic field artillery batteries, had excellent fields of fire and were supported by eight batteries of the army reserve artillery under Colonel Henry J. Hunt.

General Lee, believing this was his last opportunity to catch the retreating Federals, ordered a frontal assault by his army on Malvern Hill. The Confederate attack was not coordinated, and the fourteen separate brigades thrown at Malvern Hill were defeated piecemeal. More than half of the Confederate casualties were caused by artillery fire. At the height of the Confederate assaults, Sumner ordered two brigades of Richardson's division to his aid. Caldwell's and Meagher's brigades were rushed forward to brace the Federal lines and add their firepower to the already crumbling rebel attacks.

Malvern Hill was a failure for General Lee and a chance for General McClellan to reverse the momentum of the previous week. When the firing ceased, many Federal commanders thought that an immediate offensive would be mounted to capitalize on their victory. All were stunned when the orders came from McClellan to withdraw the army again, this time from an excellent defensive position to the safety of Harrison's Landing.

A number of Federal leaders, including Richardson, believed that McClellan made a bad decision. General Kearny was so incensed that he declared, "I, Phillip Kearny, an old soldier, enter my solemn protest against this order for retreat. I say to you all, such an order can only be prompted by cowardice or treason!"[58] McClellan, who was by now onboard the U.S. Navy gunboat *Galena*, steaming south toward Harrison's Landing, not only was physically out of touch with his commanders but also had lost the pulse of his army as well.

The retreat continued to Harrison's Landing in a tremendous rainstorm, causing the army to straggle badly and lose more soldiers and wagons to the enemy. As the Army of the Potomac went into camp, the morale of the Federals reached a low point. In a week's duration, the Federals had come from within sight of the enemy's capital to fighting by day and retreating at night to their new base of operations. Each night, enormous amounts of equipment had been destroyed or abandoned, and worst of all, their dead and wounded had been deserted on the field. On the morning of July 3, the Army of the Potomac encampment was startled by artillery fire coming from a ridgeline above the camp called Evelington Heights. Confederate cavalry led by General J. E. B. Stuart had taken control of the area and started to lob artillery shells into the Federal camp from his single piece of horse artillery. Many of these shells came down into the area assigned to Richardson's division. During this shelling, Richardson personally took charge of a couple of regiments, attempting to move them into a position to drive away the Confederate raiders. A sergeant from the 61st New York recorded, "Richardson wanted to change the location of some of us, and became very impatient at the slow movements of the men. He roared out to us, "Make haste, men! Make haste! Every minute is an hour!" and the men responded by hustling at a livelier gait."[59] The advance forced Stuart to withdraw, and the area was subsequently heavily manned to prevent further occurrences.

"He despised vanity and pomp; and measured men's greatness only by merit"

Zachariah Chandler, the Republican senator from Michigan, drew his political power from two circles: first, by teaming with Ohio senator Ben Wade in controlling the radical wing of the Republican Party and, secondly, by ardently attending to the needs of any Michigan soldier who came to him for help. Private Hiram Johnson, 16th Michigan, remembered arriving at a Washington hospital after being wounded at the Second Battle of Bull Run. The first Michigan man he met there was Senator Chandler, who sat with him and asked many questions. As he left, he handed Johnson two oranges and told him if he ever needed assistance to call on him at once.[60] Chandler built a reputation of genuine caring for Michigan soldiers, and it helped protect his political seat for decades after the war.

Since the fall of 1861, McClellan had to endure the wrath of the Radical Republicans criticizing his strategy. Now, for the first time since his assumption of command, a noticeable undercurrent of disillusionment appeared among leaders and soldiers within his army. General Kearny noted, "But McClellan's want of Generalship, or treason, has gotten us into a place, where we are completely boxed up."[61] Colonel Barlow, 61st New York, added, "It is considered generally that McClellan has been completely outwitted. . . . I think the whole army felt that it was left to take care of itself, and was only saved by their own brave fighting. . . . You have no idea of the imbecility of management both in action and out of it. . . . I think officers and men are disgusted with and have lost confidence in McClellan. . . . The stories of his being everywhere among the men in the fights are all untrue."

It seemed that the final straw for many of the young leaders of the army occurred at Malvern Hill. A captain in the 57th New York noted, "The fight at Malvern Hill was entirely favorable to our side, the enemy lost enormously, while we suffered little, and at the close of the fight, the rebel troops were dispirited and thoroughly exhausted; our corps, and the troops on the right were mostly fresh. If a grand attack of the entire army, well led, had been ordered immediately after the repulse of the enemy's last attack, who can doubt the result? But the same timid methods continued and the army was withdrawn. With such a commander, we can't hope for success. Such certainly is the opinion of a great many of our brightest officers."[62]

Although the majority of the private soldiers still had complete faith in their commanding general, within Richardson's division, respected fighters such as French, Barlow, and Zook privately voiced their lack of confidence in McClellan. There is little doubt these subordinates were echoing the thoughts of their commander, never known for his tactful personality.

His many years in the regular army, always serving in combat units in the field and never having experienced a headquarters environment, taught Richardson a more expedient way to get his point across. Perhaps it was the success in the way he publicly dealt with Colonel Miles after Bull Run, or maybe the prodding of his political ally, Senator Chandler. In his own heart, he was making a public statement that every soldier whom he identified with was saying privately. As in past experiences, he did what he felt was right for his soldiers, yet it was done in such a way that he would have a defense if his superiors challenged him for it.

Official reports of army units followed a simple format: the stated facts of an event ending with the commending of personal conduct of individuals in the performance of their duty. In the days before medals were awarded for gallantry, heroic action was recognized by the mention of specific individuals "in dispatches." Richardson's official report of the Seven Days' Battles was submitted to headquarters on July 6, 1862. The two-and-a-half-page document summarized the actions of his division in the standard format but was followed by a postscript.

The last sentence of this P.S. was his personal opinion that should have had no place in his official report. "If anything can try the patience and courage of troops it must be their fighting all day for five consecutive days and then falling back every night." It was a simple enough statement, but any military officer reading the report would instantly see it for what Richardson intended it to be, a damning criticism of McClellan's strategy and leadership.

Michigan newspapers, which published Richardson's complete report on their front pages after the campaign, contain the additional postscript paragraph that is deleted by the compilers of the *Official Records of the Union and Confederate Armies*. In the complete report, Richardson added the following sentence: "I beg leave to state that being hurried by the order compelling me to have this report in immediately, that I have been enabled to do but poor justice to my division in the last part of it—that is, in the last two actions, not even having time to read my report over."[63]

This one paragraph was Richardson's personal criticism to McClellan's strategy for all in the army to read, yet explaining that his report was rushed forward without proofreading gave him immunity from any charge of being disrespectful to his commanding general. Fifteen years of service in the Old Army, mostly in field environments away from the "flagpole," had taught Richardson some practical solutions around army regulations!

After McClellan's move to Harrison's Landing, it became clear that Lee would be content with keeping his eye on the Army of the Potomac, not risking an attack on its formidable defensive works. The crisis had passed for the moment, and priorities switched to refitting the regiments with the many supplies that had been lost. Richardson took advantage of this pause in the campaign to take sick leave and travel to Washington to see his wife and newborn son. He obtained a surgeon's certificate, endorsed by Special Order No. 45, signed by General John A. Dix at Fort Monroe. Once he had made sure that his absence was authorized, he left the Peninsula, along with his personal staff, for his rented home in Washington to see his three-month-old son, Israel Philip Augustus Richardson, for the first time.

Richardson arrived in Washington to a happy homecoming with his family during the first week of July. He entered the nation's capital at the height of his military career. To the country, and especially to the Radical Republicans, Richardson was a hero known as a "fighting general." At the same time the Lincoln administration was being heavily criticized for the lack of aggressiveness in many of its military appointees. Richardson's résumé looked impeccable.

Didn't Richardson, with his aggressiveness, open one of the first engagements of the war at Blackburn's Ford? Didn't he act as rearguard for the army, commanding the last brigade to return from the battlefield at Bull Run? Wasn't his one of the first units to enter the abandoned enemy works at Munson's Hill? On the Peninsula, wasn't he part of the corps that rushed to stave off a rout when Johnston defeated Casey and Keyes at Seven Pines? And wasn't his division key in gaining a victory the next day at Fair Oaks? During McClellan's Change of Base, didn't Sumner always assign Richardson the most difficult post of rearguard at Allen's Farm and Savage's Station? And when he fell under the command of Franklin at White Oak swamp, wasn't he also honored with the rearguard assignment? The nickname of "Rear-Guard" Richardson might have been more appropriate than "Fighting Dick"! In an army common for leaders to receive criticism from newspaper reports or the Committee on the Conduct of the War, or even fellow officers, for that matter, had there ever been any report critical of the conduct of Israel Richardson published anywhere in the country?

Upon his return to Washington, he received news of his promotion to the rank of Major General, U.S. Volunteers. The date of his commission, July 4, 1862, jumped his seniority in the army into a small group of active division and corps commanders. He became the senior military leader from the state of Michigan, and his political influence increased dramatically. The difficulty now became that Richardson's increased responsibilities and public exposure were outpacing his ability to deal in military issues with discretion, and he was still politically naive. In Washington he conferred with Zachariah Chandler about his frustrations encountered during the Peninsula campaign, which centered on the strategy and generalship of George B. McClellan. Senator Chandler was all too eager to use this information in his quest to have McClellan replaced by a "good republican" general.

Other factors in Washington were leading to a weakening of McClellan's command position in the Union army. His firm belief that the Army of the Potomac should remain based on the Peninsula, where he planned to launch another campaign against Richmond, worried Lincoln. On July 11, 1862, General Henry W. Halleck was ordered east from his post in St. Louis and was appointed general in chief of the armies, a duty that had once belonged to McClellan. Halleck won the position because of his reputation for administration (his army nickname was "Old Brains").

Armed with Richardson's criticisms, Chandler took to the U.S. Senate floor on July 16, 1862, and launched into a fiery speech that encompassed the whole lackluster history of McClellan's service as commander of the Army of the Potomac. Since the Seven Days' Battles had only occurred less than three weeks previously, with almost all of the participants still serving on the Peninsula, and because the official reports of the battle had yet to be released, it seemed probable that Chandler based many of his conclusions on private discussions with Richardson.

Chandler's speech was reprinted by all the Radical Republican newspapers and circulated throughout the country in a special pamphlet. It represented the beginning of an organized political attempt to replace General McClellan as commander of the Army of the Potomac. Lincoln, who had defended McClellan in the past, was losing confidence in his strategy. Faced with overwhelming political pressure, Lincoln sent Halleck to the Peninsula, forcing McClellan to concede to a change in plans when his own excessive estimates of enemy strength were used as an argument for the withdrawal.

Richardson gathered up his family and boarded a train for a quick trip home to Pontiac. He had left more than a year ago as a colonel and regimental commander and now made a grand return as a major general commanding a division, along with a new son to show his parents.

He remained in Pontiac for the next ten days, attending political gatherings and war meetings in support of the Union cause. The local newspapers followed his activities closely. A friend of the Richardson family recalled his visit: "I remember when attending the old Presbyterian Church in Pontiac on the Sabbath, sitting behind General Richardson. He told me that they could have taken Richmond at this time, but could not hold it without McClellan's support. Richardson was kind and gentle in nature. He would speak to a ragged boy on the street as soon as to the governor of Michigan."[64]

Richardson was entitled to his opinions; however, his position as a subordinate commander called for a certain level of loyalty. Yet while he did not openly disapprove of McClellan's tactics, it became clear to the commanding general that Richardson's behavior to him was not respectful. His after-action report on the Seven Days' Battles and the close association with Senator Chandler were more than enough to put Richardson in a precarious position. Behind the public scene, both generals jockeyed for positions that would impose conditions on the other. For the sake of self-preservation, Richardson was not above going outside the chain of command.

McClellan telegraphed orders to Pontiac for Richardson to return immediately to his command, charging him with being absent without leave. From his enthusiastic welcome by the citizens of Michigan and his newly acquired political power, Richardson, probably with the goading of Chandler, felt he could challenge McClellan. Perceiving that a cold reception awaited him on his return to the Peninsula, Richardson received assistance from Senator Chandler and the entire Michigan delegation in requesting a transfer to a different theater of operations. Radical Republican pressure was brought to bear on both the president and his secretary of war to make the change.

> July 29, 1862
> Honorable E. M. Stanton, Secretary of War
> Dear Sir,
> Brigadier General Richardson, of this State, is reported as being
> absent from duty without leave. This is not true. He is absent on

sick leave, and is not able to join his command. Will you not, in accordance with the wishes of the whole delegation, assign him to the command of Michigan soldiers now being raised? His presence here, and the assurance that he is to command, will greatly stimulate enlistments. We are proud of him as one of the best fighting generals of the army.

Very Truly Yours,
Zachariah Chandler[65]

Richardson and his family returned to Washington during the first week in August. Chandler's letter was a request that could not be simply overlooked. Michigan had been the birthplace of the Republican Party less than ten years previously, and Abraham Lincoln owed many political favors to the state founders of his own political party.

Richardson was an acquaintance of President Lincoln and had tried this approach before, when he had sought and failed to get his old brigade transferred to his new division command. Although signaling his tentative approval of the move, Lincoln left the final decision with his secretary of war and General Halleck.

Executive Mansion, Washington D. C.

August 6, 1862
Honorable E. M. Stanton, Secretary of War
Sir,
After the late battles before Richmond, we promoted General Israel B. Richardson to be a Major General. He wishes that General French may be assigned to his old Division; and that he may be assigned to a new Division from Michigan, which he thinks he can bring forward faster than any one else, & which I think, is probable. You and General Halleck must decide these things.

Yours &c,
A. Lincoln[66]

The summer of 1862 was a critical time for the Lincoln administration regarding the prosecution of the war from the points of view of both friends and enemies. Northern newspapers controlled by the Radicals editorialized the lack of talent among the senior leaders of their army, while praising the audacious rebel commanders like Lee, Jackson, and Stuart.

At the height of his success on the doorsteps of Richmond, McClellan came out openly against the corps command arrangement that the administration had imposed on him, arguing that some of his subordinates were incompetent.

He requested Lincoln to allow him to either appoint new commanders or revert to the old division command structure. This set off a howling protest among the Radicals, who had worked hard to dilute McClellan's power.

Lincoln, who was sympathetic to McClellan's problems, warned him of the political ramifications such a move would cause in Washington. In a letter on May 9, the president described the power of the Radicals, who would be greatly opposed to such a move:

"I now think it indispensable for you to know how your struggle against it is received in quarters that we cannot entirely disregard. It is looked upon as merely an effort to pamper one or two pets and to persecute and degrade their supposed rivals. Are you strong enough—are you strong enough, even with my help—to set your foot upon the necks of Sumner, Heintzelman, and Keyes all at once?"[67]

The diary of Gideon Wells, Lincoln's secretary of the navy, sums up the administration's frustration with the way the army's leadership was pursuing the war. He noted, "Some of our best educated officers have no faculty to govern, control and direct an army in offensive warfare. We have many talented and capable engineers; good officers in some respects, but without audacity, and in that respect almost utterly deficient as commanders."[68]

With the defeat of Pope's army at the Second Battle of Bull Run, on August 30, 1862, any hope of Richardson's request for transfer was dashed. The Federal armies in the east were in turmoil, and nobody knew where Lee would strike next. Rumors were rampant in Washington, as broken pieces of the defeated army straggled back to their camps. Lincoln saw Pope's failure in terms more frightening than a mere battlefield defeat. The president remarked, "Pope did well, but there was an army prejudice against him, and it was necessary he should leave. We had the enemy in our hands on Friday, and if our generals, who were vexed with Pope, had done their duty . . . all of our present difficulties and reverses have been brought upon us by these quarrels of the generals.

"I must have McClellan to reorganize the army and bring it out of chaos, but there has been a design—a purpose in breaking down Pope without regard of consequences to the country. It is shocking to see and know this, but there is no remedy at present. McClellan has the army with him."[69]

Gideon Wells remarked, "The general conviction is that Pope is a failure here, and there is a belief and admission that he has not been seconded and sustained as he should have been by McClellan, Franklin, Fitz John Porter and perhaps some others. Personal jealousies and professional rivalries, the bane and curse of all armies, have entered deeply into ours."[70]

With the political and military situation facing the Lincoln administration, it was out of the question to honor the transfer request of Richardson. If his reputation for being critical of superiors was starting to grow, it was nothing compared to the accusations that General Pope had been flinging at McClellan's friends, generals Porter, Franklin, and Smith. Whatever baggage Richardson brought with him regarding his outspoken reputation, it was more than outweighed by his aggressive leadership and his Republican Party affiliation.

On September 2, 1862, Lincoln and Halleck visited McClellan at his headquarters outside Washington and returned him to command of the Army of the Potomac. The president took a hasty visit to West Point, where he had a brief meeting with now retired general Winfield Scott and returned to Washington. Defending his decision with Gideon Wells, Lincoln believed he had no other options. "McClellan knows the ground. His specialty is to defend. He is a good engineer, and there is no better organizer. He can be trusted to act on the defensive."[71]

As Federal generals looked for guidance, the Radical Republicans made it clear where they stood. Zachariah Chandler fired off a letter to Secretary Stanton on September 10, showing his frustration with McClellan: "Is there any hope for the future? Are imbecility and treason to be sustained and promoted to the end of the chapter?"[72]

7

— •••• —

Destiny

— •••• —

"One of our best fighting generals"

During the last week in August 1862, the Army of the Potomac was withdrawn from the Peninsula. Richardson's division arrived in Alexandria on August 26. Replacements for the worn-out regiments were made, and a third division was added to the II Corps. General French was put in command of the newly formed 3rd Division, and his old brigade was given to Colonel John R. Brooke, the senior regimental commander.

On August 27 elements of Richardson's division had disembarked their ships and marched six miles toward Fredericksburg. As they came to Aquia Creek, tents were erected just before sunset. Pope's defeat caused a change in plans. Orders went out, and a flurry of activity began in each company area. Tents that moments before were set up now came down, under the excited commands of officers and sergeants. In the midst of all the confusion General Richardson appeared before Captain Janvrin W. Graves, commander of Company E, 5th New Hampshire.

"Don't you think it would be just as well, and perhaps a *little better*, to let the boys have their coffee before we start?" Richardson suggested.[1] Captain Graves thought it would be better, and learned another lesson in leadership from his division commander. The strategic initiative was once again with the Confederates, and in early September they marched north into Maryland.

McClellan's army moved south to mount a relief of Harpers Ferry, then under siege by Stonewall Jackson's corps. The night of September 13, 1862, found Sumner's corps making camp near Frederick, Maryland. The line of march lay through pleasant farm country, with fields waving with grain and corn, and the new-mown hay sending a fragrant smell into the air.

The Irish Brigade bivouacked in an open field, near a meadow full of haystacks. Captain Gosson climbed to the top of one and buried himself in the hay, sleeping comfortably until roused by reveille. He rubbed his eyes and slid down the side of the stack, landing heavily on someone beneath.

"Oh, dear!—My ribs are broken, you scoundrel; who the devil are you?" exclaimed the injured party, trying to extricate himself from the hay.

"And who the hell are you? Get up out of there," and Jack gave him the application of his boot to accelerate his movements.

He did get up in a rage, using very strong language, and faced Captain Jack. The latter fell back a pace and exclaimed, "Bless my soul, General Richardson, who the hell could think I was kicking you; I assure you I am sorry, General, an' I have a small drop, it's good, here in my flask, and the morning air is a little bitter." "Captain Jack, my dear fellow! Oh, dear, my ribs pain me; but I know you couldn't help it, or you didn't know who it was. That's good, Captain Jack—I feel better; I'll have another pull." Between them they emptied the flask, and walked off to headquarters together to have breakfast.[2]

On September 14 Lee met McClellan's cautious advance at South Mountain. As the sun was breaking, Richardson took a few minutes to write, summing up his hopes, not knowing it was to be his last letter to his wife:

> I hear, while I am writing, a cannonade in the direction of Harpers Ferry, perhaps they are attacking our garrison there; it consists of 7,000 men commanded by Col. Miles. We follow today without wagons, and three days rations in our haversacks. Now is the time to end the war if the North turns out. The South is risking everything upon their army here. They have had no rations for more than 20 days, but live off the country.
>
> My dear, it is now six in the morning, and we march at seven. I write this morning to let you know that I am well and in good spirits as I can be when I'm away from you. Hope something will soon turn, so that we can be together before long. Everything is inconvenient in camp. Doctor Taylor, McMillian and myself are all writing at a small table. The assembly has sounded and I must close. Now my dear, take good care of yourself, give my love to all in the family, also to little P. kiss him many times. Will write every possible chance.
>
> From your Affectionate and Loving Husband[3]

After marching all day, they arrived on the battlefield as the fighting was dying down. The Confederate rearguard had succeeded in holding the pass and was now slipping away in the darkness. At daylight of September 15, Richardson's division was detached from Sumner and ordered to report to Major

General Joseph Hooker. By seven o'clock, a heavy mist had cleared enough to show that the rebels had abandoned their positions. Hooker ordered Richardson to pursue but not become decisively engaged until the rest of the corps could be brought up. As Richardson moved his division forward, the rest of I Corps began to brew their coffee and have breakfast.

With Richardson leading, the division started its march through the mountain gap. At the summit, Richardson ordered a halt and sent for the 5th New Hampshire, at the rear of the division. The unit quickly came forward, passing the other regiments as they broke to the right on the road; the men called out, "There goes Richardson's foot cavalry."[4]

As the regiment passed the Irish Brigade, General Meagher complained that another unit was going in ahead of his brigade. The passing men felt quite proud as they overheard Richardson tell Meagher, "If I was going to take Hell, I should want the 5th New Hampshire for skirmishers." Colonel Cross had only recently recovered from his wounding at Fair Oaks and returned to duty. Richardson told him, "We have no cavalry nor artillery; your regiment must act as both. Deploy and sweep both sides of the road."[5]

Cross and his men led the division up the Sharpsburg turnpike for several miles, constantly exchanging shots with the cavalry of the enemy and capturing straggling rebels. Richardson, who was among the most advanced skirmishers, became upset when Captain James McMahon, detailed from the Irish Brigade to serve on his personal staff, dashed past him on horseback and up to a bridge where he and two rebels exchanged shots at point-blank range. He sent an orderly after the captain, roaring out, "Tell Captain McMahon to come back here!" which he did only after running out of ammunition. The duel showed well for the courage of Richardson's aide but poorly for his marksmanship, as neither he nor the rebels were hurt.

At ten A.M., as the skirmishers neared the Antietam Creek, they caught a glimpse of the rearmost units of Lee's army marching up the turnpike to a point on the crest of the slope. Thousands of other Confederate soldiers had deployed on either side of the road and faced Richardson's men in line of battle. Their front was spread out as far as one could see; some places they boldly stood out in plain view and others were concealed by the unevenness of the ground, marked only by a guidon or straggler. When the 5th New Hampshire advanced to the creek, rebel artillery fire began to fall among them. Richardson halted the advance, sending word to Hooker to move forward quickly.

Hooker arrived and found Richardson had opened up on the enemy with a section of artillery. The Confederates seemed well posted to prevent a crossing of the creek, and Hooker estimated their strength at close to fifty thousand. This news was sent back to McClellan as a division commanded by General

George Sykes arrived. With the Federal battery answering the rebel fire from the turnpike, Richardson posted his division to the right side of the road, and Sykes moved his division to the left.

McClellan, accompanied by a large group of staffers and escorts, arrived by the middle of the afternoon and had a hurried conference with Hooker, Porter, Richardson, and Sykes. Although every unit in the Army of the Potomac except Franklin's VI Corps was within easy marching distance, McClellan believed that it was too late to coordinate an attack on Lee's position this day. Engineers were ordered to scout the rebel positions and locate suitable fords and crossings.

At day's end Richardson detailed the 2nd Delaware to picket his front, occupying positions along the bank of Antietam Creek. Everything was quiet during the night. Captain D. L. Stricker was surprised when General Richardson appeared at dawn at the very front of the skirmish line to visually inspect the ground he expected to advance his division over. When he finished surveying the area, he ordered Captain Stricker to withdraw his picket and return to his former position.[6] But the assault would not be made. McClellan felt he could wait another day to get all his units into position and, with this gift, gave Lee another twenty-four hours to prepare for the attack.

"There is no relief in sight"

A forty-one-year veteran of the U.S. Army, Colonel Dixon S. Miles remained at home in Baltimore for six months following his court of inquiry after Bull Run. In the rapidly expanding army, all of his peers and many previous subordinates had attained general officer rank, while he remained an unemployed colonel awaiting assignment. In March of 1862 Miles received orders to command a brigade stationed at Harpers Ferry with the mission of protecting the vital Baltimore & Ohio Railroad lines in the area from attacks by Confederate cavalry and partisans. It was a backwater command, but one gladly accepted by the now humbled old soldier.

Now the fate of war had put this mediocre officer and his fourteen thousand men squarely in the path of one-third of Lee's army commanded by Stonewall Jackson. Harpers Ferry was the critical objective in the Confederate campaign plan. Lee needed a quick victory to concentrate his army before giving McClellan a chance to defeat him piecemeal. McClellan was aware of Lee's actual strength and needed Miles to defend his position as long as possible in order to keep Jackson's force from linking up with Lee.

Miles interpreted his orders to mean that Harpers Ferry was to be defended and put most of his combat strength into defensive lines around the town. The problem was that Harpers Ferry was an indefensible position once the surrounding heights were occupied and manned with artillery. By not paying attention to the strategic high ground, Miles practically gave the town with all its valuable supplies to the rapidly advancing Jackson.

At dawn on September 15 Jackson's men opened fire from the heights on all sides of Harpers Ferry. At about eight thirty A.M., Miles approached Lieutenant Fred Fout, of the 15th Indiana battery. "Orderly, cease firing. We have to surrender," Miles ordered. Corporal Johnson replied, "Colonel, we should not surrender; we came here to fight." Colonel Miles was pale and seemed the saddest man that I had ever seen. He remarked, "Jess, I would like to, but," and looking over to Maryland Heights, "there is no relief in sight." With this he pulled a white handkerchief out of his pocket, waved it at the enemy, and walked to the point where the pike crosses Bolivar Heights. At the sight of the white handkerchief, the rebels yelled and their closest guns ceased to fire. But the artillery farther away fired a few more rounds before news of the surrender reached them.[7]

Captain W. W. French, commanding Company F, 115th New York, saw the flash and heard the report of a gun up the Shepherdtown road. The sky being hazy, he could see the shell as it made its way toward him. When the time came, he ordered his men down, and the shot passed over his company line—near enough for them to feel the breeze and for his lieutenant's hat to be knocked off his head. French watched as it struck among a group of officers at the foot of the hill. The very last artillery shell fired by Jackson's men landed directly behind Miles and nearly severed his left leg.[8]

Even with his bumbling attempt to follow orders, Miles would have been successful if he could have only withstood Jackson's siege for an additional twenty-four hours. The damage to his command by Jackson's artillery was not great, and a Federal corps under General Franklin was only six miles away. The mortally wounded colonel would die the next day, some say mercifully so that he wouldn't face another board of inquiry for botching the second of his two assignments during the Civil War. The lack of action by the hapless Miles allowed Jackson to unite his command with Lee in time to meet McClellan's cautious advance.

What would these three men, Richardson, Miles, and Longstreet; whose careers had intertwined so often in the Old Army while serving in Mexico and on the frontier, have thought if they only knew how much their personal actions at this time would determine the fate of the bloodiest one-day battle ever fought on their country's soil? The act was about to be played out.

"Now is the time to end the war, if the North turns out"

Richardson's views about McClellan's decision to postpone his attack for thirty-six hours could likely be guessed. Edwin Sumner appeared at McClellan's headquarters early on the morning of September 17, impatiently waiting for permission to move forward. Sumner had ordered that his men of the II Corps be wakened at two A.M., and since then they had been busy preparing for action. In Richardson's division the men were marched to the ammunition wagons in the darkness to draw eighty rounds per man, twice the usual allotment; they accepted the grim omen in expressionless silence.[9]

Sumner heard the firing from Hooker's advance at six A.M. and felt his best course of action would be to advance with his full II Corps in support of Hooker, not "sending these troops into action in driblets," as he would later state. After McClellan's staff had him cooling his heels at headquarters for an hour, Sumner received orders to move to Hooker's support at seven. However, Richardson's division, which had been designated the army's tactical reserve, would not be allowed to move forward until a division from Porter's V Corps could replace it. Sumner had to travel two miles to reach his objective and notified Sedgwick and French to move at once. Richardson was to follow as soon as McClellan released him.

Preoccupied with his haste to advance, General Sumner made several errors that would eventually cost the Federals their chance to make any decisive gains in the Confederate center. First, although French was to follow Sedgwick and the two divisions were to attack abreast, no one from the II Corps staff was on hand to guide or coordinate the action. Immediately on receiving the order to advance, the veteran division of Sedgwick was on the move, while the green division under French, which had been organized for only two weeks, took more time to prepare. General Oliver O. Howard, who now commanded a brigade in Sedgwick's division, reported that his men began their march at seven A.M.; French reported that his division got under way at seven thirty. Perhaps Sumner felt that he had to make up for time lost in the morning delay at McClellan's headquarters; he may have reasoned that it was critical to get his men into action as fast as possible to properly support Hooker's attack. But the result of his hasty planning was that once French was ready to move out, Sedgwick's division had already marched out of sight.

French was left to generally follow the path of Sedgwick, but upon committing his division to the attack, he found himself too far to the south of Sumner and Sedgwick to offer any support. When McClellan's orders released Richardson's division, he promptly marched to the sound of the guns and tied his division neatly onto the flank of French. The result was the splitting of the strength of the II Corps, which was fighting two distinct battles. Once Sumner had finally extracted Sedgwick's battered and defeated division from the West Woods, he seemed to suffer from shock. His apparent lack of attention to his other two divisions caused him to prepare for an imaginary Confederate counterattack instead of taking advantage of Richardson's success in driving the rebels from the sunken road.

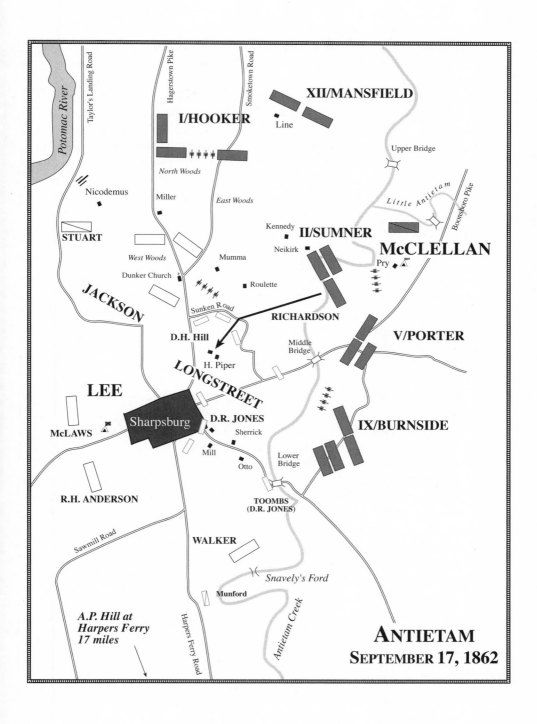

At nine A.M. the division of General George W. Morell arrived to replace Richardson's division as the army's reserve. Thomas Ward, a dispatch rider for Sumner, found Richardson immediately afterward and delivered a message: "Sir, General Sumner sends his compliments; and requests you move your division into action at once."[10] In the Irish Brigade, the order came for the unit to fall in under arms and take up a line of march, followed by Brooke's and Caldwell's brigades. General Richardson personally led his division, 4,029 officers and men strong. Moving at a rapid pace, the three brigades crossed the ford of the Antietam a mile or so to the right of their bivouac sight. As the division crossed the stream, Richardson sat astride his horse, watching each regiment as they came down the slope and waded in. As each regimental commander passed by, he cautioned them in a stern manner, "No straggling today, Colonel! Keep your men well up and in hand."

Noting the sounds of battle coming from French's attack, Richardson adjusted his advance toward the southwest, veering slightly from the westerly approach taken by the other two divisions of the Second Corps. His division marched under cover of the rising ground and depressions, keeping out of enemy sight. Arriving at a cornfield, General Richardson ordered that everything but cartridge belts be thrown off. As the brigade deployed into line of battle and he turned command back over to General Meagher, his parting words to his soldiers were "Men, follow me and where I will not go, I will not ask you to go."[11]

The division deployed about seven hundred fifty yards north of the sunken road and parallel to it. The advance would be steadily uphill, through cornfields into a cleared pasture until they reached the top of the ridge, then a gentle slope down to the sunken road eighty yards below it. Richardson ordered Meagher's and Caldwell's brigades into a line of battle, while Brooke was directed to form a second line behind the Irish Brigade as the division reserve. The Irish Brigade marched into position with the 69th New York on the extreme right flank, followed next by the 29th Massachusetts and the 63rd and the 88th New York. Caldwell's brigade followed next, with the 61st/64th New York, 7th New York, 81st Pennsylvania, and 5th New Hampshire on the far left flank.

As the regiments stepped off, a lone horseman rode across the brigade front. It was Father William Corby, one of the regimental chaplains, who gave the brigade a hasty absolution as the men marched forward. As Richardson's men cleared the cornfield and marched forward into the pasture, they came under a steady small-arms fire from Confederate troops who had moved forward from their positions to take advantage of the crest of the ridge. Their accurate firing had already affected the extreme left flank of French's advance, and now they concentrated their attention on the advancing Irish Brigade. The advance was momentarily stalled at a fence that crossed the pasture and had to be torn down for the brigade to move forward, but still Meagher did not allow his men to stop and return the enemy's fire. Passing the fence obstacle, the brigade continued its advance as the Confederate fire increased in its intensity. As the Federal advance reached about a hundred yards from the crest of the ridge, Meagher finally ordered his brigade to halt, and gave permission to open fire.

A soldier in the 29th Massachusetts reported, "The volley that played out along the line . . . was very effective, for instantly the Confederates fell back from the summit into the sunken road, receiving as they did so several other volleys."[12] When the Irish Brigade reached the crest of the ridge they could see the Confederate main defensive line anchored in the sunken road eighty yards below them on a gentle slope. Although they were very exposed in this position, skylined on top of the ridge, Meagher allowed his brigade to stand and fire five or six volleys against the semientrenched defensive line.

Standing in the open, so close to the Confederate positions, the Irish Brigade took heavy casualties from this exchange of volleys. Every regiment's color bearer went down, only to be replaced by another brave soldier, who in turn, was also wounded or killed. As the rebel fire increased, Meagher judged the time was right for the assault and shouted, "Boys! Raise the colors and follow me!" The charge had barely got under way when Meagher was thrown from his horse and crashed heavily to the ground, under the tremendous volume of fire. The stunned Meagher was carried to the rear, rumored to be more drunk than hurt, and the charge stalled after advancing only some thirty yards. Meagher, in his after-action report noted, "Having been seriously wounded and compelled to retire, the charge of bayonets I had ordered on the left was arrested, and thus the brigade, instead of advancing and dispersing the column with the bayonet, stood and delivered its fire persistently and effectively, maintaining every inch of the ground they occupied."[13] With the loss of so many key leaders, and no one stepping up to replace Meagher, the brigade became content to stand at close range with Anderson's men and trade volleys. In the 88th New York, Captain Patrick Clooney was wounded in the leg but refused to leave the field. When the color bearer went down, Clooney picked up the flag and used it as a crutch, slowly moving forward until a bullet in the chest killed him.

The brigade remained in the open, trading shots with the rebel defenders, who were partly protected by the sunken road. The casualties on both sides added up quickly. Seven color bearers from the 69th New York had already been shot down when Captain James McGee from Company F grabbed the green banner. The flagstaff was soon split in two by a bullet. When McGee bent over to pick up the banner, another bullet went through his cap. The brave and lucky captain rallied the regiment by his example and somehow lived through the day. In a short time almost 540 men from the Irish Brigade had been killed or wounded, but the remainder stayed in formation until their ammunition was almost gone.

Richardson was directing his division from behind the Irish Brigade and, because he knew they could not maintain their position without immediate support, was pushing Caldwell's brigade to make the decisive advance. The two brigades had started their advance abreast, but Caldwell moved forward more cautiously, bending back the left flank of the division's advance. Whether by skill or by luck in choosing his point of attack, Richardson was able to place four of his regiments on the undefended flank of the Confederate line. As Caldwell's brigade moved forward, they suffered only minor casualties, since they were subjected only to the fire of skirmishers and sharpshooters. Richardson, unable to find General Caldwell, and not satisfied with the progress being made on that front, dispatched an aide to Colonel Barlow directing him to tie the 61st/64th New York into the flank of Meagher's line, while he personally hiked over to Colonel Cross of the 5th New Hampshire with instructions to quickly move to the relief of the Irish Brigade and speed up the advance. Pointing toward Meagher's units, Richardson said, "Go on, Colonel, and do all you can—relieve that regiment."[14]

In hindsight, this is the point where Richardson probably made his biggest tactical error of the day. If he had only called up Colonel John R. Brooke's 3rd Brigade from their reserve position to immediately support the Irish Brigade, and used the full force of Caldwell's brigade to advance past the Confederate positions, then swing right and roll up the unsecured Confederate flank, the potential was there to sweep down the sunken lane all across his own division's frontage and even into French's zone, splitting the Army of Northern Virginia in half. Granted, it would have been an aggressive maneuver to commit his whole reserve so early into the fight; but the prize would certainly have been worth the chance.

The two men parted company as their conference came to an end, and Richardson turned to head back toward the Irish Brigade; within seconds a rebel shell exploded right on the spot where they had just been standing, knocking off Cross's hat and giving him two slight but painful wounds to his head and face. Cross immediately brushed himself off, tied a red bandanna over his head to stop the bleeding, and led his regiment to the support of Meagher.

At the same moment that Caldwell's men were coming to the rescue, the situation for the Irish Brigade had reached a desperate point. The 29th Massachusetts was the most intact regiment left in the brigade, due only to the fact that the terrain they occupied shielded them slightly from the brunt of the Confederate volleys. The other three regiments were down to half or less strength, and the soldiers were running out of ammunition. Colonel Barnes, the regimental commander, realized they could not remain in their present position and chose to make a last-resort attempt to charge the enemy. The sudden dash forward by his regiment, which was joined by the remnants of the brigade, also coincided with the opening of a heavy and accurate fire on the surprised rebels from Barlow, who had just appeared at their flank. It proved to be the tipping point for the Confederates in the sunken road. A soldier in the Irish Brigade reported, "The shouts of our men, and their sudden dash toward the sunken road, so startled the enemy that their fire visibly slackened, their line wavered, and squads of two and three began leaving the road and running into the corn."[15]

"Old Dick Richardson led us in, not merely to fill a gap, but to make gaps"

Colonel Barlow was in command of two under-strength units, the 61st and 64th New York regiments, when he received Richardson's orders to advance and relieve the Irish Brigade. Instead of merely taking over the position of the Irish Brigade, Barlow moved his regiments off to the left and rushed half the distance forward to the rebel line and opened fire. This allowed him to pour a flanking fire on the sunken road that had a devastating effect on the already weakened Confederate brigade of General George B. Anderson.

As the grimly determined Irish Brigade moved forward, the men of Caldwell's three other regiments caught up with them. Relief in place between two units is a complicated maneuver in any circumstance, let alone in the midst of an attack, while moving and under fire. Lieutenant Livermore of the 5th New Hampshire described the operation as "well ordered," but it may not have been all that precise. According to Ezra Carman, "The movement was not made with that precision described in the official reports, by breaking companies to the front. Meagher's regiments [were] breaking by companies to the rear, but the brigade (Caldwell's) was running when it reached Meagher's line, Richardson leading, swinging his hat and shouting, and without slackening pace, dashed through his ranks, passing the line by simply pushing its way through, Meagher's men quickly conforming to the movement."[16] But on the whole, little time was lost as Caldwell's men took their places and continued the advance, halting shortly before reaching the sunken road.

As the Irish Brigade was leaving the field to regroup and replenish its ammunition, General Richardson approached Lieutenant Colonel Patrick Kelly of the 88th New York. Concerned with the ever widening gap between his division and French's to his right, he grabbed the veteran officer and placed the green 108th New York under his command. Richardson ordered him forward again with his new command to support a battery a little forward of where they were previously engaged. No matter that the inexperienced 108th New York belonged to the 2nd Brigade of French's 3rd Division; the regiment had been scattered and was leaderless, struggling to reform after their initial engagement behind the ridge overlooking the sunken road, and Richardson's solution quickly put another hundred men into the fight. He was making swift tactical decisions with the judgment of a leader on the scene who could feel the pulse of battle unfolding. His staff could coordinate the action later. During the conversation, Richardson turned to the badly mauled 88th New York, the last regiment of the Irish Brigade to march off the field, and shouted, "Bravo, Eighty-eighth; I shall never forget you!"[17] The rank and file responded by giving the general three hearty cheers as Richardson sent off his aide, Major Norvell, to fetch Colonel Brooke's brigade, then turned to move forward with Caldwell's men. Small decisions, like keeping experienced leaders such as Kelly in action while sending the men back to rearm and reorganize under subordinates, were beginning to pay large dividends, as the pressure on the Confederate center was becoming unbearable.

In the midst of much confusion, Richardson was managing his division quite well. His corps commander, Sumner, was out of contact and fighting for his own life, trying to extract Sedgwick's division from the trap he had led them into. The other division of the II Corps, led by French, was running into heavy resistance and having trouble maintaining contact with Richardson's division. The Irish Brigade was moving to the rear to reform and rearm and to act as the division reserve at the same time the fresh brigade of Brooke was arriving on the scene and Caldwell's brigade was starting its advance. Richardson was using all of his units effectively, but his small staff was spread thin in coordinating the action. As a result, Richardson was working hard to personally manage the critical actions of the close fight. He covered the majority of his division's frontage on foot this day, with no more than one or two aides accompanying him at any time.

On the other side of the sunken road, Major General James Longstreet had his hands full. The Confederate center under his command was stretched to the breaking point, and all his reserves had been committed. As French's and Richardson's men slowly gained ground in their determined attack, the Confederate command and control, already weakened with key leader losses from a hard fight at South Mountain three days previous, began to fail. One of Longstreet's division commanders, Major General Richard H. Anderson, was wounded, as was his replacement, Brigadier General Ambrose R. Wright. The brigade of General Robert Rhodes, who was also wounded in the thigh, began to fall back from their defensive position in the sunken road. This retreat was not authorized by Longstreet and came as a direct result of the confusion caused by one Confederate commander after another being cut down. General George B. Anderson, who commanded the brigade on the left of Rhodes, had his ankle shattered by a minié ball and was taken out of the fight. Colonel Charles C. Tew, next in command, was shot in the head, even as he acknowledged the change in command from Colonel John B. Gordon of the 6th Alabama, who was struck in the leg at the same moment. As the remnants of Posey's brigade fell back into the sunken road from their failed counterattack, they mixed in confusion with Anderson's brigade. Under increased pressure from Caldwell's brigade now advancing, they wavered and were suddenly subjected to a flanking fire from Barlow. At that point, "the 16th Mississippi and 2nd Florida broke beyond the power of rallying. In this stampede, if we may so term it, the 4th North Carolina and 30th North Carolina also participated,"[18] reported Colonel R. T. Bennett, who had just replaced the mortally wounded Colonel Tew.

Attempting to rally his men, Colonel Gordon was struck in the face with his fifth wound of the day and collapsed, senseless for a time as his body lay wrapped in the smoke of battle. A moment before, he had been struggling with the responsibilities of holding his companies together in an almost impossible situation, and now his first confused thoughts after regaining consciousness turned to the strictly personal. "I have been struck on the head with a six pound solid shot. It has carried away my head. On the left side there is a little piece of skull left, but the brain is gone entirely; therefore I am dead. And yet, I am thinking. How can a man think with his head shot off? And yet I am thinking; I cannot be dead. And yet no man can live after his head is shot off. I may have consciousness while dead, but not motion. If I can lift my leg, then I am alive. I will try that. Can I? Yes, there it is; lifted up! I'm all right!"[19] In later years, Gordon recalled that he hesitated to lift his leg, fearing it might not move, and thereby proving to himself that he was really dead.

Racing right behind the retreating Confederates, Richardson's 1st Brigade began to pile into the sunken road and into the cornfield on the other side, pouring a devastating fire into the Confederate center. Colonel Cross described the scene: "We shot down the rebel color-bearers as fast as they could get up, killed their officers, broke their ranks and piled them in heaps among the tall corn. I never felt better in my life, and if the rebels didn't hear the Apache war-whoop that day, it was not my fault."[20] As the 5th New Hampshire entered the Confederate position, Lieutenant Livermore was surprised when he recognized the familiar voice of General Richardson cry out, "Where's General Caldwell?" He looked over his right shoulder and saw his gallant division commander advancing with the most forward of troops on the right side of the line, almost alone, afoot and with his bare sword in his hand, and his face as black as a thunder cloud. A couple of soldiers nearer to him cried out the answer, "Behind the haystack!" At this point, Richardson exploded; "God damn the field officers!" he roared and, turning toward the haystack, shouted, "General Caldwell, come up here, sir, and take command of your brigade," before continuing forward with the front ranks.[21]

Once Barlow achieved his foothold on the Confederate flank, he realized he could move his men unchallenged farther down the flank, and he positioned them, straddling the sunken road with a clear field of fire down the lane. The depleted Confederate position, faced with a fresh brigade to their front and unprotected from a devastating fire on their flank, collapsed. Barlow reported, "The portion of the enemy's line which was not broken then remained lying in a deep road, well protected from a fire in their front. Our position giving us peculiar advantages for attacking in flank this part of the enemy's line, my regiments advanced and obtained an enfilading fire upon the enemy in the aforesaid road. Seeing the uselessness of further resistance, the enemy, in accordance with our demands, threw down their arms, came in in large numbers, and surrendered. Upwards of 300 prisoners thus taken by my regiments were sent to the rear."[22]

The time was 11:45 A.M., and Richardson now had the breakthrough he had worked all morning to achieve. But he was not without problems of his own to consider. Taking the sunken lane had given him the opening he wanted, but without Caldwell in a position to coordinate the action, his brigade had essentially conducted its fight as individual regiments. As a result, while pushing the Confederates back deeper into the cornfields past the sunken road, the brigade was dangerously disjointed, with large gaps appearing between their lines.

A welcome sight was the arrival of Captain William M. Graham, Battery K, 1st U.S. Artillery, with six brass twelve pounder Napoleon guns. Assigned to the Army of the Potomac's artillery reserve, his battery had been sent forward at Richardson's request after his own divisional artillery was taken by Sumner. As Graham rode up for instructions, Richardson told him to set up on the high ground just north of the sunken road and support Caldwell's advance by driving off the Confederate batteries to his front.

Captain Frederick L. Hitchcock, of the 132nd Pennsylvania, on the far left flank of French's division, wrote that as he was watching the Irish Brigade, his attention was drawn to a heavily built general officer passing by on foot: "He came close by me and as he passed he shouted: 'You will have to get back. Don't you see yonder line of rebels is flanking you?' I looked in the direction he pointed, and, sure enough, on our right and now well to our rear was an extended line of rebel infantry with their colors flying, moving forward almost with the precision of a parade. My heart was in my mouth for a couple of moments, until the picture suddenly changed, and their beautiful line collapsed and went back as if the devil was after them. This general officer that spoke to me, I learned, was Major General Richardson, commanding the First Division."[23]

Colonel Brooke's brigade had just arrived from reserve position and Richardson rushed over to him. He ordered Brooke to divide his brigade, sending the 52nd New York and the 2nd Delaware to the right of the line, changing their front to meet this threat. As the two regiments split off from the brigade and moved forward, Captain William H. Helmbold, Company D, 2nd Delaware, remembered the scene and later remarked, "Old Dick Richardson led us in, not merely to fill up a gap, but to make gaps."[24] Brooke was also directed to take his remaining three regiments, the 57th New York, 66th New York, and 53rd Pennsylvania forward to support the spread-out regiments of Caldwell.

The rebel unit that Hitchcock described was Howell Cobb's brigade, under the command of Lieutenant Colonel William MacRae and, to his left, two regiments, the 27th North Carolina commanded by Colonel John R. Cooke[25] and the 3d Arkansas under Captain Ready. They were the only organized units left in the Confederate line and had been sent forward by D. H. Hill in an attempt to relieve the pressure on the Confederate center. Their line of advance had been well chosen, for they marched straight up the seam between the two divisions of the II Corps and had the potential to drive into the rear of the advanced position that Richardson held.

As the new Confederate attack approached, Barlow saw the confused state of his brigade after the unit had advanced into the cornfields past the sunken road. "Our troops were joined together without much order, several regiments in front of others, and none in my neighborhood having very favorable opportunities to use their fire."[26] With the Confederates advancing, Brooke's men rushed to fill the gaps. It was a patchwork solution, but Richardson had now formed his division into an inverted "L"-shaped position to meet the new Confederate threat. On his far right, anchoring the division in the sunken road, was Barlow's 61st/64th New York; then extending into the cornfields to his left were two of Brooke's regiments, the 52nd New York and the 2nd Delaware, followed by Caldwell's 7th New York. These four units were able to fire into Cobb and Cooke as the Confederate advance moved past them, aiming for the Roulette farm. Richardson also had Graham's battery shift their fire from the front to concentrate now on the Confederate attack passing their flank. Running farther to the left, at an angle, and facing what was left of the Confederate defenders from the sunken road were two more of Brooke's regiments, the 57th New York and the 66th New York, followed by two of Caldwell's regiments, the 81st Pennsylvania and the 5th New Hampshire, which anchored the left.

Longstreet came upon Captain W. B. Miller's battery of brass Napoleons in the position he had assigned him earlier that morning, posted in a orchard just past the cornfield that Caldwell's and Brooke's regiments were now putting heavy pressure on. Only two of the guns were left in action. Miller had suffered considerably from the fire of Richardson's sharpshooters. Soon Miller found himself the only officer left in his battery and with barely enough men to work his guns. In these desperate moments, Longstreet ordered his staff to help Captain Miller man his guns while he remained on horseback, holding the reins of his staff members' horses and calmly directing the battery's fire. Miller frantically charged and double-charged his guns with spherical case and canister until they leaped in the air on discharge. Longstreet later remembered that "that little battery shot harder and faster, as though it realized that it was to hold thousands of Federals at bay or the battle was lost."[27]

The officers manning these guns realized they were the only forces that stood in the way of keeping Richardson's division from punching through the thinly manned defenses. Major Thomas Walton, Longstreet's aide, was wounded in the shoulder by a rifle bullet, and Colonel Moxley Sorrel, Longstreet's chief of staff, was knocked unconscious by the concussion of a shell as they helped work the battery. At Longstreet's directions, shell after shell was fired as quickly as possible at every threatening Federal movement.

The broken Confederate divisions of D. H. Hill and R. H. Anderson retreated to the Piper buildings, where they regrouped from the sunken road withdrawal and desperately tried to form a new line in the Piper cornfields. But they were already losing ground to Caldwell's men when the additional regiments of Brooke's brigade came up. With great efforts, parts of each Confederate division rallied and another counterattack was attempted against Richardson's extended line. A stiff engagement occurred, but the disorganized Confederates, missing many key leaders, seemed uninspired and were not able to take much punishment before being forced into another retreat. With this advance, Richardson's division claimed three more captured regimental colors: the 4th and 12th Alabama and the 5th Florida, in addition to the three already taken by Barlow's men in the sunken road.

In the division center, the 57th and 66th New York, of Brooke's brigade, were able to reach the Piper house before converging fire from the two enemy batteries forced them to halt. On the division's right flank, Colonel Barlow had been advancing against Miller's battery, which was now firing double charges of spherical case and canister, when he was severely wounded in the face and groin by canister shot exploding in front of him. The accurate rebel artillery fire and persistent rifle fire seemed to intensify and, combined with the lack of cover, was making the forward positions of Richardson's advance untenable. Colonel Brooke feared his brigade, now almost 450 yards forward of the main Federal line, was becoming overextended, and finding that the enemy made no attempt to regain the field, he sent a message to Richardson asking his permission to withdraw.

For the Confederate leadership defending the center of Lee's line, the time had come to commit everyone in reserve to the fight. Both Longstreet and D. H. Hill were at their best on this day. "Longstreet's conduct on this day was magnificent," stated Colonel Moxley Sorrel, his chief of staff. There was "never a more plucky or determined fighter" than Hill, asserted Longstreet years after the battle. "It was a fearful situation," continued Longstreet; "it was easy to see that if the Federals broke through our line there, the Confederate army would be cut in two and probably destroyed, for we were already badly whipped and were only holding our ground by sheer force of desperation."[28]

When Cooke's attack was beaten back, Longstreet sent him a message that he must hold his ground at all costs. Cooke responded, "We will stay here . . . if we must all go to hell together. Tell General Longstreet to send me some ammunition. I have not a cartridge in my command, but will hold my position at the point of the bayonet."[29] All he could do in the face of another attack was to instruct his color bearers to wave their flags as if to challenge the Federals to try again.

As Longstreet was trying to manage the battle in the center, Colonel Robert H. Chilton, General Lee's chief of staff, made his way over to him, asking, "Where are the troops you are holding your line with?" Longstreet pointed to his two pieces of artillery and to Cooke's regiment and replied, "There they are; but that regiment hasn't a cartridge." Chilton's eyes popped as though they would come out of his head, he struck spurs to his horse, and away he went to find General Lee.[30]

All of the Confederate accounts at this point of the battle universally describe a sense of hopelessness in the wake of another Union advance. The Confederate center was now wrecked. "Lee's army," wrote Porter Alexander, "was ruined and the end of the Confederacy was in sight."[31] One more heavy thrust by McClellan on a widening front along the center would split beyond possible reunion the two wings of the Confederate army and would bring the Federals into the rear of both fragments.

Back in the middle of the exhausted Confederate center, Longstreet spotted a persistent Federal battery posted in a very advanced position and ordered Miller to direct his fire at it. From atop his horse, he called out the range for the gunners as they desperately fired round after round at the lone battery in hopes of stemming the Federal advance.

"No one but a soldier would understand"

Lieutenant Colonel Nelson Miles, taking over command from the wounded Colonel Barlow, struggled to hold the ground where they lay. Miles sent out three men led by Sergeant Charles A. Fuller of the 61st New York, to scout and picket the area to their front. Concealed halfway in the cornfield across from the sunken road, Fuller and his men spotted a group of rebel officers on horseback on the crest of a nearby hill observing the Federal line with binoculars. They were easily within his range, but thinking that engaging this enemy group might instigate an unwanted attack, he decided not to fire, and a short time later they left the area. His decision probably saved the lives of General Longstreet and his staff.

Richardson received the withdrawal request from Brooke and fired off another message to headquarters for more artillery support to silence the Confederate batteries and to further support his next advance. The failure of the Federal artillery to make any meaningful contribution to the battle had cost Richardson's division dearly. The chief of artillery for the II Corps, Major F. N. Clarke, was at the side of his boss, General Sumner, fighting to extract themselves from the West Woods. Sumner had taken Richardson's batteries with him when he moved forward so quickly in the morning, thinking he would be able to use them while Richardson remained behind as the army's reserve. The fire support chain of command had now broken down, and it would cause Richardson and French to conduct their fight with infantry alone. Almost three hundred pieces of Federal artillery were parked just several miles away, near McClellan's headquarters, and yet just a single battery answered Richardson's plea of support.

Once Graham arrived, Richardson personally pushed the battery as far forward as possible to engage the Confederate artillery, now the only viable enemy force left to his front. As his regiments were clearing the sunken road, Richardson followed closely, leading Graham's battery to the high ground about thirty yards behind his most forward units. From this position, he understood clearly what McClellan, with his dozens of aides, also should have known. The Confederate center would be split wide open with the next advance, and the destruction of the Army of Northern Virginia was at hand.

After Graham helped to break up the Confederate counterattack on the right flank, Richardson had him turn his attention back to the Confederate artillery that Brooke was complaining about. Richardson also sent word to Caldwell's and Brooke's brigades to suspend the advance and pull their regiments back from the southern edge of the cornfield to the sunken road area for protection from the enemy batteries, as well as for rearming and reorganizing. The badly shot-up Irish Brigade, now resupplied and under Colonel Burke of the 63rd New York, was also returning and moving into position behind the ridge to the right of Graham's battery.

When the command to withdraw and consolidate reached the farthest extended regiments, the orders were grudgingly obeyed. The 2nd Delaware had advanced into the orchard where Miller's battery had been doing so much damage to Richardson's line. Captain Hembold later wrote, "We had swept our front and there was nothing left of the enemy but about 150 men supporting the four guns of the Washington Artillery of New Orleans, which we were just on the point of charging, when we got the peremptory order from Adjutant Hatch, of the brigade staff, to come back to the line. We would have had those guns as sure as fate had not this order come."[32] When the order was passed to the 57th New York, the regiment moved back out of the cornfield past the sunken road and up the brow of a hill in the rear. The unit was hastened by a Confederate battery pouring a storm of grape and canister into the standing cornstalks. Captain Gilbert Frederick recalled, "Each explosion seemed like a rushing mighty wind and a driving hail. In the corner of a fence was discovered a pile of potatoes which the boys insisted should also fall back. It was but a temporary break in the ranks, a moment of time, and this charge also was successful, every potato being captured."[33]

The heavier firepower and rifled barrels of the Confederate artillery created a one-sided duel and prompted Captain Graham to ask General Richardson for assistance. He reported that his shots were falling short, the enemy being out of range of his smoothbore guns, and asked Richardson what he wanted him to do. Richardson ordered Graham to pull back his battery. He explained he was preparing to advance and expected a signal from General Sumner momentarily. He wanted Graham's battery intact and able to accompany the attack and support him. Just at the conclusion of the conversation, a nearby exploding airburst made Graham duck. A shell had burst above him, and he turned to see General Richardson collapse with a wound from a ball of spherical case fired from a battery that was enfilading his position from the right.[34]

During our Civil War, there were many examples of family and friends who found themselves on opposite sides of a skirmish or battle, which led to their reuniting under sorrowful circumstances. These incidents have been recounted in such a reverent way that it makes our fascination with this period of history increasingly grow. There may be no more fateful example in our Civil War than that of James Longstreet personally directing the fire of an artillery battery unknowingly at his good friend of twenty-five years, who stood near the Federal battery three hundred yards away. Not only did this represent a privately painful episode of one friend being responsible for the death of another in the name of duty, but it also makes the argument that no other act by a rebel soldier that day did more to save the Confederate center from the destruction that was a certainty if the Federal advance had continued.

Richardson was struck in the upper part of his left shoulder by a shell fragment, which passed downward, possibly penetrating his left lung, inflicting a severe wound. He struggled to get to his feet and, once over the initial shock of being hit, walked on for about ten minutes. Finally yielding to the agony, Richardson held up his right hand to summon an orderly to him. "Tell General McClellan I have been in the front rank doing the duty of a Colonel. I have done a hard day's work and have worked all day. I am wounded and he must detail someone to take my command." The orderly saluted, turned on his heel and sped off to army headquarters. He relinquished his command to his senior brigadier, General Caldwell, and was taken in an ambulance to the Philip Pry house. While being removed from the field, he told a regimental surgeon in attendance, "Tell General McClellan I have been doing a Colonel's work all day, and I'm now too badly hurt to do a General's."[35]

Lieutenant Livermore was an eyewitness to the scene and described the action in these terms: "This sending forward of infantry to cope with artillery and infantry, repeated within three days, seemed to inspire General Richardson with indignation, for the gallant man went forward with a horse battery (Graham's) to a point within three hundred yards of the enemy's artillery and a stone's throw in front of us, and there, exposed to the concentrated fire of many guns of heavier caliber, he personally overlooked its gunners in a desperate attempt to silence the enemy's batteries, and there he received his mortal wound in the side from a piece of shell; and no one but a soldier can understand our sorrow at seeing him carried off the field."[36]

Another observation by a sergeant in Richardson's 3rd Brigade indicates the feelings that the enlisted men felt for the loss of their divisional commander: "General Richardson, affectionately called 'Fighting Dick,' while directing a battery on the hill near us, was struck with a piece of shell and mortally wounded. He was a good tactician, was prompt and brave, and well deserved the sobriquet of 'Old War Horse,' given to him by his men. It was with a feeling of a personal loss that we parted with General Richardson. He was not a fuss and feather soldier. He usually wore a soft hat and fatigue dress, and looked oftenest like a uniformed farmer. But a study of his features revealed intelligence, determination, and a quiet force of character and fatherliness that made his men believe he was one of them. There has always been a halo around his head since Antietam, for the double reason that he, a general, was killed in battle at our side, and also that he was the first general officer thus lost to us."[37]

With the wounding of Richardson, command of the 1st Division passed to Brigadier General Caldwell, the next senior officer after Brigadier General Meagher had been evacuated. Indecisive and anxious with his new responsibilities, Caldwell quickly forgot any thought of continuing the advance. The new priority was to establish a strong defensive line to protect the ground that had already been taken. A short time later, Brigadier General Winfield S. Hancock, who had commanded a brigade in General William F. Smith's division, was assigned command of the division by the direct order of McClellan.

As a newcomer to the scene, Hancock immediately solicited recommendations from Caldwell and other leaders present. It was easy for the surviving junior commanders, having just experienced their toughest fight of the war to date, to feel satisfied with what they had accomplished so far. Richardson's hands-on style of command also left a void in his subordinates' minds as to their commander's own intent on how to carry on the fight. While it seems that Richardson had been gathering his units together for a final push with Sumner's approval, General Caldwell had no intention of risking any further advance. Most of the situation reports that Hancock received when he arrived painted a picture of a division that had fought itself out. "This place must be held at all hazards!" was his first order to his new division, and he busied himself making preparations for a feared enemy attack that was only a fantasy in his mind. The fighting at the center of the battlefield came to a close, and the drama for the rest of the day moved on to Burnside's attack in the south.

The Confederates were surprised and relieved when they realized that the Federals were going over to the defensive just when their own positions had come dangerously close to disintegration. Later, after reading the Federal battle reports, Longstreet was of the opinion that the Confederate center had been saved only by the "accidental artillery shots that cut down Colonel Barlow, the aggressive spirit of Richardson's right column, and General Richardson himself at his culminating moment. But for the breaking up of Richardson's aggression, this last advance could have gained the field."[38]

The Pry house, serving as General McClellan's headquarters, was on the opposite side of Antietam Creek. Richardson was not directly transported there but was taken there after going through the II Corps field hospital set up at Samuel Pry's gristmill, a three-story structure, also on the Antietam, located a half mile away. It was a good selection for a hospital, because it was less than a mile from the sunken road, but it had a drawback because the Pry Ford on the Antietam was difficult to cross and at least one wagonload of badly wounded II Corps soldiers had been dumped in the creek when an ambulance tipped over. A combination of young surgeons and bad management made this field hospital one of the worst on the battlefield. After the battle, the doctors at the Pry mill were also censured for drinking the distilled spirits that were meant to alleviate the suffering of the wounded.

As General Richardson was being carried off the field, he passed the surgeon's station of Dr. William Child, the regimental surgeon for the 5th New Hampshire. He recalled this moment later on in his journal: "His ambulance was passing the surgeon's station to a dwelling where he was to die. I well remember the pale face; death was upon him then. He was a brave, fearless, skillful officer, and a noble man. He was a favorite with the Fifth; and the feeling of high regard, mutual respect, reliance and gratitude was daily demonstrated between Colonel Cross and the brave General Richardson. It was a sad day for the Army of the Potomac when a rebel shot struck him down. If officers and soldiers ever weep, they of the Fifth did weep that day when Richardson was sacrificed on our country's altar."[39]

It was reported that Richardson lay in great suffering over four hours before his wound could be dressed. On this bloodiest day in the history of American warfare, the medical staffs of both sides were hopelessly swamped with casualties. A division commander would rate immediate attention, no matter how overburdened the hospitals had become. It seems that Major General Israel Richardson must have ordered the surgeons not to care for him ahead of his men. If so, it fit the character of the man and probably contributed to his death. After preliminary treatment at the surgeon's station, he was transported to the Philip Pry house. The medical personnel carried Richardson into an upstairs bedroom, next to one occupied by Major General Joseph Hooker, who had been shot through the foot and brought there earlier in the day.

Colonel Cross, writing in his personal journal, gave his assessment of Richardson's division fight in these terms: "I must chronicle my opinion of some of the chief actors in this eventful scene. General Richardson behaved gallantly, leading and ordering his men until he was struck by a piece of shell in the breast. Gen. Meagher was drunk as usual. Gen. Caldwell did not show himself either brave or skillful; & lost the confidence of his soldiers. Colonel Brooks of the Fifty-third Pennsylvania Volunteers did nobly, in command of the old brigade of Gen. French. My own regiment—& in fact, the entire Brigade did nobly; worthy of a better General over them."[40]

Richardson's wound was extremely painful, and he lay in bed in great suffering. While at the Pry house, in a better environment than the makeshift field hospital, the doctors tried to remove the fragment of shell that was buried deep within Richardson's chest. His surgeon, Dr. J. H. Taylor, probed seven inches for the metal but was unable to reach it. His fear and medical opinion was that the fragment had passed into the cavity of the left lung, which must eventually produce his death. Two days after the battle, an entry on September 19 in the diary of Colonel Charles S. Wainwright, the II Corps artillery commander, may have confused the wounds of Richardson and Barlow in his diary entry: "our loss is too heavy, especially in the II Corps. General Richardson lies in the same house with Hooker; he was shot through the bowels and cannot possibly live. He seemed in great pain as I could hear his groans the whole time I was in the house."[41]

As word of the battle reached Washington, and Fannie Richardson was notified of the wounding of her husband, she traveled immediately to the Pry home, near Keedysville, along with her sister-in-law Marcella, to care for him. At first the news was not good. General McClellan sent the medical director of the Army of the Potomac, Dr. Letterman, and Dr. Horace, a member of his staff, to personally examine Richardson. Both doctors came to the conclusion that the wound was not survivable. Richardson himself felt the same way, asking the doctors, "What are my chances?" He was told "one in twenty," but soon afterward Richardson's aide, Major Norvell, was told his prospects were "one in four."[42]

Doctor J. H. Taylor, medical director of Richardson's 1st Division and probably the general's best friend, was much too occupied dealing with the large number of wounded in the hospitals under his charge to be able to care for Richardson in the manner in which he would like during the first several days.

When he was able to confer with the other doctors, a disagreement developed. Dr. Letterman insisted that Taylor should tell Richardson that "he could not live"; Dr. Taylor said "that he could not, did not think it so, and it would kill Israel if he did."[43] After the first week following the battle, caring for the critical cases within the 1st Division and receiving medical help from Washington allowed Dr. Taylor to become the primary physician for Richardson, and under his care, the general began to show signs of steady improvement.

The difference in diagnosis between the doctors revolved around whether the piece of shrapnel had penetrated into the left lung or not. Early on, Richardson suffered from an attack of pneumonia, which seemed to confirm the fact that his lung had been critically damaged and the case would be fatal. When he was able to fight off the pneumonia and show progress in his recovery, the experts began to think there was a chance for his survival.

Yet it seems that Richardson was never very optimistic for his own recovery. His wife, Fannie, in a letter to her sister-in-law Marcia, noted, "He has grown very thin, and is very weak yet. He said yesterday, 'What will father say to see me so broken down?' If he would only try and think that he was improving, I think he would get better much faster. He is very much depressed, not at all like himself, and inclined to look at the dark side, much more than is good for him."[44]

Although his condition seemed to stabilize, he was in no shape to conduct any kind of army business. The 1st Division's after-action report was completed by General Hancock. Major Norvell and Dr. Taylor made sure that only close friends were allowed to visit. One exception was the officers of his beloved Irish Brigade, who were allowed to pay their respects. Father William Corby described the visit with Richardson, who explained with pride, "I placed your brigade on the ground you occupied because it was necessary to hold it, and I knew that you would hold it against all odds, and once you were there, I had no further anxiety in regard to the position."[45]

The *Detroit Free Press* noted on September 26 that "a letter from Mrs. I. B. Richardson, dated September 23rd, states that the General is now considered out of danger." He was probably close to the best condition of his recovery when he received a visit from President Lincoln on October 4. Although Richardson was still in very serious condition, he was resting easily to the point where Fannie and Marcella were in the process of making arrangements to move Israel to Washington to continue his convalescence as soon as Dr. Taylor would allow it.

During the next several weeks, as Richardson remained in the Pry house, he continued to show the stamina that protected his health throughout his army career. His sister Marcella noted, "Israel improves slowly but surely. The Dr. says he has had continual drawbacks—only slight, but still they keep him weak—and in bed, he has not set up for a week. His pulse is good, sleeps most of the time, has a little more appetite, takes very little medicine. His wound is nearly well; gives him no pain or uneasiness now. He is very patient and easy to take care of, but is very nervous and trifles trouble him very much. Israel is very anxious to be at home, and wishes to see all of you."[46]

"He has good common sense, a rare commodity apparently"

There can be no doubt that Richardson's reputation as a fighting general was highly regarded in senior political circles and by the administration in Washington. Following the battle of Antietam, Lincoln's personal secretary, John Hay, as close as anyone to the private opinions of the President, wrote in his diary, "Richardson, one of the best division commanders in the army, received a mortal hurt."

As the Northern newspapers began to disseminate the first unconfirmed stories of the greatest battle of the war to date, Richardson found himself portrayed as one of the few worthy heroes in an army of lackluster leadership. "General Richardson was everywhere conspicuous during the action up to the time he received a gunshot wound to the left breast," reported the *New York Times* somewhat inaccurately three days after the battle. The following day, the *New York Herald* stated that "his wound is painful but not dangerous; it was sufficient however to deprive the general of the pleasure of commanding his men during the remainder of the action." His professional reputation was now firmly established on the national level.

President Lincoln arrived at the Antietam battlefield on October 1 and stayed in the area for four days. He toured the battlefield, witnessed unit reviews, and visited wounded soldiers in the many hospitals. However, the real purpose for his trip may have been to make a final determination as to the future of his commanding general. Time was spent privately with General McClellan in one last effort to convince him to move his army against General Lee. Lincoln's sense of frustration with the slowness of any pursuit was exampled by his comment to his friend, Ozias M. Hatch. The two men were standing on a hill overlooking the vast campgrounds of the Army of the Potomac spread out below them. Lincoln turned to Hatch and abruptly asked whether his friend knew what he was looking at. Of course, replied Hatch, it was the Army of the Potomac. "So it is called, but that is a mistake," said Lincoln. "It is only McClellan's bodyguard."[47]

On October 4 Lincoln made a special trip to see Richardson, still bedridden at the Pry house. The only witness of the president's visit was Captain Charles Stuart Draper, one of Richardson's aides, who was also bedridden in the same room, shot through both thighs. As the president spoke to Richardson, their dialogue must have touched on subjects of friends and family, the future of the nation, and opinions on strategy and personnel. The president's opinions as to how to deal with McClellan were a definite topic confirmed by Captain Draper. During their conversation, according to Draper, the president assured Richardson that if he lived, he would undoubtedly be selected as General McClellan's successor as commander of the Army of the Potomac.[48] If the discussion occurred as Draper suggested, perhaps the subject was broached by Lincoln to elicit Richardson's views before returning to Washington.

In what will never be known with certainty, the exchange between the frustrated president and his "fighting general," now seriously wounded while giving his all to the cause, was a bitter symbol of Lincoln's current command problems. Was this just Lincoln's polite effort to comfort the dying Richardson, or did the suggestion have merit, if Richardson could have recovered? The hypothetical move would have been cheered by the Radicals, and for whatever faults Richardson had with his rough personality, he could be counted on to act as a driver on the field of battle. In many respects, his character was much like that of Ulysses S. Grant, who would come into the commanding general position one year later. Clearly, Richardson didn't have the foresight of Robert E. Lee, but, like Grant, he probably would continue moving forward tenaciously even if he were checked in his initial direction.

The *New York Herald*, a staunch Democratic paper declared, "Richardson was no holiday soldier, and had no doubt that war is earnest business." Announcing his death, the November 6 edition of the *New York Times*, a mainstream Republican paper, remarked that there had been "few battles where 'Fighting Dick' did not lead in the van." These were the exact characteristics that Lincoln was seeking.

The performance of Richardson at Antietam could not be faulted. He pushed his division harder and achieved more than any other Federal general that day. His reputation reached its zenith, and had he survived, the reward of a corps command was guaranteed. The fact that Lincoln gave clear signals that he was dissatisfied with McClellan's performance after the battle, yet waited almost six weeks, until the death of Richardson, before offering the job to Burnside the very next day is intriguing.

When Lincoln returned to Washington, the Radicals could sense a hardening of the president's attitude toward McClellan. Senator Sumner optimistically predicted that Lincoln was about to throw out his "all-parties" policy and embrace the radical platform. Colonel James A. Garfield, a future president himself, came to the same conclusion, writing to a friend that Lincoln, "having failed to buy up the Democrats by kindness, concluded he had better not drive away his friends by neglect." Senator James W. Grimes thought it was imperative to get a Republican general at the head of the loyal Western army. This general could then march his troops against McClellan if the latter attempted to make himself dictator! This perceived attitude within the political circles in Washington was just another consideration for the appointment of a commanding general who had the right political backing. Pope had been brought east for the same reasons and, in Lincoln's opinion, had done well until McClellan's cronies bushwhacked him. Why not follow the same strategy, this time using a leader familiar to the Army of the Potomac, in the likes of Israel Richardson?

By the end of October, still at the Pry house, Richardson's condition was starting to deteriorate. An infection to the wound had set in, and Dr. Taylor became very concerned. The doctor noted, "His nervous system is much shocked. So much so that he makes no effort to rally, and has himself given up all hopes for recovery." Soon it became clear that the infection would be fatal, as Richardson gradually weakened. Fannie and Marcella doted on him, staying at his bedside while he was awake. Finally, on the evening of November 3, at half past seven, Major General Israel Bush Richardson succumbed to his wound and died.

One explanation for the timing of McClellan's removal was the congressional elections in the North, on November 4. Making a change in command immediately afterward kept any political fallout from the decision to a minimum. But the fact is that the congressional campaign of 1862 revolved around many issues: dissatisfaction with the administration because of repeated military failures, the looming possibility of conscription, and the resentment of the conservatives at Lincoln's threat to proclaim emancipation. The Republicans went into the campaign disunited and listless, split by the bitter fight between their two factions, the radicals and conservatives. Lincoln's emancipation edict had repelled the conservatives without being drastic enough to draw the radicals to him.[49] Politically, Lincoln probably would have been in better shape by uniting his own party with the removal of McClellan, even at the risk of a Democratic Party backlash, before the elections.

Lincoln's dilemma was who would be the replacement? No clear front-runner had emerged from the scores of Federal generals that both politicians and military leaders could respect. Experienced corps commanders included Burnside—asked before, said he wasn't capable, didn't want it; Hooker—wanted it too badly; Sumner—too old and rigid; and Porter and Franklin—tainted by association with McClellan.

Possible division commanders who could spur aggressive life into the Army of the Potomac were Reynolds—captured asleep on the Peninsula, just exchanged and recently returned to division command; Meade—although having no prewar troop experience, was a steady fighter, wounded on the Peninsula, but was a Democrat and a political enemy of Zachariah Chandler; Sedgwick—another steady fighter, wounded at Antietam and also a Democrat; and finally, Israel Richardson—who had the reputation as the most aggressive fighter in the army, with the possible exception of Kearny, who was dead now; and with all the right political connections. Although any of these division command-ers seemed a sure bet to inject a greater sense of urgency in the Army of the Potomac, none of them, as yet, had been given any opportunity to show what initiative they possessed. In an army where seniority was jealously guarded, the field of talented candidates was small.

Would Richardson's appointment have been possible given the politically charged command structure of the Army of the Potomac? After the Peninsula campaign, a new group of senior leaders started to appear. Gone were the seniority-conscious generals like Heintzelman and Keyes. Proven warriors such as Richardson and Hancock were rising in stature. Richardson's major general's commission put him on equal footing with the majority of senior leaders now serving in the army. Although most of the rank and file in the Army of the Potomac still preferred McClellan, any officer linked closely to him was politically unacceptable to Lincoln and the Republicans as a replace-ment. In fact, Richardson's growing reputation as a successful fighter who looked after the welfare of his men, and his connections to the radical wing of Republicans, made him a viable candidate in an army that overwhelmingly admired McClellan's leadership over that of Lincoln himself.

Lincoln made his own decision privately and suddenly, although it seemed that the fate of McClellan had already been decided when the two men last visited face to face. The tensions between the two escalated when McClellan dragged his feet in continuing the Federal advance in the weeks following An-tietam. One telegram sent to the White House stated the advance could not take place as ordered because of the terrible condition of the army's horses. Lincoln responded in a scathing note, "I have just read your dispatch about sore-tongued and fatigued horses. Will you pardon me for asking what the horses of your army have done since the battle of Antietam that fatigues anything?" In what seemed to be a final warning, Lincoln wrote a long letter to McClellan, trying to prod him to advance. He concluded with an inquiry, "Are you not over-cautious, when you assume that you cannot do what the enemy is constantly doing?"[50]

Would it not be too far-fetched to believe that Lincoln was playing his cards close to his chest in his decision about McClellan's replacement in the hope that Richardson might recover from his wound and return to active service? His odds at recovery had been estimated at between five and twenty percent, as given by his doctors, so at least there was a somewhat hopeful chance for his survival. When Lincoln met with him on October 4, Richardson appeared to be gaining strength and tentative plans were being made by Fannie for him to travel to Washington for further recovery. Neither Halleck nor Stanton, of the President's inner circle, offer any insight on the selection of McClellan's replacement. It appears that the orders to Burnside to accept command of the army, without any preliminary probing to find out whether he was interested in the job, seem as if this selection was a desperate choice of last resort.

If Burnside declined the job, it would be offered to Joe Hooker. There was not a more political general serving in the Army of the Potomac. He had done a good job as a brigade and division commander on the Peninsula, and he had led a corps for only a short while before being wounded at Antietam. Hooker made use of his convalescent leave in Washington by lobbying Vice President Hamlin for the job. General Halleck, who had served with Hooker in their California days, knew firsthand of his flawed character and convinced Lincoln that he should not be the president's first choice. Burnside and Hooker didn't care for each other either, and it was the threat of Hooker getting the job that made Burnside accept it.

"The qualities that made up the man, adorned the soldier, they were one and inseparable; in that, his greatness consisted"

General Sumner was deeply saddened at the news of Richardson's death. Together, they had their most glorious days in the army at Cerro Gordo, and both acquired a brevet and their army nicknames. "Old Bull" Sumner had been Richardson's immediate commander for half a year and had never been disappointed with his service as commander of the 1st Division. Sumner stated in the *New York Times* article announcing his death to the nation that "Richardson never appeared well out of battle, but that in one he was magnificent."

The newspapers in Washington, New York, Detroit, and Chicago reported his death and ran eulogies to his service to the nation. His body, accompanied by his family, was transported home to Pontiac for burial. Senator Chandler met the family in Detroit, where a memorial service was conducted at the Fort Street Presbyterian Church. Reverend Eldridge, who had married the Richardsons only a year previously, escorted the family to Pontiac the next day and presided over the services on November 11, 1862. The newspaper text of the funeral sermon makes it clear that even with his death, the politics of the Radical Republican movement in Michigan were furthered by the address given to the hundreds of mourners at the ceremony:

"He needed no introduction to the Old Warrior (Scott) at Washington. When the Army was divided and Richmond was to be approached by way of the Peninsula, General Richardson, against some objections from high, but suspicious sources, was given command of a Division, and at last for his splendid conduct at Fair Oaks, and for his prudence and skill during the Seven Days change of base, he was promoted to Major General.

"And here let me say that there are many who have had faith in this man, and looked to him from the first of our troubles. We have watched him with anxiety from point to point, been delighted and cheered to behold him rising steadily among the foremost in command and have always felt that with his star waxing in the ascendant, the fortunes of the country could suffer no serious discomfiture. But at Antietam he fell, 'Playing the Colonel,' for the chief, in his own words to those who were bringing him to the rear, while steadying the men in the front ranks who were showing signs of wavering under the fierce artillery fire, he received the wounds from a shell bursting over him as it passed, and from which he never recovered. He is dead and gone, and we have lost him when we could ill afford to.

"When, with eagle eye, clarion voice and iron determination, he raged along the lines, like a lion; it was a spectacle never to be forgotten. But at the next turn, no man more calm and clear in council of war or full of expedient device and resource—thoughtful, wise and prudent as he was brave. Then he was found at the court-martial, while eminently square-edged, ever just and fair, magnanimous even in his construction of conduct and motive, careful of the rights and reputations of his brother officers.

"He was also though rigid in the essentials of discipline, kind and considerate toward his men, seldom forgetful of their necessity and hardships, never exposing them to needless dangers and trials so that they came to march and fight under him with the strong assurance not only he could carry them through, but that he would never expose them where it was madness to go, or he was not ready to lead the way. All true patriots in the Army from General Scott to the smallest drummer boy, believed in our own Richardson, and they who knew him the longest and best, the most implicitly."[51]

The body of Richardson lay in state at the courthouse in Pontiac and was visited by hundreds of people. The body was in a remarkable state of preservation, having been embalmed; "the features were as natural as life, though he looked somewhat worn down, owing to the loss of blood and the pain to which he was subjected to [sic] prior to death." At eleven o'clock, the services began within the courthouse, which was full to capacity, while hundreds of people remained outside and accompanied the casket in a procession to the final funeral ceremony and burial at Oak Hill Cemetery.

From the moment he was laid to rest, the memory of Richardson's contributions to his country began to slowly fade. He was quietly forgotten as a new generation of leaders stepped forward to replace his peers, who fell one after another as the war continued. General Sumner instilled a warrior ideal in his subordinates, who tried to follow his professional conduct under fire. It was no accident that both his division commanders, Richardson and Sedgwick, went down with wounds, while leading their commands from the front, and died later.

One of the reasons for the lack of historical accounts of Israel Richardson after the war might have been the fact that very few of his intimate peers survived the conflict themselves. Sumner lasted only five months longer, dying at the home of his son-in-law in Syracuse, New York. Sedgwick, his contemporary division commander, would live only a year and a half longer, falling victim to a sharpshooter at Spotsylvania while inspecting his lines. Warned of his exposed position, Sedgwick answered with the last words he would speak, "They couldn't hit an elephant at this distan—."

The 1st Division suffered heavy casualties in the ill-conceived assault ordered by Burnside at Fredericksburg a month after Richardson's death. The everlasting glory of the Irish Brigade charge was bought at a terrible cost, and its colorful commander, Thomas F. Meagher, would soon resign. When Hancock was promoted to II Corps commander, the 1st Division fell to the command of General Caldwell, and the finest of its officers and men were killed as the division was decimated in the wheat field at Gettysburg.

The unit that Richardson and his peers had built into what could well be argued the best and most experienced division within the Army of the Potomac finished July 2, 1863, by relieving the hard-pressed III Corps and narrowly stopping the Confederate advance, but it would never recover from the losses suffered that day. The division would continue to serve in the toughest battles with the Army of the Potomac in the future, but it would only be a shell of the division it had once been.

At Gettysburg Colonel Cross, commanding the 1st Brigade, would be mortally wounded while leading an attack and would die the next day. He recalled the service under his old commander with pride: "You know, 'Old Richardson,' as we called him, styled us the 'Fire Proofs,' and the boys have earned the title."[52] His final words were, "I think the boys will miss me." Before the Irish Brigade went into action, Colonel Patrick Kelly let Father William Corby gather the men together to lead them in prayer. Kelly would be killed at the battle of Petersburg the following year. Brigadier General Samuel K. Zook was also mortally wounded, shot off his horse while leading the 3rd Brigade. Colonel John R. Brooke was severely wounded but remained in the field, commanding the 4th Brigade, and for a portion of the day commanded the division, as well, when General Caldwell disappeared from the action again.

By the end of the war, the 1st Division, II Corps, Army of the Potomac, had the distinction of losing more men killed in action than any other Federal division. When McClellan replaced the wounded Richardson with Hancock on September 17, 1862, the division began a new chapter in its glorious history. In time, Hancock would make his mark as one of the finest division commanders in the Army of the Potomac, but in the eyes of the men of the 1st Division, he had a very large pair of boots to fill in replacing Richardson. Sergeant Seth G. Evans of the 57th New York summed up the rank-and-file opinion in a letter home: "General Richardson is dead I know, but it is his Div. yet until it is given to some one else. We are proud of his name; he was a brave man and one we shall always remember. I felt as if my best friend was gone when we got word that he was dead."[53]

While the 1st Division was fortunate in the selection of a talented leader such as Hancock to replace Richardson, no changes in the division's operating procedures were necessary. The unit was blessed with an abundance of talented subordinate leaders, and the staff was run efficiently. Hancock was cut of the same aggressive mold as Richardson, except that he might have been a little more refined. From the time of its first engagement at Fair Oaks until its last at Appomattox, the division fought with the same intensity that its first commander, Israel "Fighting Dick" Richardson, spurred into the organization from the beginning. Just as Richardson had been taught how to lead men as a young lieutenant in the Mexican War, a new generation of officers learned their skills from the example set by their beloved division commander. New commanders emerged and tactics changed as the war continued, but the example of fighting spirit set for the young leaders under Richardson lived on for the duration of the war.

The final consideration in this study of Israel Richardson should be a description of his personal traits. The old adage that "you can't fool the troops" is very appropriate. No commander can be successful without surviving the scrutiny of his soldiers who are entrusting their lives to him. They can tell very early whether a leader truly cares about them or is merely going through the motions. Richardson was a genuine leader of men because his past experiences as a company grade officer never left him as he attained higher responsibilities. He lived his personal life that way also.

The *Philadelphia Press* ran a eulogy of Richardson, which was written by his intimate friend and physician, Dr. J. H. Taylor. Many examples related in this text corroborate Taylor's description of Richardson's character and act as a final illustration that Richardson's success on the field of battle was brought about by the lack of distinction between the human qualities of the man and those of the soldier.

"Among the many eulogies to the memory of the late Maj. Gen. Richardson, few, if any, have paid tribute to his sterling qualities as a man. The world acknowledges the hero and history will do honor to his fame; but only those who knew him as a man, and had learned to love him, can appreciate his noble character.

"He possessed the kindest heart and the most unselfish nature; ever careful and considerate where others were concerned, yet as guileless as a child. His intellect was clear, vigorous and comprehensive, and his perceptions so intuitive as almost to appear prophetic.

"Possessing a singleness of purpose in the conscientious of every duty, he despised sophistry and duplicity in all their forms, and went straight to his work with a firm and honest heart. He was earnest in all he undertook, and integrity was so strongly marked in every act, that faith in the man was irresistible. Impartial and just in his conclusions, lenient in his judgments, firm in the right, and unswerving in his duty, he impressed his manhood upon you. The most humble could approach him, sure of an attentive hearing and a sincere interest in their wants; and the affectionate respect with which he was regarded by every soldier in his division is an evidence of his considerate care for their welfare.

"They all felt and appreciated the true nobility and grandeur of his character. Despising all vain pretensions, pomp and show, he recognized greatness only by its worth. With manly independence of thought and action, he was urbane and deferential to honest difference of opinion, but fearless in the expression of his own. The innate kindness of his heart made him tolerant and charitable. He looked at the world through his own unselfish nature, trusted to that integrity in others, which was but a counterpart of himself.

"Life to him was earnest, and he felt as though it must be so to all; thus his trust and confidence in human nature. The qualities that made up the man adorned the soldier, they were one and inseparable; in that, his greatness consisted. He carried his manhood ever with him, and lived out the honest promptings of his heart. No one could be in daily intercourse with him and not feel his worth. Frank, cordial and genial, and unpretending; where he trusted, he confided.

"A close observer of men and events, a concise reasoner, possessed of a wonderful memory, and an analytical mind, his conclusions were carefully and accurately drawn. In council, as in the field, he was ever the same fearless, independent man, conscious of the right, and steadfast in its maintenance. His character was marked by strong contrasts, but the same generous impulses prompted every act, whether by the family hearth or on the tented field. It is in accordance with perfect manhood that it should be so.

"At home, the dutiful son, the devoted husband, and affectionate brother, and kind friend; thoughtful and ever mindful of those he loved, guarding them with jealous care and tender solicitude. But as he was kind and gentle in retirement, so was he stern and invincible in war; and, as he lived for others, so did he die."[54]

Notes

Bibliography

Index

Notes

1. Novice

1. David Humphreys, *An Essay on the Life of Major General Israel Putnam* (Boston: Samuel Avery, 1818), 57.

2. Application file of Israel B. Richardson, letter dated Mar. 19, 1832, U.S. Military Academy Archives.

3. Ibid.

4. IBR to Susan Richardson, Feb. 11, 1836, D. Duffy Lane Collection, in the possession of Thomas Lane, Summerville, S.C.

5. IBR to Susan Richardson, Feb. 11, 1836, Lane Collection.

6. IBR to Israel P. Richardson, July 26, 1838, Lane Collection.

7. IBR to Susan Richardson, Oct. 6, 1838, Lane Collection.

8. IBR to Susan Richardson, Dec. 31, 1837, Lane Collection.

9. Demerit Roster, entry dated July 28, 1838, U.S. Military Academy Archives.

10. IBR to Susan Richardson, Feb. 2, 1837, Lane Collection.

11. IBR to Susanna H. Richardson, Dec. 20, 1839, Lane Collection.

12. IBR to Israel P. Richardson, July 29, 1840, Lane Collection.

13. IBR to Marcia Richardson, Apr. 4, 1840, Lane Collection.

14. IBR to sister, Apr. 4, 1841, Lane Collection.

15. IBR to Marcia Richardson, Nov. 4, 1841, Lane Collection.

16. IBR, "Twelve Years Service in the U.S. Army" (unpublished manuscript), Lane Collection, 14–15.

17. Ibid., 23.

18. IBR to Marcella Richardson, Dec. 4, 1841, Lane Collection.

19. IBR, "Twelve Years Service in the U.S. Army," Lane Collection, 24.

20. Ibid., 16.

21. IBR to Marcella Richardson, Dec 4, 1841, Lane Collection.

22. Washington, D.C., *National Tribune*, June 15, 1899, 3.

23. IBR to Marcia Richardson, Aug. 24, 1842, Lane Collection.

24. IBR, "Twelve Years Service in the U.S. Army," Lane Collection, 20.

25. Ethan A. Hitchcock, *Fifty Years in Camp and Field*, ed. W. A. Croffut (New York: Putnam, 1909), 167.

26. IBR, "Twelve Years Service in the U. S. Army," Lane Collection, 28.

27. IBR to Israel P. Richardson, Aug. 11, 1842, Lane Collection.

28. Ethan A. Hitchcock, *Fifty Years in Camp and Field*, ed. W. A. Croffut (New York: Putnam, 1909), 172.

29. IBR to Israel P. Richardson, Apr. 4, 1843, Lane Collection.

30. Ethan A. Hitchcock, *Fifty Years in Camp and Field*, ed. W. A. Croffut (New York: Putnam, 1909), 181.

31. Richard S. Ewell, *The Making of a Soldier: Letters of General R. S. Ewell*, ed. P. G. Hamlin (Richmond, Va., 1935), 52.

32. IBR, "Twelve Years Service in the U. S. Army," Lane Collection, 36.

33. Ibid., 37.

34. IBR to Susan Richardson, June 7, 1845, Lane Collection.

35. IBR to Susanna H. Richardson, July 17, 1845, Lane Collection.

36. Ulysses Simpson Grant, *Personal Memoirs of U. S. Grant* (New York: Webster, 1894), 41.

37. IBR to Israel P. Richardson, July 29, 1845, Lane Collection.

38. William Seaton Henry, *Campaign Sketches of the War with Mexico* (New York: Harper, 1847; New York: Arno, 1973), 43. Citations are to the Arno edition.

39. IBR, "Twelve Years Service in the U. S. Army," Lane Collection, 41.

40. Douglas S. Freeman, *Lee's Lieutenants*, vol. 1 (New York: Scribner, 1944), 347.

41. Hitchcock, *Fifty Years in Camp and Field*, 215.

42. Abner Doubleday, *My Life in the Old Army*, ed. Joseph E. Chance (Fort Worth: Texas Christian University Press, 1998), 49.

43. IBR to Israel P. Richardson, Dec. 19, 1845, Lane Collection.

44. IBR to family, Feb. 7, 1846, Lane Collection.

45. Letter from Robert Hazlitt, Mar. 20, 1846. Robert Hazlitt file, U.S. Military Academy Archives.

46. IBR to Israel P. Richardson, Apr. 6, 1846, Lane Collection.

47. IBR, "Twelve Years Service in the U. S. Army," Lane Collection, 59.

48. Napoleon J. T. Dana, *Monterrey Is Ours! The Mexican War Letters of Lieutenant Dana, 1845–1847*, ed. Robert H. Ferrell (Lexington: University Press of Kentucky, 1990), 5.

49. IBR, "Twelve Years Service in the U. S. Army," Lane Collection, 64.

50. IBR to Israel P. Richardson, May 20, 1846, Lane Collection.

51. IBR to Israel P. Richardson, May 18, 1846, Lane Collection.

52. IBR, "Twelve Years Service in the U. S. Army," Lane Collection, 77.

53. IBR to Israel P. Richardson, May 10, 1846, Lane Collection.

54. U. S. Grant, *The Papers of Ulysses S. Grant*, vol. 1, ed. John Y. Simon (Carbondale: Southern Illinois University Press, 1967), 96.

55. Henry, *Campaign Sketches of the War with Mexico*, 158.

56. IBR to Israel P. Richardson, May 11, 1846, Lane Collection.

57. George Meade, *The Life and Letters of George Gordon Meade, Major General, United States Army*, vol. 1 (New York: Scribner, 1913), 91.

58. IBR to Israel P. Richardson, Aug. 24, 1846, Lane Collection.

59. Henry, *Campaign Sketches of the War with Mexico*, 96.

60. IBR to Israel P. Richardson, May 18, 1846, Lane Collection.

61. Robert Hazlitt to his sister, Sept. 16, 1846, Robert Hazlitt file, U.S. Military Academy Archives.

62. IBR to Israel P. Richardson, Aug. 24, 1846, Lane Collection.

2. Apprenticeship

1. John R. Kenly, *Memoirs of a Maryland Volunteer* (Philadelphia: Lippincott, 1873), 119.

2. Justin H. Smith, *War with Mexico*, vol. 1 (New York: Macmillan, 1919), 249–50.

3. IBR to Israel P. Richardson, Oct. 7, 1846, D. Duffy Lane Collection, in the possession of Thomas Lane, Summerville, S.C.

4. William F. Gotezmann, ed., "Our First Foreign War: Letters of Barna Upton, 3rd U.S. Infantry," *American Heritage* 17 (1966): 94.

5. William Seaton Henry, *Campaign Sketches of the War with Mexico* (New York: Harper, 1847; New York: Arno, 1973), 194. Citations are to the Arno edition.

6. Henry, *Campaign Sketches of the War with Mexico*, 194–95.

7. Ulysses Simpson Grant, *Personal Memoirs of U. S. Grant* (New York: Webster, 1894), 68.

8. John S. D. Eisenhower, *So Far from God: The U. S. War with Mexico 1846–1848*. New York: Doubleday, 1989, 138.

9. IBR to Israel P. Richardson, Oct. 7, 1846, Lane Collection.

10. Gotezmann, *Our First Foreign War*, 95.

11. William Preston Johnston, *The Life of General Albert Sidney Johnston* (New York: Appleton, 1878), 139.

12. Henry, *Campaign Sketches of the War with Mexico*, 244.

13. IBR to Israel P. Richardson, Oct. 7, 1846, Lane Collection.

14. Grant, *Personal Memoirs*, 81.

15. IBR to Israel P. Richardson, Oct. 7, 1846, Lane Collection.

16. IBR, "Twelve Years Service in the U.S. Army," Lane Collection, 162.

17. Henry, *Campaign Sketches of the War with Mexico*, 204.

18. IBR to Israel P. Richardson, Sept. 23, 1846, Lane Collection.

19. Eisenhower, *So Far from God*, 141.

20. IBR, "Twelve Years Service in the U.S. Army," Lane Collection, 174.

21. Ibid., 208.

22. Henry, *Campaign Sketches of the War with Mexico*, 237.

23. *Philadelphia Press*, Eulogy of Israel Richardson by Dr. J. H. Taylor, Nov. 4, 1862.

24. IBR, "Twelve Years Service in the U. S. Army," Lane Collection, 211.

25. Hitchcock, *Fifty Years in Camp and Field*, 124.

26. Grant, *Personal Memoirs*, 114.

27. Louis S. Craig, from Virginia, was a second lieutenant of the 2nd Dragoons in 1837 but transferred to the 3rd Infantry the following year. He became a first lieutenant in 1840, obtained a captaincy in June 1846, and won a brevet majority Sept. 23, the same year, for gallant and meritorious service in several conflicts at Monterrey. He was brevetted to lieutenant colonel for further gallantry in the battles of Contreras and Churubusco on Aug. 20, 1847. He was appointed officer in charge of the military escort for the boundary survey between the United States and Mexico in August 1850. His senseless murder by deserters in the desert on June 6, 1852, ended a long and honorable career.

28. IBR to Israel P. Richardson, Feb. 16, 1847, Lane Collection.

29. IBR to Israel P. Richardson, Mar. 24, 1847, Lane Collection.

30. K. Jack Bauer, *The Mexican War, 1846–1848* (New York: Macmillan, 1974), 252.

31. IBR, "Twelve Years in the U. S. Army," Lane Collection, 243.

32. Ibid., 299.

33. George Ballantine, *An English Soldier in the U.S. Army* (New York: Stringer and Townsend, 1853; Townsend, 1860), 163. Citations are to the 1860 edition.

34. William W. Averill, *Ten Years in the Saddle*, ed. Edward K. Eckert and Nicholas J. Amato (San Rafael, Calif.: Presidio, 1978), 126.

35. Douglas S. Freeman, *Lee* (New York: Macmillan, 1991), 61.

36. IBR, "Twelve Years in the U.S. Army," Lane Collection, 306–7.

37. Ballantine, *An English Soldier in the U.S. Army*, 180–82.

38. IBR, "Twelve Years in the U.S. Army," Lane Collection, 308–9.

39. IBR to Israel P. Richardson, Apr. 20, 1847, Lane Collection.

40. T. F. Rodenbough, *From Everglade to Canon: A History of the 2nd Dragoons* (New York: Van Nostrand, 1875), 141.

41. Washington, DC, *National Tribune*, Apr. 18, 1901, 1.

42. IBR to Israel P. Richardson, Apr. 20, 1847, Lane Collection.

43. IBR, "Twelve Years in the U.S. Army," Lane Collection, 311–12.

44. Gotezmann, *Our First Foreign War*, 98.

45. IBR to Israel P. Richardson, Apr. 20, 1847, Lane Collection.

46. U.S. Congress, Executive Document No. 1, 30th Cong., 2d sess., Captain E. B. Alexander, Third Infantry Regiment, After-action Report, Jalapa, Mexico. Apr. 20, 1847, 293–94.

47. IBR to Israel P. Richardson, Apr. 20, 1847, Lane Collection.

48. Grant, *Personal Memoirs*, 129.

49. Steven W. Sears, *George B. McClellan: The Young Napoleon* (New York: Ticknor & Fields, 1988), 22.

50. U.S. Congress, Executive Document No. 1, 30th Cong., 2d sess., Captain L. S. Craig, 3rd U.S. Infantry, After-action report, San Angel, Mexico, Aug. 27, 1847, 83–84.

51. IBR to Israel P. Richardson, no date or location, Lane Collection.

52. Hitchcock, *Fifty Years in Camp and Field*, 298.

53. IBR to Israel P. Richardson, Oct. 25, 1847, Lane Collection.

54. Ibid. This war trophy was in the possession of Marcia Richardson, who mentioned it in a newspaper story in the *Pontiac Press* in 1915.

55. IBR to Israel P. Richardson, Jan. 12, 1848, Lane Collection.

56. There does not seem to be a primary source for the quote. The 3rd Infantry Regiment was one of the first units to march into the main plaza of Mexico City, and the fact that it was the oldest infantry regiment in the army was known, so the story is plausible. In the early 1920s, Colonel A. W. Bjornstad, who decided on the design and use of the "cockade" and the "buff strap" formalized the various 3rd Infantry traditions and probably declared the Scott story to be true. The story appears in the 1922 Organization Day program.

57. IBR to Israel P. Richardson, Apr. 7, 1848, Lane Collection.

3. Adversity

1. IBR to Marcia Richardson, Sept. 8, 1848, D. Duffy Lane Collection, in the possession of Thomas Lane, Summerville, S.C.

2. IBR to Israel P. Richardson, Aug. 1, 1849, Lane Collection.

3. M. H. Thomlinson, *The Garrison at Fort Bliss, 1849–1916* (El Paso: Hertzog and Resler, 1945), 4.

4. Marcella Richardson journal entry, May 25, 1851, Lane Collection.

5. Paul Teetor, *A Matter of Hours* (Rutherford, N.J.: Farleigh Dickinson University Press, 1982), 17.

6. William W. Averill, *Ten Years in the Saddle*, ed. Edward K. Eckert and Nicholas J. Amato (San Rafael, Calif.: Presidio, 1978), 193–94.

7. Henry Harrison Walker was born in Sussex County, Virginia, on Oct. 15, 1832, and was appointed to West Point in 1849. After serving in New Mexico with Richardson,

he was stationed in Kansas and California. He resigned his commission on May 3, 1861, and returned to his native state, where he received a commission of lieutenant colonel in the 40th Virginia Infantry Regiment. During the Seven Days' Battles, he distinguished himself in his first action at Mechanicsville. The next day, while commanding his regiment in the center of the Confederate assault at Gaines Mill, he was wounded twice. Later, as a brigadier general, commanding a brigade in Heth's division, his foot was shattered in the fighting at the Po River on May 10, 1864, in the Spotsylvania Campaign. His foot was amputated the next day, and his career on the battlefields came to an end. He was assigned to administrative commands until the end of the war.

8. National Archives, Record Group 393, Letters Received, M1102, R6, Craig to Scott, Sept. 4, 1851.

9. National Archives, Record Group 94: Adjutant General's Office, Letters Received, File 138-S (AGO), 1852. Richardson's Report, Feb. 8, 1852.

10. Jerry D. Thompson, ed., "With the Third Infantry in New Mexico, 1851–1853: The Lost Diary of Private Sylvester W. Matson," *Journal of Arizona History*, Winter 1990, 361–62.

11. National Archives, Record Group 94: Adjutant General's Office, Letters Received, File 138-S (AGO), 1852, Richardson's Report, Feb. 8, 1852.

12. Thompson, "With the Third Infantry in New Mexico, 1851–1853," 364–65.

13. National Archives, Record Group 94: Adjutant General's Office, Letters Received, File 138-S (AGO), 1852, Richardson's Report, Feb. 8, 1852.

14. IBR to Marcella Richardson, Feb. 11, 1852, Lane Collection.

15. National Archives, Record Group 94: Adjutant General's Office, Letters Received, File 138-S (AGO), 1852, Sumner's Report, Apr. 1, 1852.

16. National Archives, Record Group 393: Records of U. S. Army Continental Commands, Part 1, Entry 5568, Letters Sent, Fort Webster, N.M., Mar. 24, 1852.

17. IBR to Marcella Richardson, Mar. 7, 1854, Lane Collection.

18. Ibid., 86.

19. Thomas T. Fauntleroy (1795–1883) was commissioned a lieutenant during the War of 1812 and served in the Mexican War and in Indian fighting before resigning in 1861 as colonel of the 1st U.S. Dragoons. He offered his services to the Confederacy but was not accepted, and he retired from active duty.

20. IBR to Marcella Richardson, July 5, 1855, Lane Collection.

21. IBR to Marcella Richardson, July 15, 1855, Lane Collection.

22. IBR to Israel P. and Susanna H. Richardson, Aug. 7, 1855, Lane Collection.

23. National Archives, Record Group 98: Dept. of New Mexico Orders, vol. 9, 390–91.

24. Chris Emmett, *Fort Union and the Winning of the Southwest* (Norman: University of Oklahoma Press, 1965), 192–93.

25. National Archives, Record Group 94, Records of the Adjutant General's Office, Letters Received, File R-400 (1855).

26. Ibid.

27. Ibid.

4. Tutor

1. Robert Garth Scott, ed., *Forgotten Valor* (Kent, Ohio: Kent State University Press, 1999), 250.

2. Jonathan Robertson, comp., *Michigan in the War* (Lansing, Mich.: W. S. George, 1882), 203–4.

3. IBR to Governor Levi Underwood, 18 May 1861, D. Duffy Lane Collection, in the possession of Thomas Lane, Summerville, S.C.

4. Howard Coffin, *Full Duty: Vermonters in the Civil War* (Woodstock, Vt.: Country-man, 1993), 59. George J. Stannard's distinguished combat career included capture and exchange at Harpers Ferry in 1862 and severe wounding in action at Gettysburg in 1863, at Cold Harbor, and again two weeks later at Petersburg. Finally, a fourth wound cost him his right arm in the capture of Fort Harrison on September 29, 1864. He ended the war as a brevet Major General, U.S. Volunteers.

5. Ibid., 15.

6. Washington, D.C., *National Tribune*, July 7, 1887, 1.

7. Stephen W. Sears, *For Country, Cause and Leader* (New York: Ticknor & Fields, 1993), 143.

8. Ibid., 13.

9. George G. Meade, *The Life and Letters of George Gordon Meade, Major General, United States Army* (New York: Scribner, 1913), 214, 248.

10. Robert W. Hodge, ed., *The Civil War Letters of Perry Mayo* (East Lansing: Michigan State University, 1967), 17.

11. Washington, D.C., *National Tribune*, Jan. 4, 1906, 3.

12. Harold Petzold, *Memoirs of the Second Michigan* (Ann Arbor: University of Michigan, Bentley Historical Library, 1897), 7.

13. IBR to family, June 25, 1861, Lane Collection.

14. *Appleton's Cyclopedia*, "Israel B. Richardson" entry.

15. Petzold, *Memoirs of the Second Michigan*, 8.

16. Hodge, *The Civil War Letters of Perry Mayo*, 21.

17. Sears, *For Country, Cause and Leader*, 29.

18. Charles B. Haydon Diary, Michigan Historical Collection, University of Michigan, Ann Arbor, June 19, 1861.

19. Henry F. Lyster, *Recollections of the Bull Run Campaign* (Detroit: Wm. S. Ostler, 1888), 115. McCreery entered service May 25, 1861, with the Flint Union Greys, which became Company F, 2nd Michigan Infantry. Appointed sergeant at the time of enlistment, McCreery was soon promoted to captain, and on November 20, 1862, he was transferred to the 21st Michigan Infantry with the rank of lieutenant colonel. He became colonel of the regiment February 3, 1863.

At the Battle of Chickamauga, the 21st Michigan was part of Lytle's Brigade. Mc-Creery was wounded by a bullet in his leg and another in his arm when he saw his brigade commander, Brigadier General William H. Lytle, fall. With the help of three other men, McCreery picked up General Lytle's body and started with it to the rear. They had not gone far when a Confederate shell exploded nearby. A fragment of the shell slammed into McCreery's back, and he blacked out. When he awoke he found himself a prisoner. Six months later he tunneled out of Libby Prison and escaped with fifty other officers. His injuries forced him to resign September 14, 1864.

20. IBR to Israel P. and Susanna H. Richardson, July 15, 1861, Lane Collection.

21. Lyster, *Recollections of the Bull Run Campaign*, 114.

22. Sears, *For Country Cause and Leader*, 32.

23. Washington, D.C., *National Tribune*, May 16, 1907, 3.

24. Charles C. Perkins Diary, July 17, 1861, 39, in the possession of Fredrick Clark, Marblehead, Mass.

25. Jerome J. Robbins Diary, Michigan Historical Collection, University of Michigan, Ann Arbor, July 17, 1861.

26. Sears, *For Country, Cause and Leader*, 29.

27. John T. Setright Papers, Michigan Historical Collection, University of Michigan, Ann Arbor, July 28, 1862.

28. William C. Davis, *Battle at Bull Run* (Baton Rouge: Louisiana State University Press, 1977), 114.

29. Washington, D.C., *National Tribune*, June 26, 1884, 5.

30. Ibid., Jan. 4, 1906, 3.

31. *Report of the Joint Committee on the Conduct of the War*. Richardson testimony, 37th Congress, Third session (Washington, D.C.: Government Printing Office, 1863), 20.

32. Edward Porter Alexander, *Fighting for the Confederacy: The Personal Recollections of General E. P. Alexander*, ed. Gary W. Gallagher (Chapel Hill: University of North Carolina Press, 1989), 46. General James Longstreet, in his book *From Manassas to Appomattox* (Philadelphia: Lippincott, 1896; New York: Mallard, 1991), p. 38, states that the first shots fired in the engagement at Blackburn's Ford were aimed at the batteries emplaced close to Bull Run. Porter's account is more convincing because of his detailed description of the unfolding events.

33. Davis, *Battle at Bull Run*, 130.

34. Washington, D.C., *National Tribune*, Sept. 8, 1898, 8.

35. Longstreet, *From Manassas to Appomattox*, 39.

36. Washington, D.C., *National Tribune*, June 26, 1884, 5.

37. *Report of the Joint Committee on the Conduct of the War*, Richardson's testimony, Dec. 24, 1861, 21.

38. William Todd, *Seventy-Ninth Highlanders* (Albany, 1886), 24–25.

39. Adolphus Wesley Williams was commissioned Major, 2d Michigan, on Apr. 25, 1861; Lieutenant Colonel, 2d Mich., on Mar. 6, 1862; and Colonel, 20th Mich., July 26, 1862. He was promoted to brevet Brigadier General, USV, for war service and was discharged on Nov. 21, 1863. He was wounded in action at Yorktown in April 1862; at Williamsburg on May 5, 1862; and at Fair Oaks on May 31, 1862. He died in 1879.

40. Lyster, *Recollections of the Bull Run Campaign*, 119. Dr. Lyster was a member of one of Detroit's most prominent families, and he became a recognized leader in the medical profession. Henry Lyster entered the University of Michigan and graduated with a medical degree in 1860. He entered the army as an assistant surgeon attached to the 2nd Michigan at the time of its organization on April 25, 1861. He was commissioned surgeon, 5th Michigan, on July 15, 1862. The following year he became brigade surgeon. He participated in many important engagements in Virginia and was wounded in the Battle of the Wilderness. After the war, he became a member of the University of Michigan medical school faculty and became one of the founders of the Wayne State University medical school. Dr. Lyster died in Niles, Michigan, on October 3, 1894.

41. Sears, *For Country, Cause and Leader*, 54.

42. Ibid., 54.

43. Ibid., 54.

44. In 1995 the remains of six men believed to have belonged to the 1st Massachusetts were discovered in shallow unmarked graves while land was being cleared for the construction of a McDonald's restaurant in Centreville. The bones remained on a shelf at the Smithsonian Institute for a decade until researcher Dalton Rector identified them as those of the Massachusetts men. The six received a proper military burial at the National Cemetery in Bourne, Massachusetts, on June 10, 2006.

45. Haydon Diary, 28.

46. *Report of the Joint Committee on the Conduct of the War* (Washington, D.C.: Government Printing Office, 1863), Richardson's testimony, 22.

47. IBR to Israel P. and Susanna H. Richardson, July 15, 1861, Lane Collection.

48. Ibid., 24.

49. Allen R. Foote, *Some of My War Stories*. Military Order of the Loyal Legion of the United States, vol. 9 (Wilmington, N.C.: Broadfoot, 1993), 25.

50. *Report of the Joint Committee on the Conduct of the War*, Richardson's testimony, Dec. 24, 1861, 24.

51. Ibid., 378.

52. *Report of the Joint Committee on the Conduct of the War*, Colonel Thomas A. Davies' testimony, Jan. 14, 1862, 179.

53. Jubal A. Early, *Autobiographical Sketch and the Narrative of the War Between the States* (Philadelphia: Lippincott, 1912), 17.

54. *Report of the Joint Committee on the Conduct of the War*, Richardson's testimony, Dec. 24, 1861, 24.

55. Ibid., 24.

56. Court of Inquiry Proceeding of Colonel D. S. Miles, War Department, Dec. 14, 1861, 28.

57. *Report of the Joint Committee on the Conduct of the War*, Colonel Thomas A. Davies' testimony, Jan. 14, 1862, 180.

58. Sears, *For Country, Cause and Leader*, 57.

59. Lyster, *Recollections of the Bull Run Campaign*, 122–24.

60. Robert Brethschneider Papers, Bentley Historical Library, University of Michigan, Mf 359c.

61. Washington D.C., *National Tribune*, Jan. 4, 1906, 3.

62. *Court of Inquiry Proceedings of Colonel D. S. Miles*. U.S. War Department, Dec. 14, 1861.

63. Davis, *Battle at Bull Run*, 242.

64. Petzold, *Memoirs of the Second Michigan Infantry*, 11.

65. Sears, *For Country, Cause and Leader*, 59.

66. Robert Brethschneider Papers, Bentley Historical Library, University of Michigan, Mf 359c.

67. Several contrary versions to these events have been recorded: Thomas J. Goree of Longstreet's staff states in a letter dated November 1861, "I would not detract from the noble dead, but from all I can gather, both Generals Bee and Bartow went themselves, and carried their men into places on July 21, which they could and would have avoided, had they been entirely free from the influence of liquor." The "stone wall" comment was explained by Major Thomas Rhett, of Jackson's staff, who spent the evening comforting the mortally wounded Bee, that its description was meant by Bee as one of anger at Jackson for standing like a stone wall and not moving to his assistance while his command was being destroyed.

68. IBR to his family, July 27, 1861, Lane Collection.

69. Stephen W. Sears, *George B. McClellan: The Young Napoleon* (New York: Ticknor & Fields, 1988), 114.

70. Letter from IBR to his family, Aug. 17, 1861, Lane Collection.

71. Court of Inquiry Proceedings in the case of Colonel D. S. Miles, War Department, Dec. 14, 1861, 5–7.

72. Ibid., 56.

73. IBR to his family, Aug. 18, 1861, Lane Collection.

74. Washington, D.C., *National Tribune*, Mar. 3, 1892, 3.

5. Opportunity

1. George A. McClellan, *McClellan's Own Story* (New York: Webster, 1887), 139.

2. Stephen W. Sears, *For Country, Cause, and Leader* (New York: Ticknor & Fields, 1993), 73.

3. Ibid., 78.

4. IBR to Israel P. and Susanna H. Richardson, Sept. 11, 1861, D. Duffy Lane Collection, in the possession of Thomas Lane, Summerville, S.C.

5. James Longstreet, *From Manassas to Appomattox* (Philadelphia: Lippincott, 1896), 59.

6. Poe had a distinguished service record during the war. At the head of the 2d Michigan, he participated in the Peninsula campaign of 1862, winning a citation for bravery and promotion to Brigadier General, U.S. Volunteers. Poe's volunteer commission expired March 4, 1863, but the Senate refused to grant confirmation when renewal was recommended because of partisan politics. Poe reverted to his regular army rank of captain. His services as an engineer, however, were in demand, and he was soon acting as engineer officer of the XXIII Corps, building fortifications at Knoxville, whose defense he directed during the siege of 1863. He became chief engineer for General William T. Sherman, on whose staff he remained until the end of the war. He ultimately regained his rank of brevet brigadier general.

After the war, Poe returned to Detroit, having general supervision in the Corps of Engineers over work on the upper Great Lakes. For a while he also represented the army in the construction of the transcontinental railroads. In 1883 he was made superintending engineer of improvement of rivers and harbors on lakes Superior and Huron. He was responsible for designing and constructing the Poe Lock in the St. Mary's River at Sault St. Marie.

7. Charles Carleton Coffin, *The Boys of '61* (Boston: Estes and Lauriat, 1925), 56.

8. Russel H. Beatie, *The Army of the Potomac; Birth of Command*, vol. 1 (Da Capo Press, 2002), 489–90.

9. Washington, D.C., *National Tribune*, March 27, 1884, 1.

10. Sears, *For Country, Cause, and Leader*, 98–99.

11. Stephen W. Sears, *George B. McClellan: The Young Napoleon* (New York: Ticknor & Fields, 1988), 116.

12. IBR to Marcella Richardson, Oct. 10, 1861, Lane Collection.

13. *Official Records of the Union and Confederate Armies* (*OR*; Washington, D.C.: Government Printing Office), series I, vol. 5, chap. 14, p. 249.

14. Sears, *For Country, Cause, and Leader*, 121.

15. T. Harry Williams, *Lincoln and the Radicals* (Madison: University of Wisconsin Press, 1941), 80.

16. Sears, *For Country, Cause, and Leader*, 143.

17. Ibid., 103.

18. Robert W. Hodge, *The Civil War Letters of Perry Mayo* (East Lansing: Michigan State University, 1967), 25.

19. Daniel G. Crotty, *Four Years Campaigning in the Army of the Potomac* (Grand Rapids, Mich.: Dygert, 1874), 34.

20. Sears, *For Country, Cause and Leader*, 151.

21. Washington, D.C., *National Tribune*, July 7, 1887, 1.

22. Sears, *For Country, Cause and Leader*, 142.

23. Ibid., 122.

24. Washington, D.C., *National Tribune*, June 30, 1887, 1.

25. Philip Kearny, *Letters from the Peninsula, the Civil War Letters of General Philip Kearny*. Ed. William B. Styple (Kearny, N.J.: Belle Grove, 1988), 43.

26. IBR to Susanna H. Richardson, Nov. 15, 1861, Lane Collection.

27. Kearny, *Letters from the Peninsula*, 30.

28. Ibid., 52, 127, 129, 146.

29. Sears, *For Country, Cause and Leader*, 202, 206.

30. William Child, *A History of the Fifth Regiment of New Hampshire Volunteers* (Bristol, N.H.: Musgrove; repr., Van Sickle Military Books, 1988), 47.

31. Thomas L. Livermore, *Days and Events, 1860–1865* (Boston: Houghton Mifflin, 1920), 50.

32. Jacob H. Cole, *Under Five Commanders* (New Jersey: Paterson, 1907), 19–20.

33. Josiah Marshall Favill, *The Diary of a Young Officer* (Chicago: Donnelley, 1909), 72–73.

34. Cole, *Under Five Commanders*, 87–88.

6. Distinction

1. Oliver Otis Howard, *Autobiography of Oliver Otis Howard, Major General, United States Army* (New York: Baker and Taylor, 1908), 1:208.

2. David Power Conyngham, *The Irish Brigade and Its Campaigns* (Boston: Patrick Donahoe, 1869), 119.

3. Christian G. Samito, ed., *"Fear Was Not in Him": The Civil War Letters of Major General Francis C. Barlow, USA* (New York: Fordham University Press, 2004), 32.

4. Thomas L. Livermore, *Days and Events, 1860–1865* (Boston: Houghton Mifflin, 1920), 61.

5. Conyngham, *The Irish Brigade and Its Campaigns*, 119–21. The woman in the anecdote was most likely "Big Mary" Gordon, whose husband served in Co. H, of the 88th New York. Father William Corby, a chaplain in the Irish Brigade, mentioned in his memoirs that Mary Gordon especially distinguished herself in caring for the wounded. General Sumner saw her at work at the hospital at Savage's Station and made her brigade sutler as a reward for her bravery. This gave her permission to pass freely to Washington and back in all government boats. This reward might have led to her downfall. Another soldier from the Irish brigade mentioned in his diary that Mrs. Gordon was "sent to a prison in Washington" and her husband court-martialed for "smuggling liquor and selling it to enlisted men in late 1863."

6. Washington, D.C., *National Tribune*, Sept. 29, 1887, 3.

7. Charles A. Fuller, *Personal Recollections of the War of 1861* (Sherburne, N.Y.: News Job, 1906), 14–15.

8. Jacob H. Cole, *Under Five Commanders* (New Jersey: Paterson, 1907), 18–19.

9. John A. Carpenter, *Sword and Olive Branch, Oliver Otis Howard* (Pittsburgh: University of Pittsburgh Press, 1964), 32.

10. Josiah M. Favill, *The Diary of a Young Officer . . .* (Chicago: Donnelly, 1909), 97–98.

11. Ibid., 103.

12. Ibid., 103.

13. Stephen W. Sears, *To the Gates of Richmond: The Peninsula Campaign* (New York: Ticknor & Fields, 1992), 135–36.

14. William Child, *A History of the Fifth Regiment of New Hampshire Volunteers* (Bristol, N.H.: Muskgrove, 1893), 78.

15. Washington, D.C., *National Tribune*, Feb. 14, 1884, 7.

16. Mike Pride and Mark Travis, *My Brave Boys: To War with Colonel Cross and the Fighting Fifth* (Hanover: University Press of New England, 2001), 80.

17. Brigadier General David E. Birney was court-martialed by his fiery division commander, Kearny, and acquitted of the charge of "halting his command a mile from the enemy" at Fair Oaks. He later commanded Kearny's division after he was killed at Chantilly. At Gettysburg he commanded the III Corps after Sickles was wounded, and he received two wounds himself. He died of malaria on October 18, 1864.

18. Gustavus W. Smith, "Two Days of Battle at Seven Pines (Fair Oaks)," in *Battles and Leaders of the Civil War*, ed. Robert U. Johnson and Clarence C. Buel (New York: Century, 1888), 2:256.

19. *Official Records of the Union and Confederate Armies* (*OR*; Washington, D.C.: Government Printing Office, 1901), series I, vol. 11, 765.

20. Favill, *The Diary of a Young Officer*, 111–12.

21. Smith, "Two Days of Battle at Seven Pines (Fair Oaks)," in Johnson and Buel, *Battle and Leaders of the Civil War*, 2:258.

22. *OR*, series I, vol. 11, 765.

23. Pride and Travis, *My Brave Boys: To War with Colonel Cross and the Fighting Fifth*, 82.

24. Washington, D.C., *National Tribune*, Feb. 14, 1884, 7.

25. Child, *A History of the Fifth Regiment of New Hampshire Volunteers*, 82.

26. D. L. Gilbert, 53rd Pennsylvania, June 7, 1862, Richmond National Park Battlefield Museum.

27. *OR*, series I, vol. 11, 777.

28. Ibid., 783.

29. *New York Daily Tribune*, June 16, 1862.

30. Sears, *To the Gates of Richmond*, 150.

31. Favill, *The Diary of a Young Officer*, 122.

32. Evans (Seth Gilbert) Papers, June 14, 1862, 1861–64, Pearce Civil War Collection, Navarro College, Corsicana, Texas.

33. Francis C. Barlow, letter, June 18, 1862, Massachusetts Historical Society, Boston.

34. Favill, *The Diary of a Young Officer*, 157.

35. T. Harry Williams, *Lincoln and the Radicals* (Madison: University of Wisconsin Press, 1941), 138–39.

36. Edward M. L. Ehlers, 52nd New York, diary entry, June 14, 1862, Richmond National Park Battlefield Museum.

37. Livermore, *Days and Events*, 72.

38. Cyrus H. Forwood, 2nd Delaware, journal entry, June 13, 1862, Delaware Public Archives.

39. Douglas Southall Freeman, *Lee's Lieutenants* (New York: Scribner, 1943), 1:271.

40. IBR to Israel P. Richardson, June 23, 1862, D. Duffy Lane Collection, in the possession of Thomas Lane, Summerville, S.C.

41. Ibid.

42. Clifford Downey and Louis H. Manarin, eds., *The Wartime Papers of R. E. Lee* (Boston: Little, Brown, 1961), 216–17.

43. Freeman, *Lee's Lieutenants.* 1:547.

44. James Cooper Miller, "Serving under McClellan on the Peninsula." *Civil War Times Illustrated* 8, no. 3 (June 1969): 27–28.

45. Cole, *Under Five Commanders*, 19.

46. Daniel Hand, *Reminiscences of an Army Surgeon*, Military Order of the Loyal Legion of the United States, vol. 26 (Wilmington, N.C.: Broadfoot, 1993), 294.

47. William B. Franklin, "Rearguard Fighting during the Change of Base," In Johnson and Buel, *Battles and Leaders of the Civil War*, 2:375.

48. Sears, *To the Gates of Richmond*, 276.

49. George B. McClellan, *The Civil War Papers of George B. McClellan: Selected Correspondence, 1860–1865*, ed. Steven W. Sears (New York: Ticknor & Fields, 1989).

50. Ibid.

51. Washington, D.C., *National Tribune*, Jan. 22, 1885, 1.

52. Thomas W. Hyde, *Civil War Letters by General Thomas W. Hyde* (privately printed, 1933).

53. Livermore, *Days and Events*, 84.

54. Washington, D.C., *National Tribune*, July 19, 1888, 3.

55. Livermore, *Days and* Events, 86.

56. Favill, *The Diary of a Young Officer*, 143.

57. Daniel H. Hill, "McClellan's Change of Base and Malvern Hill," in Johnson and Buell, *Battle and Leaders of the Civil War*, 2:388.

58. Sears, *To the Gates of Richmond*, 338.

59. Fuller, *Personal Recollections of the War of 1861*, 45.

60. Washington, D.C., *National Tribune*, Sept. 8, 1910, 5.

61. Philip Kearny, *Letters from the Peninsula: The Civil War Letters of General Philip Kearny*, ed. William B. Styple (Kearny, N.J.: Belle Grove, 1988), 125–30.

62. Favill, *The Diary of a Young Officer*, 158–59.

63. *Detroit Free Press*, July 23, 1862.

64. *Pontiac Press*, Nov. 25, 1915.

65. *Zachariah Chandler, His Life and Public Services* (Detroit: Post and Tribune, 1880), 259–60.

66. Roy P. Basler, ed., *The Collected Works of Abraham Lincoln* (New Brunswick, N.J.: Rutgers University Press, 1953), 5:360.

67. Williams, *Lincoln and the Radicals*, 135–36.

68. Gideon Welles, *Diary of Gideon Welles* (New York: Houghton Mifflin, 1911), 1:85–86.

69. Ibid., 1:536–37.

70. Ibid., 1:104.

71. Ibid., 1:125.

72. Williams, *Lincoln and the Radicals*, 180.

7. Destiny

1. William Child, *A History of the Fifth Regiment of New Hampshire Volunteers in the American Civil War, 1861–1865* (Bristol, N.H.: Muskgrove, 1893), 105.

2. David Power Conyngham, *The Irish Brigade and Its Campaigns* (Boston: Patrick Donahoe, 1869), 293–94.

3. IBR to Fannie Richardson, Sept. 14, 1862, D. Duffy Lane Collection, in the possession of Thomas Lane, Summerville, S.C.

4. Child, *A History of the Fifth Regiment of New Hampshire Volunteers*, 101.

5. Ibid., 118.

6. *OR*, series I, vol. 19, 300.

7. Washington, D.C., *National Tribune*, Sept. 19, 1901, 4.

8. Ibid., July 24, 1902, 3.

9. Bruce Catton, *Mr. Lincoln's Army* (Garden City, N.Y.: Doubleday, 1954), 155.

10. Washington, D.C., *National Tribune*, March 12, 1908, 5.

11. Jacob H. Cole, *Under Five Commanders* (New Jersey: Paterson, 1907), 19.

12. William A. Osborne, *The History of the Twenty-Ninth Regiment of Massachusetts Volunteer Infantry in the Late War of Rebellion* (Boston: Albert J. Wright, 1877), 186.

13. *OR*, series I, vol. 19, 296.

14. Mike Pride and Mark Travis, *My Brave Boys: To War with Colonel Cross and the Fighting Fifth* (Hanover: University Press of New England, 2001), 134.

15. Osborne, *The History of the Twenty-Ninth Regiment of Massachusetts Volunteer Infantry in the Late War of Rebellion*, 186–87.

16. Ezra A. Carman, Carman Papers, copy at Antietam National Battlefield Collection.

17. *OR*, series I, vol. 19, 298.

18. Ibid., 1047–48.

19. Washington, D.C., *National Tribune*, March 3, 1879, 1.

20. Ibid., July 20, 1893, 4.

21. Thomas L. Livermore, *Days and Events, 1860–1865* (Boston: Houghton Mifflin, 1920), 137–38. Livermore would rise to the rank of colonel and command the 5th New Hampshire by the end of the war; he later wrote, "I shall never cease to admire that magnificent fighting general who advanced with his front line, with his sword bare and ready to use, and his swarthy face, burning eye, and square jaw."

22. *OR*, series I, vol. 19, 289.

23. Frederick L. Hitchcock, *War from the Inside* (Philadelphia: Lippincott, 1904), 64.

24. Robert G. Smith, *A Brief Account of the Services Rendered by the Second Regiment Delaware Volunteers in the War of the Rebellion* (Wilmington: Historical Society of Delaware, 1909), University of Delaware Library, Newark, Delaware, 10–11.

25. The gallant conduct of Colonel Cooke on this occasion deservedly won him promotion to the grade of brigadier general. His losses in this engagement were terrible. Of twenty-six commissioned officers in his regiment, the 27th North Carolina, who went into action, eighteen were killed or wounded. The losses were equally as great in the 3rd Arkansas.

26. *OR*, series I, vol. 19, 290.

27. James Longstreet, "The Invasion of Maryland," in Robert U. Johnson and Clarence C. Buel, eds., *Battles and Leaders of the Civil War*, (New York: Century, 1887–88), 2:669.

28. Ibid.

29. Douglas Southall Freeman, *Lee's Lieutenants: A Study in Command* (New York: Scribner, 1943), 2:216.

30. James Longstreet, "The Invasion of Maryland," in Johnson and Buel, *Battles and Leaders of the Civil War*, 2:669.

31. Freeman, *Lee's Lieutenants*, 2:213.

32. Smith, *A Brief Account of the Services Rendered by the Second Regiment Delaware Volunteers in the War of the Rebellion*, 11.

33. Gilbert Frederick, *The Story of a Regiment, being a Record of the Military Service of the Fifty-Seventh New York State Volunteer Infantry in the War of the Rebellion* (Chicago: Fifty-Seven Veteran Association, 1895), chap. 8, 2.

34. *OR*, Series I, vol. 19, 343–44.

35. *New York Times*, Sept. 20, 1862; Washington, D.C., *National Tribune*, Oct. 7, 1909, 5.

36. Livermore, *Days and Events*, 144–45.

37. Cole, *Under Five Commanders*, 86.

38. James Longstreet, *From Manassas to Appomattox* (Philadelphia: Lippincott, 1896), 252.

39. Child, *A History of the Fifth Regiment of New Hampshire Volunteers*, 126–27.

40. Walter Holden, William Ross, and Elizabeth Slomba, eds., *Stand Firm and Fire Low: The Civil War Writings of Colonel Edward E. Cross* (University of New Hampshire: University Press of New England), 51.

41. Charles S. Wainwright, *A Diary of Battle: Personal Journals of Colonel Charles S. Wainwright, 1861–1865*, ed. Allan Nevins (New York: Harcourt, 1962), 104.

42. Fannie Richardson to Marcia Richardson, October 1862, Lane Collection.

43. Ibid.

44. Ibid.

45. William Corby, *Memoirs of Chaplain Life* (Notre Dame, Ind.: Scholastic, 1894), 373.

46. Marcella Richardson to Marcia Richardson, Oct. 20, 1862, Lane Collection.

47. Emanuel Hertz, ed., *Lincoln Talks: A Biography in Anecdote* (New York: Viking, 1939), 465.

48. Captain Draper's account was recorded by Mrs. Winifred Lyster, wife of the 2nd Michigan's surgeon, Dr. Henry F. Lyster, and sister to Colonel Orlando Poe, the 2nd Michigan commander following Richardson's promotion. Draper was assigned to Richardson's staff on April 1, 1862. He resigned from the army on March 19, 1863, and practiced law in Saginaw until his death in 1892. Michigan Pioneer and Historical Society, *Historical Collections*, vol. 35 (Lansing, Mich.: Wynkoop Hallenbeck Crawford, 1907), 162.

49. T. Harry Williams, *Lincoln and the Radicals* (Madison: University of Wisconsin Press, 1941), 187.

50. Carl Sandburg, *Abraham Lincoln: The War Years*, vol. 1 (New York: Harcourt, 1939), 599.

51. *Detroit Advertiser and Tribune*, Nov. 12, 1862, p. 3.

52. Holden, Ross, and Slomba, *Stand Firm and Fire Low: The Civil War Writings of Edward E. Cross*, 129.

53. Evans (Seth Gilbert) Papers, 1861–1864, Nov. 13, 1862, Pearce Civil War Collection, Navarro College, Corsicana, Texas.

54. Rootsweb. www.rootsweb.ancestry.com/~vermont/franklinfairfax_2.html.

Bibliography

Newspapers

Detroit Advertiser and Tribune, November 5, 8, 12, 1862.
Detroit Free Press, July 6, 23, 1862; September 26, 1862; November 5, 9, 11, 12, 1862.
National Tribune, Washington, D.C., 1880–1910.
New York Daily Tribune, June 16, 1862.
New York Times, September 20, 1862; September 26, 1862; November 6, 1862.
Pontiac Gazette, March 27, 1862; November 11, 1862.
Pontiac Press Gazette, November 25, 1915.

Official Compilations

U.S. Congress. Executive Document No. 4. *The President's Message to the Two Houses of Congress, December 8, 1846.* 29th Cong., 2nd sess. Washington, D.C.: Ritchie & Hess, 1846.
———. Executive Document No. 1. *Message from the President of the United States to the Two Houses of Congress. With accompanying documents.* 30th Cong., 2nd sess. Washington, D.C.: Wendell & Van Benthysen, 1848.
———. Executive Document No. 24. *Major J. Van Horn, After-action Report, El Paso, Texas.* 31st Congress, 1st sess.
———. Executive Document No. 8. *Court of Inquiry, Colonel D. S. Miles.* 37th Congress, 2nd sess.
———. *Report of the Joint Committee on the Conduct of the War.* 3 vols. Washington D.C.: Government Printing House, 1863.
U.S. Military Academy. Admissions Archives. West Point, N.Y.
———. Special Collections Div. Israel Richardson File. West Point, N.Y.
U.S. National Archives. Record Group 94. Records of the Adjutant General's Office. *Letters received—File-R400 1855, Richardson correspondence.*
———. Record Group 107. Records of the Office of the Secretary of War. *Letters received—File-A131 (WD) 1847.*
———. Record Group 393. Records of the U.S. Army Continental Commands, Part I, Entry 5572, Letters Received, Western Div. (File 10-R-1852).
U.S. War Department. *The War of the Rebellion: A Compilation of the Official Records of the Union and Confederate Armies.* 70 vols. Washington, D.C.: Government Printing Office, 1880–1901.

Manuscripts and Papers

Brethschneider (Robert) Papers. Bentley Historical Library, University of Michigan. Mf 359c.

Carman (Ezra) Papers. Copy at Antietam National Battlefield.

Evans (Seth Gilbert) Papers, 1861–64. Pearce Civil War Collection, Navarro College, Corsicana, Texas.

Forwood (Cyrus H.) Papers. 2nd Delaware. Delaware Public Archives.

Haydon (Charles B.) Papers. Michigan Historical Collection, University of Michigan, Ann Arbor.

Richardson, Israel B. "Twelve Years Service in the U. S. Army." Unpublished manuscript. D. Duffy Lane Collection, in the possession of Thomas Lane, Summerville, S.C.

Richardson (Israel B.) Papers. D. Duffy Lane Collection.

Robbins (Jerome J.) Diary. Michigan Historical Collection, University of Michigan, Ann Arbor. July 17, 1861.

Setright (John T.) Papers. Michigan Historical Collection, University of Michigan, Ann Arbor.

Books and Articles

Agnew, James B. "General Barnard Bee." *Civil War Times Illustrated,* December 1975.

Alexander, Edward Porter. *Fighting for the Confederacy: The Personal Recollections of General Edward Porter Alexander.* Ed. Gary W. Gallagher. Chapel Hill: University of North Carolina Press, 1989.

Ambrose, Stephen E. *Halleck: Lincoln's Chief of Staff.* Baton Rouge: Louisiana State Press, 1962.

Averill, William W. *Ten Years in the Saddle.* Ed. Edward K. Eckert and Nicholas J. Amato. San Rafael, Calif.: Presidio, 1978.

Ballantine, George. *An English Soldier in the U.S. Army.* New York: Stringer and Townsend, 1853. Reprint, Townsend, 1860.

Bandel, Eugene. *Frontier Life in the Army, 1854–1861.* Ed. Ralph P. Bieber. Glendale, Calif.: Clark, 1932.

Barbour, Philip, and Martha Barbour. *The Journals of Major Philip Norbourne Barbour and His Wife Martha Isabella Hopkins Barbour.* Ed. Rhoda Van Bibber Tanner Doubleday. New York: Putnam, 1936.

Basler, Roy P., ed. *The Collected Works of Abraham Lincoln.* 9 vols. New Brunswick, N.J.: Rutgers University Press, 1953.

Bauer, K. Jack. *The Mexican War, 1846–1848.* New York: Macmillan, 1974.

Beatie, Russel H. *The Army of the Potomac.* Vol. 1, *Birth of Command.* Cambridge, Mass.: Da Capo, 2002.

Bender, Averam B. *The March of Empire: Frontier Defense in the Southwest, 1848–1860.* New York: Greenwood, 1968.

Bennett, James A. *Forts and Forays: A Dragoon in New Mexico, 1850–1856.* Ed. Clinton E. Brooks. Albuquerque: University of New Mexico Press, 1948.

Bilby, Joseph G. *Remember Fontenroy! The 69th NY and the Irish Brigade in the Civil War.* Hightstown, N.J.: Longstreet, 1985.

Boatner, Mark Mayo, III. *The Civil War Dictionary.* New York: McKay, 1959.

Bridges, Hal. *Lee's Maverick General: Daniel Harvey Hill.* New York: McGraw-Hill, 1961.

Carpenter, John A. *Sword and Olive Branch: Oliver Otis Howard.* Pittsburgh: University of Pittsburgh Press, 1964.

Casdorph, Paul D. *Prince John Magruder: His Life and Campaigns.* New York: Wiley, 1996.

Catton, Bruce. *Mr. Lincoln's Army.* Garden City, N.Y.: Doubleday, 1954.

———. *Terrible Swift Sword.* Garden City, N.Y.: Doubleday, 1963.

Chamberlain, Samuel E. *My Confession.* New York: Harper, 1956.

Chance, Joseph E. *Jefferson Davis's Mexican War Regiment.* Jackson: University Press of Mississippi, 1992.

Chase, Salmon P. *Inside Lincoln's Cabinet: The Civil War Diaries of Salmon P. Chase.* Ed. David Donald. New York: Longmans, 1954.

Child, William. *A History of the Fifth Regiment of New Hampshire Volunteers in the American Civil War, 1861–1865.* Bristol, N.H.: Muskgrove, 1893.

Clowes, Walter F. *The Detroit Light Guard.* Detroit, 1900.

Coffin, Charles Carleton. *The Boys of '61.* Boston: Estes and Lauriat, 1925.

Coffin, Howard. *Full Duty: Vermonters in the Civil War.* Woodstock, Vt.: Countryman, 1993.

Coffman, Edward M. *The Old Army, A Portrait of the American Army in Peacetime, 1784–1898.* New York: Oxford University Press, 1986.

Cole, Jacob H. *Under Five Commanders.* Paterson, N.J.: News Printing, 1907.

Commanger, Henry Steele, ed. *The Blue and the Gray.* Indianapolis: Bobbs-Merrill, 1950.

Conyngham, David Power. *The Irish Brigade and Its Campaigns.* Boston: Patrick Donahoe, 1869.

Corby, William. *Memoirs of Chaplain Life.* Notre Dame, Ind.: Scholastic, 1894.

Cox, Jacob D. *Military Reminiscences of the Civil War.* 2 vols. New York, 1900.

Cox, Merlin G. *John Pope, Fighting General from Illinois.* University of Florida, 1956.

Crotty, Daniel G. *Four Years Campaigning in the Army of the Potomac.* Grand Rapids, Mich.: Dygert, 1874.

Cudworth, Warren H. *History of the First Massachusetts Infantry.* Boston, 1866.

Cullen, Joseph P. *The Peninsula Campaign of 1862: McClellan and Lee Struggle for Richmond.* Harrisburg, Pa.: Stackpole, 1973.

Cullum, George W. *Biographical Register of the Officers and Graduates of the U.S. Military Academy.* 3 vols. Boston: Houghton, 1891.

Dana, Napoleon J. T. *Monterrey Is Ours! The Mexican War Letters of Lieutenant Dana, 1845–1847.* Ed. Robert H. Ferrell. Lexington: University Press of Kentucky: 1990.

Davis, William C. *Battle at Bull Run.* Baton Rouge: Louisiana State University Press, 1977.

———. *The Confederate General.* Vol. 1. National Historical Society, 1991.

De Peyster, John W. *Personal and Military History of Philip Kearny, Major General, United States Volunteers.* New York: Rice and Gage, 1869.

Detroit Post and Tribune. *Zachariah Chandler: His Life and Public Services.* Detroit: Post and Tribune, Publishers, 1880.

Dowdey, Clifford. *The Seven Days: The Emergence of Lee.* Boston: Little, Brown, 1964.

Early, Jubal A. *Autobiographical Sketch and Narrative of the War between the States.* Philadelphia: Lippincott, 1912.

Eisenhower, John S. D. *So Far from God: The U. S. War with Mexico, 1846–1848.* New York: Doubleday, 1989.

Eisenschimel, Otto. *The Celebrated Case of Fitz John Porter: An American Dreyfus Affair.* Indianapolis: Bobbs-Merrill, 1950.

Eliot, Charles W. *Winfield Scott: The Soldier and the Man.* New York: Macmillan, 1937.

Emmett, Chris. *Fort Union and the Winning of the Southwest.* Norman: University of Oklahoma Press, 1965.

English, William H. *Life and Military Career of Winfield Scott Hancock.* Philadelphia: McCurdy, 1880.

Ewell, Richard S. *The Making of a Soldier; Letters of General R. S. Ewell.* Ed. Richmond, Va.: Captain Percy Gatling Hamlin, 1935.

Favill, Josiah M. *The Diary of a Young Officer Serving in the Armies of the United States during the War of the Rebellion.* Chicago: Donnelley, 1909.

Foote, Alan R. *Some of My War Stories.* Military Order of the Loyal Legion of the United States, vol. 9. Wilmington, N.C.: Broadfoot, 1993.

Foote, Shelby. *The Civil War: A Narrative.* 3 vols. New York: Random, 1958, 1963, 1974.

Frassanito, William A. *Antietam.* New York: Scribner, 1978.

Frederick, Gilbert. *The Story of a Regiment, being a Record of the Military Service of the Fifty-Seventh New York State Volunteer Infantry in the War of the Rebellion.* Chicago: Fifty-Seven Veteran Association, 1895.

Freeman, Douglas Southall. *Lee's Lieutenants: A Study in Command.* 3 vols. New York: Scribner, 1943.

———. *R. E. Lee.* 4 vols. New York: Scribner, 1949.

French, Samuel Gibbs. *Two Wars: An Autobiography.* Nashville: Confederate Veteran, 1901.

Fry, James B. *McDowell and Tyler in the Campaign of Bull Run.* New York, 1884.

Fuller, Charles A. *Personal Recollections of the War of 1861.* Sherburne, N.Y.: News Job, 1906.

Gibbon, John. *Personal Recollections of the Civil War.* New York: Putnam, 1928.

Gordon, John B. *Reminiscences of the Civil War.* New York: Scribner, 1903.

Gotezmann, William F., ed. "Our First Foreign War: Letters of Barna Upton, 3rd U.S. Infantry." *American Heritage,* vol.17, 1966.

Grant, Ulysses Simpson. *Personal Memoirs of U.S. Grant.* Vol.1. New York: Webster, 1885.

Hancock, Ada. *Reminiscences of Winfield Scott Hancock.* New York: Webster, 1887.

Hassler, Warren W., Jr. *General George B. McClellan: Shield of the Union.* Baton Rouge: Louisiana State University Press, 1957.

Hay, John. *Lincoln and the Civil War in the Diary and Letters of John Hay.* Ed. Tyler Dennett. New York: Dodd, Mead, 1939.

Henderson, G. F. R. *Stonewall Jackson and the American Civil War.* New York: Longmans, Green, 1936.

Hennessy, John J. *Return to Bull Run.* New York: Simon, 1993.

Henry, Robert Selph. *The Story of the Mexican War.* New York: Fredrick Unger, 1950.

Henry, William S. *Campaign Sketches of the War with Mexico.* New York: Harper, 1847. Reprint, New York: Arno Press, 1973.

Herbert, Walter H. *Fighting Joe Hooker.* Indianapolis: Bobbs-Merrill, 1944.

Hesseltine, William B. *Lincoln and the War Governors.* New York: Knopf, 1948.

Hitchcock, Ethan Allen. *Fifty Years in Camp and Field.* Ed. W. A. Croffut. New York: Putnam, 1909.

Hitchcock, Frederick L. *War from the Inside.* Philadelphia: Lippincott, 1904.

Hodge, Robert W., ed. *The Civil War Letters of Perry Mayo.* East Lansing: Michigan State University, 1967.

Holden, Walter, William Ross, and Elizabeth Slomba, eds. *Stand Firm and Fire Low: The Civil War Writings of Colonel Edward E. Cross.* Hanover, N.H.: University Press of New England, 2003.

Hood, John B. *Advance and Retreat.* Edison, N.J.: Blue and Gray, 1985.

Howard, Oliver Otis. *Autobiography of Oliver Otis Howard, Major General, United States Army.* 2 vols. New York: Baker and Taylor, 1908.

Johnson, Robert U., and Clarence C. Buel, eds. *Battles and Leaders of the Civil War.* 4 vols. New York: Century, 1888.

Johnston, William Preston. *The Life of General Albert Sidney Johnston.* New York: Appleton, 1878.

Kearny, Philip. *Letters from the Peninsula: The Civil War Letters of General Philip Kearny.* Ed. William B. Styple. Kearny, N.J.: Belle Grove, 1988.

Kendall, George W. *Narrative of an Expedition from Texas to Santa Fe.* London: David Bogue, 1855.

Kenly, John R. *Memoirs of a Maryland Volunteer.* Philadelphia: Lippincott, 1873.

Keyes, E. D. *Fifty Years Observation of Men and Events, Civil and Military.* New York: Scribner, 1885.

Lanman, Charles. *The Red Book of Michigan.* Detroit: E. B. Smith, 1871.

Le Duc, William G. *Recollections of a Civil War Quartermaster: The Autobiography of William G. Le Duc.* St. Paul, Minn.: North Central, 1963.

Lewis, Lloyd. *Captain Sam Grant.* Boston: Little, Brown, 1950.

Livermore, Thomas L. *Days and Events, 1860–1865.* Boston: Houghton, 1920.

Longacre, Edward G. *The Man behind the Guns.* South Brunswick, N.J.: Barnes, 1977.

Longstreet, James. *From Manassas to Appomattox.* Philadelphia: Lippincott, 1896. Reprinted New York: Mallard, 1991.

Lowry, Thomas P. *Tarnished Eagles.* Mechanicsburg, Pa.: Stackpole, 1997.

Luvaas, Jay, and Harold W. Nelson. *The U.S. Army War College Guide to the Battle of Antietam.* New York: Harper, 1988.

Lyster, Henry F. *Recollections of the Bull Run Campaign.* Detroit: Wm. S. Ostler, 1888.

Malone, Dumas, ed. *Dictionary of American Biography.* New York: Scribner, 1935.

Maury, Dabney Herndon. *Recollections of a Virginian in the Mexican, Indian and Civil Wars.* New York: Scribner, 1894.

McCall, George A. *Letters from the Frontier.* Philadelphia, 1868.

———. *New Mexico in 1850: A Military View.* Ed. Robert W. Frazier, Norman: University of Oklahoma, 1968.

McClellan, George B. *McClellan's Own Story.* New York: Webster, 1887.

———. *The Mexican War Diary of General George B. McClellan.* Ed. William Starr Myers. Princeton: Princeton University Press, 1917.

McConnell, H. H. *Five Years a Cavalryman.* Freeport, N.Y., 1888; reprinted 1970.

Meade, George G. *The Life and Letters of George Gordon Meade, Major General, United States Army.* New York: Scribner, 1913.

Miles, Nelson A. *Serving the Republic: Memoirs of Nelson A. Miles.* New York: Harper, 1916.

Miller, James Cooper. "Serving under McClellan on the Peninsula." *Civil War Times Illustrated* 8, no. 3 (June 1969).

Mitchie, Peter S. *General George Brinton McClellan.* New York: Appleton, 1901.

Morrison, James V. *"The Best School in the World": West Point, the Pre-Civil War Years 1833–1866.* Kent, Ohio: Kent State University Press, 1986.

Murfin, James V. *The Gleam of Bayonets: The Battle of Antietam and the Maryland Campaign of 1862*. New York: Yoseloff, 1965.

Nevin, David. *The Mexican War*. Alexandria, Va.: Time-Life, 1978.

Nichols, Edward J. *Zach Taylor's Little Army*. Garden City, N.Y.: Doubleday, 1963.

Nicolay, John, and John Hay. *Abraham Lincoln: A History*. 10 vols. New York: Century, 1890.

Oliva, Leo E. *Soldiers on the Santa Fe Trail*. Norman: University of Oklahoma Press, 1967.

Osborne, William A. *The History of the Twenty-Ninth Regiment of Massachusetts Volunteer Infantry in the Late War of the Rebellion*. Boston: Albert J. Wright, 1877.

Palfrey, Francis W. *The Antietam Campaign and Fredericksburg*. New York: Scribner, 1882.

Patrick, Marsena. *Inside Lincoln's Army: The Diary of Marsena Rudolph Patrick, Provost Marshal General, Army of the Potomac*. Ed. David S. Sparks, New York: Yoseloff, 1964.

Petzold, Herman. *Memoirs of the Second Michigan*. Ann Arbor: University of Michigan, Bentley Historical Library, 1897.

Pride, Mike, and Mark Travis. *My Brave Boys: To War with Colonel Cross and the Fighting Fifth*. Hanover, N.H.: University Press of New England, 2001.

Reese, Timothy. *Sykes' Regular Infantry*. Jefferson, N.C.: McFarland, 1990.

Reilly, Oliver T. *The Battlefield of Antietam*. Hagerstown, Md.: Hagerstown, 1906.

Ripley, R. S. *The War with Mexico*. 2 vols. New York: Burt Franklin, 1970.

Robertson, Jonathan. *Michigan in the War*. Lansing, Mich.: W. S. George, 1882.

Rodenbough, T. F. *From Everglade to Canon: The History of the Second Dragoons*. New York: Van Nostrand, 1875.

Samito, Christian G., ed. *"Fear Was Not in Him": The Civil War Letters of Major General Francis C. Barlow, USA*. New York: Fordham University Press, 2004.

Sandburg, Carl. *Abraham Lincoln: The War Years*. Vol. 1. New York: Harcourt, 1939.

Schildt, John W. *Antietam Hospitals*. Chewsville, Md.: Antietam, 1987.

Scott, Robert Garth, ed. *Forgotten Valor*. Kent, Ohio: Kent State University Press, 1999.

Scott, Winfield. *The Memoirs of Lieutenant General Winfield Scott*. 2 vols. New York: Sheldon, 1864.

Sears, Stephen W. *For Country, Cause and Leader*. New York: Ticknor & Fields, 1993.

——. *George B. McClellan: The Young Napoleon*. New York: Ticknor & Fields, 1988.

——. *Landscape Turned Red: The Battle of Antietam*. New York: Ticknor & Fields, 1983.

——. *To the Gates of Richmond: The Peninsula Campaign*. New York: Ticknor & Fields, 1992.

Sedgwick, John. *Correspondence of John Sedgwick, Major General*. 2 vols. New York: privately printed, 1903.

Sherman, William T. *Home Letters of General Sherman*. Ed. De Wolfe Howe. New York: Scribner, 1937.

Smith, E. Kirby. *To Mexico with Scott: Letters of Ephraim Kirby Smith to his Wife*. Cambridge: Harvard University Press, 1917.

Smith, Justin H. *The War with Mexico*. 2 vols. New York: Macmillan, 1919.

Smith, Robert G. *A Brief Account of the Services Rendered by the Second Regiment Delaware Volunteers in the War of the Rebellion*. Wilmington: Historical Society of Delaware, 1909. University of Delaware Library, Newark, Delaware.

Smith, William F. *Autobiography of Major General William F. Smith, 1861–1864*. Ed. Herbert M. Schiller, Dayton, Ohio: Morningside, 1990.

Sorrel, G. Moxley. *Recollections of a Confederate Staff Officer*. New York: Neale, 1905.

Stackpole, Edward J. *From Cedar Mountain to Antietam*. Harrisburg: Stackpole, 1959.

Stanley, F. *E. V. Sumner: Major General United States Army, 1797–1863*. Texas, Hess, 1969.

Stevens, Hazard. *The Life of Isaac Ingalls Stevens*. Boston, 1900.

Stine, J. H. *History of the Army of the Potomac*. Philadelphia: Rogers, 1892.

Swinton, William. *Campaigns of the Army of the Potomac*. Boston: Ticknor, 1889.

Teetor, Paul R. *A Matter of Hours*. Rutherford, N.J.: Farleigh Dickinson University Press, 1982.

Thomlinson, M. H. *The Garrison at Fort Bliss, 1849–1916*. El Paso: Hertzog & Resler, 1945.

Todd, William. *The Seventy-Ninth Highlander New York Volunteers in the War of the Rebellion*. Albany, 1886.

Trefousse, Hans L. *The Radical Republicans: Lincoln's Vanguard for Radical Justice*. New York: Knopf, 1969.

Utley, Robert M. *Fort Union and the Santa Fe Trail*. El Paso: Texas Western Press, 1989.

———. *Frontiersmen in Blue: The United States Army and the Indian, 1848–1865*. Lincoln: University of Nebraska Press, 1967.

Vinson, John Adams. *The Richardson Memorial*. Portland: B. Thurston, 1876.

Wainwright, Charles S. *A Diary of Battle: The Personal Journals of Colonel Charles S. Wainwright, 1861–1865*. Ed. Allan Nevins. New York: Harcourt, 1962.

Walker, Francis A. *History of the Second Army Corps*. New York: Scribner, 1886.

Warner, Ezra J. *Generals in Blue: Lives of the Union Commanders*. Baton Rouge: Louisiana State University Press, 1964.

———. *Generals in Gray: Lives of the Confederate Commanders*. Baton Rouge: Louisiana State University Press, 1959.

Webb, Alexander S. *The Peninsula: McClellan's Campaign of 1862*. New York: Scribner, 1881.

Weigley, Russell F. *Quartermaster General of the Union Army: A Biography of M. C. Meigs*. New York: Columbia University Press, 1959.

Welles, Gideon. *Diary of Gideon Welles*. Ed. Howard K. Beale. 3 vols. New York: Houghton Mifflin, 1911.

Wert, Jeffry D. *General James Longstreet*. New York: Simon, 1993.

Whilden, Charles E. *Letters from a Santa Fe Army Clerk, 1855–1856*. Ed. John Hammond Moore. *New Mexico Historical Review* 40, no. 2, 1965.

Wilcox, Cadmus M. *History of the Mexican War*. Washington, D.C.: Church News, 1892.

Williams, T. Harry. *Lincoln and His Generals*. New York: Knopf, 1952.

———. *Lincoln and the Radicals*. Madison: University of Wisconsin Press, 1941.

Woodford, Frank B. *Father Abraham's Children: Michigan Episodes in the Civil War*. Detroit: Wayne State University Press, 1961.

Woodworth, Steven E., ed. *Leadership and Command in the American Civil War*. Campbell, Calif.: Savas Woodbury, 1995.

Index

Page numbers in italics indicate maps.

Jack C. Mason lives in Waterford, Michigan, and works for the Tank and Automotive Life Cycle Management Command as a Department of Army civilian. He is a lieutenant colonel in the U.S. Army Reserve and a graduate of the U.S. Army Command and General Staff College and the Canadian Land Force Militia Command and Staff College. He has more than thirty years of enlisted and commissioned service, including active duty tours with U.S. Central Command in Afghanistan. He currently serves as a faculty member for the Command and General Staff College and has written several historical case studies for the professional journal of the U.S. Army, *Army* magazine.